THE PEOPLE AS ENEMY

THE PEOPLE AS ENEMY

The Leaders' Hidden Agenda in World War Two

John Spritzler

BLACK
ROSE
BOOKS

Montréal/New York/London

Black Rose Books No. GG320

National Library of Canada Cataloguing in Publication Data
Spritzler, John
The people as enemy : the leaders' hidden agenda in world war two / John Spritzler

Includes bibliographical references and index.
Hardcover ISBN: 1-55164-217-4 (bound) Paperback ISBN: 1-55164-216-6 (pbk.)

1. World War, 1939-1945--Social aspects. 2. Working class--Government policy--History--20th century. 3. Elite (Social sciences)--Political activity--History--20th century. 4. Social control--Political aspects--History--20th century. I. Title.

D743.S67 2003   940.53'1   C2002-904812-5

Posters reproduced herein are in the public domain, but we wish, nonetheless, to thank the National Archives and Records Administration (http://www.archives.gov/exhibit_hall/powers_of_persuasion) and the Minneapolis Public Library (http://digital.lib.umn.edu/warposters) for providing broad access.

Cover design: Associés libres

BLACK ROSE BOOKS

C.P. 1258	2250 Military Road	99 Wallis Road
Succ. Place du Parc	Tonawanda, NY	London, E9 5LN
Montréal, H2X 4A7	14150	England
Canada	USA	UK

To order books:
In Canada: (phone) 1-800-565-9523 (fax) 1-800-221-9985
email: utpbooks@utpress.utoronto.ca

In United States: (phone) 1-800-283-3572 (fax) 1-651-917-6406

In the UK & Europe: (phone) London 44 (0)20 8986-4854 (fax) 44 (0)20 8533-5821
email: order@centralbooks.com

Our Web Site address: http://www.web.net/blackrosebooks

A publication of the Institute of Policy Alternatives of Montréal (IPAM)

Printed in Canada

CONTENTS

to David, William and Abram

ACKNOWLEDGMENTS

THIS BOOK WOULD NOT HAVE BEEN POSSIBLE WERE IT not for the enormous efforts of historians who went to primary source materials such as diaries, letters, archived documents and newspapers as well as other secondary sources to write histories of the war period that included the actions and the voices of ordinary people. In particular I am indebted to Gabriel Kolko, Tim Mason, Sergio Bologna, Ian Kershaw, Detlev Peukert, Andrew Gordon, Robert Service, Nicolas Werth, Jeremy Brecher, Hugh Thomas, John W. Dower, and Thomas Fleming. This book would also not have been possible without the inspiration and personal encouragement I received from David Stratman, whose book, *We CAN Change The World*, gave me the confidence to challenge the standard story of the origin and significance of World War Two.

WORLD WAR TWO **POSTERS**

In order to rally support for the war effort and defuse discontent, all governments knew that to win the 'hearts and minds' of their people was imperative. Relying on the immediate emotional appeal of posters, aggressive propaganda campaigns were launched—the form and content of which, meant to control and discourage discussion or dissent.

United States

United States

United States

United States

Germany ("The Reich will never be destroyed if you are united and loyal.")

United States

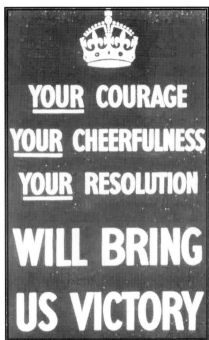

Great Britain

United States

Unites States

Germany ("Mother fight for your children.")

Canada

United States

United States

Great Britain

Canada

Italy ("The enemy listens here, be silent.")

Germany ("The enemy is listening.")

United States

United States

United States

United States

Germany ("The Jew, the inciter of war, the prolonger of war.")

United States

France

United States

United States

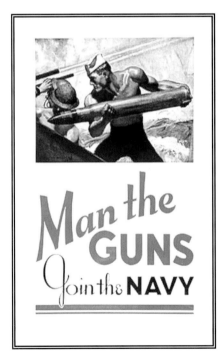

United States

Canada

I INTRODUCTION

FIFTY-FIVE MILLION PEOPLE—TWENTY-FIVE MILLION SOLDIERS and thirty million civilians—died in the second world war, not counting more than five million Jews and possibly a half-million Gypsies whom the Nazis singled out to kill during the Holocaust. The Soviet Union lost more than 20 million lives, China 13 million, Germany 7.3 million, Poland 5.4 million, Japan 2.1 million, Yugoslavia 1.6 million, Romania 0.7 million, France 0.6 million, the British Empire and Commonwealth 0.5 million, the United States 0.4 million, Italy 0.4 million, Hungary 0.4 million and Czechoslovakia 0.3 million.[1] Whole cities were bombed for the express purpose of killing civilians by the hundreds of thousands. And yet this war is known as "the good war" on the grounds that the aim of the Allied nations of Great Britain, the United States, the Soviet Union and China, and the outcome of the war, was to save the world from being enslaved by the Axis (Fascist[2]) nations of Germany, Italy and Japan who intended to establish a "master race" tyranny worse than anything the world had ever seen. But there weren't just two possible outcomes of the war—an Axis or an Allied victory; there was a third possibility that many people fought for and which the leaders of both the Allied and Axis governments opposed—a seizure of power by ordinary working people, and the creation of a very different kind of society from one dominated by wealthy and powerful elites. Many working people in the United States, and in Resistance movements against the Nazis in Europe and against the Japanese invaders in Asia, fought for this goal, and were attacked not only by Fascists, but by the British and American and Soviet governments.

The films, books and television shows about World War II that are currently so prevalent in the United States tell a story of the war which fits into the officially approved myth—that the leaders of capitalism in the West defended people against those who would oppress them. The lesson we are told to draw from the official mythology of WWII is that the world will be ruled either by ultra-Evil forces like Fascism (or Communism or Terrorism), or by the leaders of Western capitalism who, for all of their faults, are our protectors against the far worse alternative. In the name of preventing the triumph of ultra-Evil, we are required to give up all hope for a humane society that is based on equality, democracy and solidarity instead of corporate power, inequality and competition. We are told to renounce the very idea of democratic revolution. Everything that capitalist leaders are doing to strengthen their control over working people, we are supposed to accept as the price we must pay to avoid a greater evil. The corporate leaders who are depriving workers of job security by outsourcing jobs and moving capital and factories around the world to set whole nations of workers in competition with one another, and the governments and multinational corporations who, under cover of "free trade," are compelling workers in "under-developed" nations to work so hard and for so little pay in sweat shops, that we are now hearing of teenage girls in China literally dropping dead from exhaustion in Western-owned factories making things like stuffed animal toys—these elites are cast by the mythology of WWII as our past champions against Fascism and, by extension, our protectors against the "real" enemy today.

We need to penetrate the myths to reveal what World War II was truly about. To create a democratic alternative to our increasingly undemocratic and unequal world, we need to understand why the "good war" story is a myth and how that myth is used today as a central legitimizing idea for capitalism. Beneath the layers of myth is a story of World War II that reveals revolutionary possibilities for making a far better world than what Fascists, Communists or liberal capitalists will ever willingly allow.

Before the fall of Communism the masters of our "new world order" claimed the moral high ground by pointing to the "Evil Empire" as the "only alternative." After Communism's demise, capitalists stood more exposed than ever as the ones responsible for the trampling of democracy and equality. Increasingly larger and more explicitly anti-capitalist demonstrations against the World Trade Organization occurred in cities around the world from Seattle to Genoa, forming the basis of an internationalist and potentially revolutionary movement. Corporate and government leaders can barely conceal their delight that "Terrorism" has emerged just in the nick of time to take on the role previously played by Communism. Once again they have an enemy frightful enough to make them look good in comparison. The "war against terrorism," which President Bush tells us will last for decades, and in which, he warns us, "You are either with us or against us,"[3] provides him the perfect pretext to restrict the rights and freedoms of ordinary people in the United States, to question the patriotism of workers who go on strike or of anybody who dissents from the official dogma, and to send armed forces to attack people anywhere in the world who are hostile to U.S. corporate power.

The ideological framework that our leaders use to justify this brave new world is based on the mythology that enabled Allied leaders during WWII to use people's rightful hatred of Fascism to mobilize them for goals that had nothing to do with defeating Fascism. By labeling Fascism simply as "Evil," (a concept divorced from any concrete social and political context), the mythology hid the role of Fascism as a means by which German and Japanese upper classes suppressed their own working classes. This concealment of Fascism's class nature was, as I shall demonstrate, necessary for leaders like Franklin Delano Roosevelt, because without it they would not have been able to carry out their hidden agenda—to attack working people at home and abroad, all under the cover of fighting "the good war."

After the First World War, people everywhere were disgusted by the carnage of war and cynical that it had only been fought for ulterior motives of war-profiteers and others. During WWII world leaders told their people that *this* war was different because it was, depending on the nation in question, either for the everlasting glory and redemption of the race, or for the defeat of the greatest evil that ever existed. The basic elements of the Allies' WWII ideology are employed as much today as in the past: that there is a supremely "Evil" threat with motives so irrational that only its "evilness" can explain them; that the threat is strictly foreign, and its defeat therefore requires that we all unite with our leaders; that solidarity, patriotism and loyalty mean supporting every action and making every sacrifice demanded by our leaders because nothing short of all-out war will suffice. ("Evil" can never be appeased, so we must never repeat the folly of "Munich.") The current version of this ideology merely substitutes for Hitler a Saddam Hussein or an Osama bin Laden. Thus, George W. Bush declared shortly after the September 11 attack on the Pentagon and World Trade Center: "What happened at Pearl Harbor was the start of a long and terrible war for America. Yet out of that surprise attack grew a steadfast resolve that made America freedom's defender. And that mission, our great calling, continues to this hour as the brave men and women of our military fight the forces of terror in Afghanistan and around the world."[4] World War II is central to the way we are told to understand our world today.

How successfully we meet the challenge posed by corporate and government leaders' attacks on working people during our new century's "war against terrorism" will determine the future of the human race—will we be forever pitted against each other in a dog-eat-dog competition overseen by the world's financial plutocracy, forced to accept outrageous inequalities in living standards,

health care, education and justice, and sent to fight and kill each other in wars
whose true purpose we are never told, or will we create a very different and humane world? The future is ours to determine. But until we get the past straight,
it is hard to get a handle on the future. We need clarity about World War II.

TWO VERY DIFFERENT VIEWS OF THE WAR

There is a standard story of the war, an official view—the one we have all been
taught—and a very different view presented here. The official view is prevalent
not because it is right but because history is written by the victors. The alternative view presented here—what I will refer to in this book as the "social control" view because it understands elite actions in the war primarily as an
attempt to control ordinary people—is based on understanding what ordinary
people in countries like Germany and Japan and the United States were really
like—what they wanted in life and what they were striving for, what they believed was right and what they felt was wrong; also who opposed them, why
and how. This is what makes it possible to truly understand the war, and this is
precisely what the official view covers up with stereotypes and lies. This book
looks at three major myths about the war, each of which is a reflection of the
key element in the official view—the notion that in the great contest between
good and evil that was called forth by Fascist aggression, whole nations were
on one side or the other, and hence the war was for all practical purposes a
conflict of nation versus nation. These myths are outlined below, and in the
following sections this book explores them in greater detail by looking at the
history of the war period from a working class point of view.

The official view of the war is based on denying a simple and powerful
fact: within every country, societies during World War II were (like today) divided into different classes with conflicting values and desires. In the official
view, all we hear about is nations—"Americans," or "Japanese" ("Japs" as they
were called then), or "Germans" etc.—as if they were an undifferentiated mass
of people on behalf of whom their government was fighting the war; as if the entire population had the same stake in the outcome; and as if, depending on the
country, they were all either "our friends" or "the enemy."[5] This profoundly deceptive view of the world can be summed up in one word—nationalism. The
fact is that regardless of the country, ordinary people hated being bossed
around and exploited; they didn't like it when a few people got special privileges; they wanted things to be more equal and democratic, and they fought to

make their desires reality to the extent they thought possible. And in every country there was an elite class who bossed people around and exploited them, enjoyed special privileges, controlled the government, wanted an extremely unequal and undemocratic world, and—when they felt their grip on power slipping—deliberately pushed their people into a war as a means of controlling them.

Intense war-time propaganda about Japan being "one hundred million hearts beating as one" and Germans being all pro-Nazi "militarists" created an intimidating atmosphere for Americans. Anyone who, from experience and commonsense, thought that maybe ordinary people in "enemy" nations were not fundamentally different from most Americans with respect to basic values and hopes, must have either wondered if they were crazy for even having such thoughts, or at least thought twice about expressing their opinions out loud, for fear of seeming unpatriotic. During the war business and government leaders promoted nationalism intensely; they called on Americans to be "patriotic" and "loyal," and they always defined "loyalty" as loyalty to the American government and corporate elite, not fellow working people of all countries. This is how the elite used nationalism during the war to control people.

Myth #1—Conflicts between nations caused the war. In the official view "the Germans" and "the Japanese" were inspired by Fascist demagogues to believe they were superior races, and they set out to conquer other nations. In response, the Allies declared war on the Fascists to save the world from tyrannical thugs. This view covers up the fact that German and Japanese Fascists embarked on their aggressive wars to prevent working class revolutions in their own countries. Before the war, elites in Germany and Japan were so frightened by the possibility of working class revolutions that they believed that the only thing that could save them was extreme anti-working class repression. The methods they used were draconian. In Japan they dissolved the labor unions and arrested dissidents. In Germany they placed working class leaders and all other dissidents, (and, later, Jews) in concentration camps. This repression required a war-like environment so that "national defense" could be used as a pretext. For the Japanese elite, the "threat" was the white race; for Hitler the "threat" was Britain, France, Bolsheviks, and Jews. War, in other words, played a very functional role for these elites to control their own rebellious working classes. German and Japanese Fascists used racist propaganda not because it was particularly effective among their general populations but rather because it served to recruit and motivate a relatively small minority of followers whom the Fascists relied upon to attack working people and any-body else who dissented.

The official view also covers up the reason why the leaders of the Allied nations entered the war. Saving the world from tyranny had nothing to do with it. Except insofar as public opinion had to be taken into account, Ameri-can, British and Soviet leaders did not consider the brutality of the Nazis and the Japanese militarists against working people to be an important factor in judging whether to ally with these Fascist nations or not. Stalin for example, on April 18, 1939, tried to ally with France and Great Britain against Germany[6] only to sign a non-aggression pact with Hitler four months later on August 23. Within the United States and within Great Britain, there were major disagree-ments among the elite about whether to ally with the Soviet Union against Germany and Japan or to ally with Germany and Japan against the Soviet Un-ion. Many of the British nobility were openly anti-Semitic and pro-Nazi, in-cluding the Duke of Westminster, the wealthiest man in the Empire.[7] The British Prime Minister, Neville Chamberlain, was inclined to see Nazi Ger-many as a positive force if it attacked the Soviet Union and Eastern Europe and left Western Europe alone, and he worked hard to encourage Hitler to do just that. (Earlier, in 1934, Chamberlain thought that Great Britain should ally with the Japanese militarists who had just invaded northern China, because they would threaten the Soviet Union.[8]) Churchill, on the other hand, thought it was necessary to ally with the Soviet Union against Hitler because he believed Hitler would attack the West. In the United States, people like Joseph Kennedy Sr. and Henry Ford (who owned Ford Motor Company) as well as the DuPonts (who controlled General Motors) admired Hitler and did not believe he posed a threat to U.S. power. Others, like President Franklin Roosevelt, dis-agreed and felt that the U.S. needed to fight Germany and Japan.

Despite their disagreements about whether to ally with Fascists or Com-munists, however, individuals on both sides of this issue served together in the same U.S. and British government administrations because they shared a com-mon and overriding fear. What they feared was working class revolution in their own countries especially, but also anywhere else in the world, including the obvious places such as the British Empire and the American Pacific sphere of influence centered in the Philippines. Furthermore, American and British leaders found it natural to ally with Stalin because he feared working class revo-lution in his own country as much as the Western leaders feared it in theirs. In the pre-war years working people in the Allied nations posed a revolutionary threat to their supposedly democratic ruling elites. Britain's two future Prime Ministers, Winston Churchill and Neville Chamberlain, greatly disagreed about what stance to take towards Hitler, but their responses to the 1926 General Strike in Great Britain reveal their common fear of the British working class. Winston Churchill, Chancellor of the Exchequer (Treasurer) at the time, called for generously paying auxiliary police to put down the strike and warned those in the government who disagreed that, "If we start arguing about petty details, we will have a tired-out police force, a dissipated army and bloody revolution." Neville Chamberlain, Minister of Health at the time, wrote of the strike, "constitutional government is fighting for its life...it would be the revolution [if the strikers won a victory] for the nominal leaders would be whirled away in an instant."[9] In the U.S. a wave of sit-down strikes during the Great Depression followed regional general strikes and violent confrontations between federal troops and armed workers, leading politicians and newspapers to say openly that they feared a revolution. Stalin's reign of terror in the 1930s was designed to make sure that workers and peasants were terrified of the government, because he feared that otherwise the peasants would revolt against their extreme exploitation in large collective farms and workers would revolt against the Bolshevik usurpation of the genuine power workers once held in the factories. This is why Stalin forcibly deported, between 1930 and 1931, 1.8 million peasants to inhospitable regions without sufficient supplies to survive, and why, in the Great Terror of 1937 to 1938, he executed (according to official records) 681,692 people. In the years leading up to the war, the leaders of Great Britain, the Soviet Union and the United States were extremely worried about the possibility of domestic revolution that would end their very existence as ruling elites. Nothing else could possibly concern them as much as this.

FDR led the U.S. into the war because he knew there was no other way to control the American working class that was growing increasingly revolutionary. Just as for the Fascist leaders, the function of war for American leaders was not to defend against a threat from foreign nations, but to serve the needs of domestic social control. The repression against working people in the Allied nations during the war—making unions promise not to strike in the U.S. for example—could not have been implemented without a war and the justification of "national defense." Only in wartime can capitalist leaders hope to rally rebellious working people behind their corporate and government masters. Roosevelt used lies and manipulation to get the United States into the war, even secretly provoking the Japanese to attack the U.S., because he had an ulterior motive that he dared not openly reveal—social control, not national defense. If the Fascists hadn't presented themselves as the perfect enemy, some other "crisis" would no doubt have been invoked. The official view of the war covers up the shared anti-working class goals of the Allies and the Fascists. But the origin of the war cannot be fully understood with this framework. (See section II, "Origins of the War" for further discussion.)

Myth #2—The top priority goal of the Allies in Europe and Asia was to defeat the Fascists. What were the actual aims of the Allied government and military leaders overseas during the war? We're told that their objective was simple: defeat the Fascist military forces as quickly as possible. What we're not told is why, in France, Italy, Greece, Yugoslavia, the Philippines, and China, to name just some examples, the Allies treated the anti-Fascist working class Resistance armies as hostile (in many cases attacking them militarily) and gave support to the very people who collaborated with the Fascists. The official view covers this up because otherwise it would be more evident what the real goal of Allied leaders was during the war. The goal of the Allied leaders (including Stalin with respect to Eastern Europe and East Asia) outside their own borders, a goal which of course they never revealed to the men and women who died or lost loved ones fighting in the war, was to replace Fascist control of the working class with U.S. or British control, the top priority being to prevent working people themselves from seizing power anywhere. Whenever the choice was between supporting working class power or Fascist power, the Allies chose Fascist power. (See section III, "Allied War Objectives In Europe And Asia" for a closer look at how and why the Allies fought the anti-Fascist Resistance movements in the occupied nations.)

Myth #3—The Allies bombed civilians to defeat the Fascists. Why did the Allies use incendiary bombs (conventional bombs at first and later atomic bombs) to deliberately kill hundreds of thousands of German and Japanese civilians in cities some of which were acknowledged not to be militarily significant targets? The official explanation is that the slaughter was necessary to make "Germany" and "Japan" admit defeat and surrender. Covered up by this explanation is the fact that many and arguably most of the people who were killed by the bombs were opposed to both their Fascist governments and the war. They would have welcomed help in overthrowing their governments if they had been convinced that the help was from people who were clearly on the side of working people and not just another elite power that might be even worse. But instead of helping these people fight the Fascists, Allied leaders tried to kill them. Roosevelt and Churchill viewed German and Japanese civilians as the enemy for the same reason they viewed anti-Fascist workers and peasants in countries like Italy and Greece and China and rebellious workers in their own countries as the enemy—the shared aspirations of ordinary people, and the possibility they would support each other across national and racial divisions, threatened elite power and made it necessary that they be cowed into submission and convinced that they were each other's mortal enemy. Fighting Fascism was the excuse, not the reason why Allied leaders killed so many civilians during the war. (See section IV, "Why The Allies Bombed Civilians" for a close look at working people in Germany and Japan during the war years and discussion of why the Allies were so intent on killing them.)

Notes

1. This enumeration of fatalities is not exhaustive and it is necessarily only an estimate. Accounts differ on the number of deaths in World War II. Martin Gilbert, in *The Second World War: A Complete History* (revised edition, 1989, Henry Holt & Co, New York) says "more than forty-six million soldiers and civilians perished" (pg. 1). See: "World War II," Microsoft®® Encarta®® Online Encyclopedia, http://encarta. msn.com/encnet/refpages/RefArticle.aspx?refid=761563737&para=131#p131

2. In this book I use the word "Fascist" very loosely to refer to the rulers of the Axis nations, without intending to define fascism precisely, and with apologies to scholars who aim to give the word a precise definition and critically evaluate whether, for example, the Japanese government during WWII is rightly labeled "fascist."

3. CNN, November 6, 2001.

4. American Forces Press Service, Dec. 7, 2001, http://www.defenselink.mil/news/ Dec2001/ n12072001_200112074.html

5. David Kaiser, in *Politics and War: European Conflict from Philip II to Hitler*, speaks of "one of the essential beliefs of modern politics: that governments fight wars on behalf of the whole people, and that the people share an enormous stake in the outcome." [p. 280]

6. *Ibid.*, 219.

7. *Ibid.*, 224.

8. Clement Leibovitz and Alvin Finkel, p. 59 regarding Chamberlain's views on Japanese aggression on China, and the entire book on Chamberlain's desire to encourage Hitler to attack the Soviet Union.

9. Clement Leibovitz and Alvin Finkel, *In Our Time: The Chamberlain-Hitler Collusion*, Monthly Press Review, New York, 1997, pp.46-7.

II ORIGINS OF THE WAR

THE OFFICIAL STORY OF WORLD WAR TWO EXPLAINS the war's origins entirely in terms of conflicts between the various nations: Axis nations aiming to rule over the world as a master race verus Allied nations determined to protect freedom, or Axis nations imposing dictatorships versus Allied nations defending democracy (this latter view requires an especially great leap of faith when it comes to explaining why Stalin fought with the Allies against Hitler.) The war is also described sometimes in so-called *Realpolitik* terms, as a conflict of material interests between the nations, regardless of the type of governments they had. Nowhere does the class conflict between working people and elites enter into the official explanation of why nations went to war, especially not class conflict within the warring nations themselves. And yet, there is strong evidence for this social control view of the war's origins—that the reason Germany, Japan and even the United States went to war at this time was largely because their leaders viewed war as the only solution to their number one problem: how to keep control over their own working classes. The ruling classes of these nations certainly considered other factors—the danger of losing colonies or spheres of influence to the elites of other nations, the risk of losing a war and being overthrown (as happened to Tsar Nicholas II of Russia during WWI), and the threat of working class revolutions in their colonies and spheres of influence, to cite just a few concerns—but staying in power inside their own nation was of necessity their most important objective and in this section we will see how they came to use war to accomplish it.

Are there "smoking gun" admissions by the rulers of any nation in World War II that they went to war to suppress domestic working class revolution? There are actually some cases where the elite in Germany and Japan are recorded speaking relatively candidly about how this was their real reason for going to war. U.S. rulers, on the other hand, seem to have been more discreet, perhaps because they knew this was necessary in a system in which the legitimacy of their authority required that they win elections and tolerate some exposure in the press. The bulk of the evidence for the social control view of the origin of the war presented here is the overall historical record and logical inference from it.

In all the nations that had fought in World War I, the years after that war leading up to the Second World War witnessed extremely sharp class struggles that made the elites believe that extraordinary measures were necessary to hold onto power. The Great Depression didn't take place until after these struggles were well under way, but it added fuel to the fire. The Soviet Union aside, the Great Depression made the elites even more anxious about their ability to control the economy, and therefore people, with conventional methods. We will look at events inside Germany, Japan and the United States prior to and during World War II that reveal three key facts that the official view of the war covers up: 1) class conflict in these pre-war years was raging at an extreme level that threatened elite power; 2) the elites were clearly very frightened by the possibility of working class revolution in their own countries, and 3) the elites used the war as a pretext for suppressing their own workers.

The actions of the leaders of Germany, Japan and the United States at the beginning of World War II were not primarily driven by foreign policy considerations, either aggressive or defensive; for these leaders the war was primarily a solution to their far more pressing domestic problem. This is a story we have not been told. In the standard story, for example, the United States was forced into the war because of Japan's unexpected attack on Pearl Harbor. But in the weeks prior to Pearl Harbor, President Roosevelt, as we shall see, cut off the flow of oil from the U.S. to Japan and abruptly halted negotiations on the issue at the same time that he knew, from intelligence sources, that this policy would lead inevitably and imminently to Japan's rulers launching a war against the United States. Long before Pearl Harbor, FDR intended to use a Japanese attack on the U.S. to convince Americans to wage a war in Asia and Europe.

While the leaders of Great Britain, France and Italy were also concerned about containing their own working classes, this discussion does not focus on their role in the origin of the war, in part to limit the scope of this work, and in part because the story of these nations with respect to the fundamental factors leading to the war is not essentially different from the story which emerges from looking at the United States, Germany and Japan.

In the light of the facts we will examine in Germany, Japan and the US, it will be difficult to continue to believe the official story of the origin of the war—that the warring governments were acting on behalf of their own populations, that the German and Japanese people just happened to choose to be aggressive, and that America's leaders were shocked by Pearl Harbor into seeing the need to stop Fascist aggression. One would have to insist that national rulers who were frightened by domestic threats to their power and who used the war to defeat those threats nonetheless made the decision to go to war for entirely unrelated reasons. This view is especially unconvincing because, as we shall see in section III, "Allied War Objectives In Europe And Asia," the Allies' stated goal—defeating the Fascists and liberating their victims—does not fit the facts. We also look closely at the Soviet Union between the First and Second World War, not primarily to understand the origin of the war, but to understand the origin of Stalin's key role as an anti-working class force in the anti-Fascist alliance during the war.

GERMANY

That Hitler viewed war as a means of social control is indicated by his recorded remarks to his military leaders in November 1937 (below) in which he argued that war—i.e., "solving the need for space (*Lebensraum*)"—was necessary to maintain the Nazi totalitarian regime—i.e., "Germany's future"—because in the current peacetime the people's enthusiasm for Nazi rule and their willingness to sacrifice for the glory of the Aryan race—i.e., "Germanism"—was in decline and that people were instead pursuing working class goals—i.e., "sterility was setting in":

> To arrest the decline of Germanism (*Deutschtum*) in Austria and Czechoslovakia was as little possible as to maintain the present level in Germany itself. Instead of increase, sterility was setting in, and in its train disorders of a social character must arise in course of time, since political and ideological ideas remain effective only as long as they furnish the basis for the realization of the essential vital demands of a people. Germany's future was therefore wholly conditional upon solving the need for space (*Lebensraum*.)[1]

To fully appreciate the meaning of Hitler's words, we must look at the sweep of events in Germany before and after these remarks.

World War I—Rebellion In The Ranks

In August, 1918, WWI was nearly over. German troops knew Germany was the loser, and they detested their generals and the entire German elite who refused to negotiate a peace and instead ordered the soldiers to continue their suffering and dying. In October, "sailors on warships based at Kiel refused to obey orders, leading to arrests, violence involving about 40,000 partly armed soldiers, sailors, and workers, and a soldiers' and sailors' council takeover of Kiel on November 4," which in turn "stimulated the formation of soldiers' and workers' councils throughout Germany." The troops took it upon themselves "to surrender in large numbers, simply return home, or create councils far more extensive than those that existed among the workers." For a short time "the streets of many cities were the scene of continuous meetings and demonstrations."[2] The Kaiser was forced to abdicate (leading many to refer to this period as the "Revolution of 1918") and the military chiefs explicitly calculated that the only way to stop a real working class revolution was to install the most conservative leaders from the working class-based socialist party—the Social Democratic Party (SPD)—in power in a new parliamentary type of government that came to be known as the Weimar Republic.

The subsequent years of the Weimar Republic were marked by growing class war in the electoral arena and in the streets. There were two parties whose support came almost entirely from the industrial working class, each with associated trade unions and even militias. The SPD was led by Marxists who supported the German war effort in World War I, did not call for revolution against capitalism, and filled many positions in the government of the Weimar Republic. The Communist Party (KPD) was smaller and it was led by Marxists who followed the Bolshevik leaders of the Communist revolution in Russia (Lenin and later Stalin); the KPD opposed Germany's fighting World War I, and it fought the Weimar Republic with calls for revolution against capitalism on the model of the very undemocratic Soviet Union. (See the section, "Soviet Union.")

Workers Versus Nazis In The Weimar Republic

The working class militia organizations defended against attacks from government controlled anti-working class forces such as the Free Corps[3] (Freikorps) as well as the Nazi's private SA militia. On May Day 1929 the Communist Party challenged a ban declared on demonstrations in the streets of Berlin by the Berlin police chief (who was a member of the Social Democratic Party.) The Communists announced that, "We do not accept the ban. We shall demonstrate in the streets, and if the police try to attack we shall call a general strike for the next day." The police made a deliberate attack and violence broke out. The Communists called for a general strike and were pressured by many militant workers to distribute weapons, which they did not do. But workers set up barricades in the quarters of Neukolln and Wedding and the police had to lay siege to the areas for three days before they were able to restore capitalist "order." Thirty demonstrators died in the fighting and 200 were wounded; 1,200 people were arrested. The Prussian Minister of the Interior used the event as an excuse to ban the mass organizations of the Communist Party.[4]

In the large May Day struggle and in numerous smaller fights the working class asserted its control over entire local areas. The Communist Party was a paramilitary organization and it had mass organizations that were also paramilitary and focused on self-defense of working class neighborhoods. One such organization was the *Kampfbund gegen den Faschismus*, which at the end of 1931 had 100,000 members, 7,000 in Berlin. Communist party membership itself rose from 135,000 in 1929 to 381,000 in 1931.[5] In addition, 400,000 workers in the building trades, textiles, and later engineering and mining, belonged to another radical and militant organization—the anarcho-syndicalist *Freie Arbeiter Union.*[6]

In the German province of Prussia alone, between June 1 and June 20, 1932, there were 461 pitched street battles between workers and Nazis, in which eighty-two people died and four hundred were wounded.[7] In his classic account, *The Nazi Seizure of Power: The Experience of a Single German Town*, William Allen gives a detailed account of events from 1930 to 1935 in a small German rural town with a population of 10,000 mainly middle-class Lutherans. Allen describes a typical incident. Three weeks before the July 31, 1932 Reichstag elections, twenty-five men in the Reichsbanner (a Social Democratic Party militia organization) got into a fight with sixty Nazi SA (militia) men while crossing a bridge in opposite directions. Homeless people in a nearby Army compound rushed to help the Reichsbanner, and when police arrived there was a surging crowd of about eighty persons pelting the Nazis with stones.[8]

In the years of the Great Depression (1929-33) when unemployment rose to 30 percent, fighting broke out daily between the unemployed and government officials. The welfare system was designed to humiliate the unemployed and make them submissive. Unemployed people had to report sometimes daily and at least monthly to the authorities and beg. Welfare recipients went from being submissive, however, to being aggressive, and were backed up by the Communist Party. It was an everyday occurrence for welfare claimants to get into "episodes of assaults, clashes and threats to benefits officers, and the police repeatedly being called."[9]

In addition to the police, the Nazis (not yet in control of the government) made a concerted attempt to subjugate workers in the working class neighborhoods. Nazi gangs threatened the owners of taverns where unemployed workers gathered, demanding that the taverns cater to Nazis and not the workers.[10] Nazi SA men would walk into tenement houses and urinate in the hallways and wave their pistols at children and threaten to shoot into people's windows.[11] Against such criminality, the people in the poorest quarters preferred to organize vigilante squads rather than ask the equally hated police to intervene. And similarly, people organized groups to physically defend people being evicted.

Hitler Was Never Elected

Hitler, contrary to today's popular misconception, was never elected; he was appointed Chancellor by President Hindenburg on January 30, 1933. (The germ of truth in the misconception is that Hitler did in fact become Chancellor constitutionally, since the constitution permitted the President to appoint the Chancellor.) The only times Germans had an opportunity to vote for Hitler, the Nazi leader failed to capture even a plurality: In the Presidential election March 13, 1932 there were four candidates including the incumbent Hindenburg, and Hitler received only 30.1% of the vote versus Hindenburg's 49.6%. In the runoff election April 10 between Hindenburg, Hitler and a third candidate, Hindenburg received 53% versus Hitler's 36.8% of the votes.[12]

In the November 6, 1932 Reichstag (Parliament) election, the last one before President Hindenburg appointed Hitler Chancellor, the Nazis won 196 deputies, while the Social Democratic Party and the Communist Party—both Marxist, both rooted in the working class, and both explicitly opposed to anti-Semitism[13]—won between them 25 more seats than the Nazis for a total of 221 seats.[14] After this election the Nazis were in steep decline. The party was literally bankrupt and unable to make the payroll of its functionaries or pay its printers. In provincial elections in Thuringia on December 3, the Nazi's vote dropped by 40 percent. Gregor Strasser, a top Nazi who had led the party during Hitler's time in prison, concluded that the Nazis would never obtain office through the ballot.[15] In his diary the last week of December, Hitler's right-hand man, Joseph Goebbels, wrote: "[T]he future looks dark and gloomy; all prospects and hope have quite disappeared."[16] This was only two months before Hindenburg, in response to pressure from industrialists, bankers, large landowners and military leaders,[17] would appoint Hitler Chancellor.

Germany's rulers feared not only working class votes, but a general strike that could lead to civil war. On December 2, General Kurt von Schleicher told the current Chancellor, Franz von Papen, "The police and armed services could not guarantee to maintain transport and supply services in the event of a general strike, nor would they be able to ensure law and order in the event of a civil war."[18] Hindenburg subsequently dismissed Papen and appointed Schleicher as Chancellor, telling Papen: "I am too old and have been through too much to accept the responsibility for a civil war. Our only hope is to let Schleicher try his luck."[19]

Schleicher, responding to the same Great Depression and the same kind of working class militancy that forced FDR to offer Americans a New Deal, tried to pacify the German working class with similar promises, but workers did not trust him. After just fifty-seven days in office the elite decided that only Hitler could do what had to be done. Twenty-six days before Hitler's appointment as Chancellor, Baron Kurt von Schroeder, a Cologne banker, had a private meeting with Hitler, three other Nazi leaders, and Papen. During this meeting Papen and Hitler agreed that Social Democrats, Communists, and Jews had to be eliminated from leading positions in Germany, and Schroeder promised that German business interests would take over the debts of the Nazi Party. Twelve days later, Goebbels reported that the financial position of the (previously bankrupt) Nazi party had "fundamentally improved overnight."[20]

When members of Germany's elite prevailed upon Hindenburg to appoint Hitler as Chancellor January 30, 1933, the reason was because they were convinced that only Hitler would do whatever was necessary decisively to defeat workers' power.

Chancellor Hitler Fails To Tame His Workers

Within two months of being appointed Chancellor, Hitler arrested four thousand leaders of the Communist Party along with others in the Social Democratic and liberal parties, including members of the Reichstag, and carted them off to be tortured and beaten. Hitler got away with this because of a suspiciously convenient fire that burned down the Reichstag building February 27, 1933. (Although the trial of the suspected arsonist came too late to affect events, historian William Shirer writes that "the trial, despite the subserviency of the court to the Nazi authorities, cast a great deal of suspicion on Goering and the Nazis.") Hitler used the fire as an excuse to gag and arrest his opponents. The Nazis accused a communist of starting the fire, and did everything they could to create panic and fear of Communists. The day after the fire Hitler got President Hindenburg to sign a decree "For the Protection of the People and the State." Shirer notes the act was described as a "defensive measure against Communist acts of violence endangering the state." It imposed restrictions on personal liberty, free expression of opinion including freedom of the press, rights of assembly and association; and violations on the privacy of postal, telegraphic and telephonic communication. Also it declared that warrants for house searchers, orders for confiscations and restrictions on property were permissible beyond the pre-existing legal limits. And it imposed the death sentence for new categories of crime including "serious disturbances of the peace" by armed persons.

Hitler had scheduled elections to the Reichstag for the following week, March 5, and tried to use the fire to frighten Germans into believing that they had to vote for Nazis to prevent the Communists from taking over and completely destroying the nation. "Truckloads of storm troopers roared through the streets all over Germany, breaking into homes, rounding up victims and carting them off to S.A. barracks, where they were tortured and beaten. The Communist press and political meetings were suppressed; the Social Democrat newspapers and many liberal journals were suspended and the meetings of the democratic parties either banned or broken up. Only the Nazis and their Nationalist allies were permitted to campaign unmolested." Hitler naturally expected the Nazis to win handily. But in a show of resistance to the Nazis that is almost always overlooked by standard 21st century accounts, Germans under these extraordinary circumstances gave the Nazi Party only 44% of the total vote.[21] The Nazis could not obtain a majority even with Hitler installed as Chancellor and their opponents in prison!

On May 2, 1933 Nazis occupied all trade union headquarters, confiscated their funds, dissolved the unions, arrested the leaders and beat and sent many to concentration camps; any known working class radicals were put in prison camps or went into hiding. Hitler outlawed strikes, and appointed "labor trust-ees" to maintain "labor peace." Dr. Robert Ley, the man Hitler chose to take over the unions, promised "to restore absolute leadership to the natural leader of a factory—that is, the employer."[22] By July more than 25,000 enemies of the regime, mostly socialists and communists and not mainly Jews, were in concentration camps or prisons.[23] William Shirer writes that "the purpose of the concentration camps was not only to punish enemies of the regime but by their very existence to terrorize the people and deter them from even contemplating any resistance to Nazi rule."[24] By 1938 tens of thousands of working class leaders were in the concentration camps or prison and hundreds had been killed. Eventually the Nazis rounded up three million political prisoners.[25]

When the Nazis gained control of the government with Hitler's appointment as Chancellor, the unprecedented scale of repression against the working class meant that overt resistance became far more difficult and dangerous. "After 1934 the Gestapo system was refined and ruthless, also relatively unobtrusive"[26] in the sense of attacking individuals rather than groups acting publicly; it was used to arrest, incarcerate and torture any individuals whose behavior made it seem likely that they would organize or lead any form of mass protest. Any opposition to Nazi rule was illegal. Few underground organizations survived more than two years. The Gestapo used many informants and systematically tortured all suspects. The Gestapo appeared whenever workers went on strike, and from 1938 on it used terroristic surveillance over workers who were 'unreliable' at their jobs. The Nazis were so fearful of working class opposition at the factory level that they established 165 miniature concentration camps (*Arbeitserziehungslager*) attached to major industrial firms.[27] At the Folke-Wolfe aircraft factory accounts of workers describe the atmosphere as being one in which "it took only a minor infraction, a lateness, an unjustified absence or an angry word for a worker to end up in a concentration camp; thus it sometimes happened that one's workmates would disappear for months at a time, with no explanation offered, and when they returned they were obliged to maintain silence as to where they had been."[28] The Nazi police state was, as Timothy Mason describes it, "tactically and strategically always on the offensive."[29]

For the Nazis to carry out such extreme repression of the most radical and militant workers and at the same time neutralize opposition among the rest of the population to their unprecedented actions, they needed to play the "Reich in danger" card—claim they were only doing what was necessary for the security of the nation in a time of great peril from a grave external threat. Hitler identified this threat as Bolsheviks (i.e., Communists) and Jews and Britain and France, all of whom, he said, wanted Germany to remain weak and crippled by the Versailles Treaty imposed on Germany after World War I. Hitler said Germany had to go to war against these enemies to obtain the "living space (Lebensraum)" that the German race needed. To create the required warlike and intimidating atmosphere, Hitler began the systematic persecution of Communists and Jews and he began militarizing Germany and increasing arms production. For Germany to remain at peace was politically impossible for the Nazi regime, because the authority of the Fuehrer was based on the idea that the nation needed a strong leader to rally it and unify it against its national enemies. While the Nazis had in fact gone to war against the German working class, they needed the public to perceive it as a war against external enemies. War and the preparation for war were therefore a necessary part of domestic social control, rather than a means for obtaining foreign policy objectives. Hitler's war aims were thus always vague (Lebensraum) and never articulated as specific and limited objectives, because a war for limited objectives might conclude with a peace agreement, and the Nazis knew that peace and Nazism could not long coexist.

The history of Germany from 1933 to 1939 is essentially the story of how Hitler tried to mobilize Germans behind the Nazi vision of a Fuehrer-led master race setting out to enslave inferior races and solve its need for space by perpetual war, and how the German working class resisted this goal and fought for its own, very different goals. Hitler initially expected that he could build up sufficient weapons to successfully wage war in Europe by some time between 1943 and 1945.[30] In fact, the Fuehrer was forced to attack Czechoslovakia in October 1938 and, in what marks the beginning of World War Two, attack Poland September 1, 1939, when he did not have nearly enough weapons to defeat his enemies. The explanation lies in the nature of the struggle between Hitler and the German working class. The central problem Hitler (and the industrialists and aristocrats behind him) faced was that, on the one hand, he needed Germany to go to war in order to create an ideological framework for controlling the German working class; but on the other hand he could not initiate the war until he had greatly increased Germany's weapons stock, and doing this meant forcing workers to give up butter for guns which only increased their opposition to the regime and made them harder to control. The dilemma became especially acute after weapons production transformed the high unemployment of the Depression years into such a tight labor market that workers no longer feared losing their jobs. As we shall see, Hitler responded to this predicament by gambling that he could win quick *blitzkrieg* victories to plunder weapons and forced labor from conquered nations, thereby obtaining the social control benefits of war before risking the loss of social control that he feared would occur if he forced German workers to make sacrifices to arm Germany during peacetime. This is the context in which to understand what happened in Germany under Hitler in the 1930s.

Despite all of the Gestapo terror, workers did engage in some overt resistance to the Nazis and much covert resistance. A strike wave broke out between 1935 and 1936. There were at least 260 work stoppages, most on road building sites or other public works projects.[31] Then between January 1936 and July 1937 there were, according to a report by the Nazi trade union organization, *Deutsche Arbeitsfront (DAF)*, "more than 200 work stoppages...On June 25, 1936 236 workers in the Body Plant [of Opel in Russelsheim] went on strike. [At] Auto Union in Berlin...600 trim workers went on strike; and in the shipyards at Bremen...[a] Communist organizer, Ernst Novak, was arrested and tortured to death." Altogether during this period 11,687 people were arrested for strike actions.[32]

Even when unsuccessful in winning demands, the strikes built morale. An SDP member, reporting on a three hour work stoppage by glass workers at Bayerischer Wald in February 1937, said the job action was regarded by the workers themselves "as a moral victory which has given back to them again the feeling of their own strength...Nobody cut himself off and no one denounced [a fellow worker]; the Nazi bosses faced closed ranks which were not shaken by threats [and one worker said of the Nazis] 'This lot should just not play about with us. The day will come when we don't give in any longer.' "[33]

By the end of the 1930s thousands of young people were resisting the Nazis by avoiding mandatory membership or activities in the Hitler Youth. An SDP informant reported that, "Young people are causing the relevant Party agencies much anxiety. Both boys and girls are trying by every means possible to dodge the year of Land Service. In Greater Berlin in May 1938 a total of 918 boys and 268 girls were reported missing, having secretly run away from home because they did not want to go away on Land Service. Police patrols in the Grunewald, the Tegel Forest and the Wannsee district periodically round up whole lorry-loads of young people, some Berliners, some from the provinces."[34]

Blitzkrieg—How To Wage War When Your Workers Won't Produce Weapons

The Nazi's great fear of the working class was the key reason why the regime was unable to increase armaments production as rapidly as it wished in the late 1930s. By 1937 the regime had reversed the unemployment of the Depression through greatly increased government spending on armaments and there was now a labor shortage, especially in the key industries of construction, metals and mining.[35] "In December 1938 the Minister of Labor announced the economy was short about one million workers."[36] Workers took advantage of the labor shortage by reducing their productivity, causing the Nazis to report a decline in "work-morale." "The owner of a tannery in Dresden described the attitude of his workers as a 'strike in disguise.' "[37] Other employers complained of a declining discipline at work, of open rebelliousness, unpunctuality, absenteeism and poor performance.[38]

As all German and foreign observers, including the Gestapo, agreed, the attempt to make the German population enthusiastic about the political aims of the Nazis, and to "enlist their spontaneous and obedient cooperation, was completely unsuccessful."[39] As a result, the regime realized that the only way it could keep any hold on the working class was by not provoking it with any severe reduction in its material standard of living. Hitler by now understood that relying on German workers to produce all of the weapons for the coming war was not possible, but that the war was nonetheless necessary and therefore some other way had to be found to make it possible. In May, 1939 the Fuehrer made it clear that if he couldn't rely on German workers to arm Germany then he would use war itself to capture the weapons needed to wage war, declaring:

> The ideological problems have been solved by the mass of 80,000,000 people. The economic problems must also be solved. To create the economic conditions necessary for this is a task no German can disregard. The solution to the problems demands courage. We must not allow the principle to prevail that one can accommodate oneself to the circumstances and thus shirk the solution of problems. The circumstances must rather be adapted to suit the demands. This is not possible without breaking into other countries or attacking other people's property.[40]

The refusal of German workers to respond to Nazi exhortations to produce for war was evident, for example, in the government's failure to solve the labor shortage problem. The obvious solution was to conscript women into the labor force, but the regime knew this was politically impossible. In fact, the government was forced by a fear of low morale among its soldiers in the field to introduce very high levels of support payments for their families, which led to "a steep rise in the number of marriages in the late summer of 1939" and the mass desertion of these new "war wives" from their jobs, resulting in a drop in the number of women in the workforce of 450,000 between June 1939 and March 1940.[41] When the Nazis finally tried to shift production from butter to guns at the outbreak of the war they abolished paid holidays and higher rates for overtime pay. But this "produced so much bitter discontent and absenteeism" that the "decrees had to be annulled in the winter of 1939-40."[42] Hitler's generals worried that the uncooperative German working class was making the pursuit of war impossible. General Thomas, in November 1939, remarked that "we are never going to conquer England with radios, vacuum cleaners and kitchen equipment."[43] In his detailed discussion of this topic, the historian Timothy Mason concludes, "Until the political leadership was in a position to fall back on that deceptive slogan, 'Reich in danger,' it did not have the courage to present its people with the bill for its rearmament policy."[44] David Kaiser, an historian at the U.S. Naval War College, agrees, writing that arms production in the first years of war from 1939 to 1941 "increased far more rapidly than at any other time during the Nazi regime. The increase, moreover, was accomplished largely at the expense of domestic consumption, which dropped significantly, supporting Mason's claim that the war enabled the government to demand more from the civilian population."[45]

Even the 'Reich in danger' slogan had a limited effect in bringing the working class to heel. In September, 1939 the government tried to set the German economy on wartime conditions by imposing a wartime income tax that would affect 40% of the industrial working class, abolish all wage supplements, cut wages 10% on average across the board, cancel all holiday entitlements, and restrict companies' social obligations to their workers. But these measures died by December of the same year as the regime realized how politically unpopular they were. The working class opposed the war and these economic attacks on their lives by a wave of passive resistance. Pre-war indiscipline escalated to what one government official called "sabotage" and "the government, taken aback and deeply worried about the reliability of the home front as well as the supplying of the Wehrmacht, caved in immediately."[46] The resistance of the German working class prevented the Nazis from diverting resources from butter to guns to such an extent that on October 8, 1939 the staff of the quartermaster-general of the German armed forces reported that, "munitions stocks were sufficient only to keep one-third of the divisions combat-ready for another four weeks at the most. On top of this the Luftwaffe's reserves of bombs were almost exhausted and the motorized divisions of the army and the supply system were mostly out of fuel, tires and spare parts, and the shortage of vehicles for an invasion of France ran into five figures. The level of armaments had only just sufficed for the rapid defeat of Poland."[47] Hitler's need for war as an instrument of social control at this time is described by David Kaiser who writes, "By 1938, economic problems in many sectors had become serious, and police and other sources reported increasing discontent. Unless Hitler cut back on rearmament, all of these problems would get worse, not better—and far from reducing rearmament, Hitler was insisting that it be drastically increased...In this context, the political and economic significance of a series of crises and small wars becomes clear. Crisis and war provided some excuse for the hardships imposed upon the German people...Any prolonged period of peace would surely have called into question the need for the further disruption of the economy."[48]

On the eve of World War II Hitler ruled a nation in which the working class had posed such a threat to elite power in 1933 that the elite felt it necessary to rely on the unprecedented ruthlessness of the Nazi party to defeat it. Hitler's Nazi method of rule required that Germany go to war. Hitler originally intended to build up an armaments superiority by 1943 to 1945 and to delay going to war until that time. Domestic working class resistance to policies aimed at shifting the economy from butter to guns, however, prevented Hitler from achieving his armaments goals. The result, as Timothy Mason demonstrates, was that Hitler was forced to take a big gamble by launching *Blitzkrieg* attacks on Czechoslovakia, Poland and France which had to win immediate victories and secure by plunder the war *materiel* that he could not coerce the German workers to produce. The gamble worked and Hitler captured enormous quantities of raw materials, foodstuffs, industrial products and plant as well as forced foreign labor[49] and war *materiel*. From Czechoslovakia alone Hitler acquired 500 trainloads of war supplies "sufficient to arm five new German divisions." Knowing exactly how inadequate domestic German armaments production was, Hitler, on August 22, 1939, argued for the need to attack Poland by telling his top generals, "We have nothing to lose. We have everything to gain. Because of our limitations our economic situation is such that we can only hold out for a few more years. Göring [Hermann Göring, Commander -in-Chief of the Luftwaffe] can confirm this. We have no other choice, we must act."[50]

The inter-war history of Germany shows that the Nazi foreign aggression that initiated the Second World War was not an act taken by the German people as a whole, but was an act taken by German rulers whose draconian suppression of the German working class required a war to succeed. Even the premature timing and the novel nature of the *Blitzkrieg* attacks were driven by the fact that Hitler feared rebellion by his own working class so much that he dared not force them to produce the quantity of armaments that he initially counted upon. German workers living under constant Gestapo terror and working in factories with attached concentration camps were, along with other European workers, the real enemy that the Nazis most feared in World War II.

JAPAN

Scholars of Japanese history before World War II have investigated the reasons why Japanese rulers chose war and aggression. Andrew Gordon, Assistant Professor of History at Duke University, in *Labor and Imperial Democracy in Prewar Japan* writes:

> I believe the relationship between labor and social problems and the 'big story' of the ascendance of the military and fascism in the 1930s has been insufficiently studied and its significance underappreciated. The existence of such a 'relationship,' for example between the repudiation of party rule in 1932 and the social turmoil of the previous three years, is difficult to prove. No radical push from below, either of the left or the right, directly ousted the parties; Admiral Saito did not proclaim that the nation was turning to military rulers because radical unions were too powerful. Yet a range of evidence examined below, from diaries and memoirs to newspaper and magazine articles, suggests that a relationship did exist. We shall see, first, that the newly ascendant military men and bureaucrats, among many others, truly feared that domestic social order might collapse during and after the depression, and second, that this fear informed, and at times propelled, a wide range of new domestic and foreign policies.[51]

Based on the diary of one of Japan's key army leaders, Lieutenant General Suzuki Teiichi, Gordon writes:

> Suzuki's diary from 1933 to 1934 notes numerous lengthy discussions on the subject with Army Minister Araki, as well as with the ministers of finance, foreign affairs, and agriculture, and also reports on the deliberations at several cabinet meetings. It records a consistent military chorus at such meetings, echoed by reform-oriented bureaucrats in the Home Ministry such as Goto Fumio: "domestic unrest" was a great problem, impeding national defense...Suzuki repeatedly told his associates that "a great war would fundamentally strengthen the people and their nationalism."[52]

The background to this evidence that Japan's rulers viewed war as a means of preventing working class revolution, or "collapse of domestic social order," is the intense class struggle that existed in Japan for decades prior to World War II, which we review here.

A Groundswell Of Anti-Capitalism

The end of World War I, in which Japan fought alongside of Great Britain and the U.S. against Germany, was marked by "rice riots" throughout Japan. World War I had produced inflation which caused the price of rice to shoot up much faster than wages in the closing years of the war. A small demonstration by fisherwomen in Toyama Prefecture on July 23, 1918, in protest against the shipping of rice out of their district, ignited a national outbreak of popular anger against Japan's rulers. In numerous major cities there were pitched battles between tens of thousands of rioters and the police, with the army being called out in many instances. To people in Osaka on August 12, 1918, for instance, it felt "as though a revolution had really come." People seized stores of rice and smashed stores. The government arrested 578 people, but it found itself no longer firmly in control; there were too many disturbances for it to be able to concentrate its forces and smother the protests one at a time.[53]

These "rice riots" came at the end of a period of similar riots that took place nine times between 1905 and 1918. Japan was ruled by an oligarchy of feudal lords in a constitutional framework. The government consisted of an "imperial bureaucracy" controlled by elite ministers who acted in the name of the Emperor. As a result of the riots, the oligarchy decided to allow political parties to play an important role in the government, but did not allow even universal male suffrage until 1925 and women's suffrage was only introduced in 1931. Yamagata Aritomo, Japan's premier in 1900 and later President of the Privy Council and the power behind the throne, and known as a man not given to displays of emotion or fear, was described by a visitor as "terribly upset" by the rice riots and convinced that he had no choice but to turn reluctantly to the "once-upstart commoner Hara [a party politician] as the only man who could control the masses."[54]

In the 1920s many Japanese workers in the new and growing labor movement repudiated both imperialism and capitalism and denounced the new parliamentary democracy as a sham. In 1920 the largest labor union, Sodomei, dropped the word "Greater" from its name (Greater Japan Federation of Labor) to express its opposition to the imperialist aims of the government. The Sodomei union opposed the Japanese military's Siberian expedition that began in 1918, and in 1923 it opposed Japanese imperial aims in Korea when it called for self-government in Korea and printed an article in its union magazine supporting the cause of female labor in Korean rubber factories. In another article it lamented that children at play shouted "Soldiers, soldiers!" at a procession of workers carrying union flags en route to a rally. At a rally held February 11, 1920 workers carried posters that read, "Our enemy is the capitalist" and "Destroy the zaibatsu [the big industrial conglomerates]" and "From slavery to humanity." Leaders of the labor movement claimed that suffrage was no longer an important goal and they rejected the tactic of using the vote as a means to longer-term revolutionary mobilization. Instead they advocated direct action and a general strike as primary labor tactics.[55] Additionally, "in the 1920s all of the proletarian parties opposed Japanese imperialism and expansionism, criticizing the aggressive 'send-in-the-troops' China policy of the [ruling] Seiyukai, and supporting the Chinese people against the Japanese military in speeches and slogans."[56]

The government strictly controlled all working class assemblies by requiring that a policeman stand or sit at the side of the stage at all labor gatherings. The policeman stopped any speech in mid-sentence if it crossed the boundary of tolerated discourse. At a rally in 1921 of the Sodomei's Electric and Machine Workers' Union attended by 800 people, police halted fifteen of the twenty-two speeches. Some of the offending utterances were:

1. Capitalists are ...[speech halted]
2. We workers first must destroy...[halted]

3. The only course is to build the road to freedom with our own strength ... [halted]

4. We have absolutely no freedom. At dawn I had a dream. I was advancing down the road to freedom carrying a sword, when I fell into a deep crevice. This is a crevice that captures those who speak the truth ...[halted]

5. To discover how, and with what, to destroy this system is our objective ...[halted]

6. One after another the speakers have been unjustly halted ... [halted]

7. For example, a revolution...[halted][57]

A June 1921 editorial printed by the Pure Laborers' Union (with a membership of 1000 in six locals) claimed that workers had a mission to create a new society, separate from capitalist society and opposed to its values. A year later the allied consumers' "Cooperative Society" declared:

- We will not tolerate exploitation. We will resist the commercial system.
- The bourgeois commercial system is deformed. We will destroy it.
- Ours is an autonomous workers' consumer cooperative that will not only destroy the old society; with our ideal of a new society, we will construct a new society.[58]

These unions led fierce strikes against the capitalists that were explicitly for working class values of solidarity. For example, following a strike of 27,000 workers at the Kawasaki and Mitsubishi shipyards in Kobe in July and August of 1921, workers at the Ishikawajima shipyard began a strike that lasted five weeks. Management had agreed to a raise, but tried to undermine worker solidarity by insisting that it depend on assessments of individual performance. The majority of union members opposed any such selective raise and demanded a uniform wage hike. The workers began a slowdown on October 7 and the company locked them out on October 14. Seven major demonstrations took place between October 16 and November 3, each one turning into confrontations between massed policemen and workers, occasionally turning violent with workers throwing rocks at the police. After five weeks of a lockout, during which the company had foremen visit the workers' homes and offer double pay for the duration if they would return to work, the company was finally able to sneak in 60 strikebreakers to resume limited operations in a shipyard that normally employed 3000 workers. Managers confidently predicted that 2000 of the 3000 workers would be on the job by November 11, but by the 14th only 400 had returned.[59]

An indication of how greatly Japan's rulers feared the working class can be seen in the actions they took to repress it. When the great earthquake struck Tokyo on September 1, 1923, the police took advantage of the chaos to murder ten of the labor movement's most radical leaders, along with several hundred Koreans in the city, while feeding the newspapers hysterical lies claiming that "Koreans and socialists are planning a rebellious and treasonous plot."[60] In 1924 the Sodomei union split over the question of "support for parliamentary political actions and accommodation with the institutions of capital and the state." The "realists" were afraid that "unity with the revolutionary left would invite repression and prove more damaging than the disunity of a split." The revolutionaries were ousted and went on to form the Hyogikai federation which claimed 15,000 national members, including Communists, by 1925.[61] Alarmed by the growth of the revolutionaries, the government on March 3, 1928, "ordered the mass arrest of over 1000 suspected Communists nationwide and simultaneously dissolved the Hyogikai," forcing revolutionaries to go underground.[62]

During the years of the Great Depression which began in 1929, social conflict in working-class districts intensified dramatically and their actions profoundly frightened Japan's rulers. In the industrial section of Tokyo called Nankatsu, which Andrew Gordon studied in detail, "workers at virtually every major textile producer responded by striking."[63] In 1930 at Toyo Muslin in the center of Tokyo young women (who, only a short time earlier, had not even been allowed out of their factory dormitories except for supervised shopping and to work) "marched in the streets and literally fought police and company guards," which "shocked both management and the public. These combative textile girls were neither the pitiful victims portrayed in muckraking magazines nor the satisfied brides-to-be of company public relations campaigns."[64] During the strike on the night of October 24 there was a famous "riotous demonstration" organized by the revolutionary, Kato Kanju, as part of an "effort to build a regional general strike." Authorities turned off the street lights, whereupon "the demonstrators marched through darkened streets towards the Toyo Muslin factory singing the Internationale, shouting slogans. They threw stones, smashed streetcar windows, and fought police, who arrested 197 demonstrators, including four of the women. Over 20 workers were injured" in what became known as "the street war."[65]

"We Shudder As We Observe This Situation"

In response to the Toyo Muslin strike, Zen Keinosuke, former manager at Yahata Steel and executive director of the Japan Industrial Club, gave a speech about the fighting at the textile mill. He said these were not properly economic actions, but politically inspired acts; the organizers had created regional networks and were promoting a general strike.[66] Toyo Muslin's president, Umemura Kenkichi, said the union had a revolutionary agenda and had provoked the street fight and that "we shudder as we observe this situation." His women employees had been, he said, transformed; in addition to joining the riot, "several hundred" had trampled guards who sought to remove the belongings of fired women from the dorms. He was "aghast." He warned that the passage of a union bill [that was being debated and which would give unions more rights] would "sanction such organizations and give workers a new sense of 'rights.'" And he demanded that the police act more firmly to protect company assets.[67] Across Japan, capitalists were voicing exactly the same concerns. They called on the government to act more firmly against radical labor, "to prohibit sympathy strikes, and outlaw participation of minors or public employees in strikes...prohibit demonstrations, third-party involvement in strikes" and even to prohibit any "obstruction of an enterprise" which would have meant essentially making any strike illegal.[68] All of these demands were in sharp contrast to the earlier stance of businessmen which had been that government intervention in labor disputes would do more harm than good. Gordon writes that, "The explanation for the change lies in the new atmosphere of fear that gripped owners and managers trying to stave off bankruptcy and cope with labor militance even among women and men in small companies."[69]

War And Fascism To The Rescue

In the early 1930s leading figures in the military, the civil bureaucracy, and business began supporting and organizing Fascist unions and other supposedly "grass roots" organizations which used their backing by the state to weaken the radical working class organizations. The Fascist groups called for replacing disputes and polarization with a spirit of sacrifice and national loyalty. They supported capitalism, but only so long as capital with labor ("fused in an inseparable solidarity") focused on national glory. Fascist political parties were formed, but very revealingly, not a single Fascist party ever won even modest electoral support in Japan.[70]

In September 1931 Japan's Kwangtung Army instigated the "Manchurian Incident"—militarily occupying China's Manchuria territory and creating a Japanese puppet state called Manchukuo. This was the beginning of Japan's march toward military rule at home and world war abroad. The link between the Manchurian aggression and the domestic labor crisis faced by Japan's elite was thoroughly appreciated by Japan's rulers and elite intellectuals; they viewed foreign aggression as a necessary means of controlling an increasingly radical working class by creating an atmosphere of nationalism that would define any working class objections to elite rule as unpatriotic. For example, "one contributor to *Chuo koron*, a respected forum of intellectual and elite opinion, writing just days before the Manchurian Incident, felt that the military could potentially represent the popular will and redirect concern with domestic problems abroad. Another referred to the 'domestic and foreign impasse' and called for 'a new political force with a critical awareness of the needs of the Japanese race.' " Oyama Ikuo predicted that "social fascism" would come "when both rulers and social democratic parties turned to imperialism in the face of domestic tension." A right-wing organization, the Radical Patriotic Labor Union Federation, just before the Manchurian Incident, wanted to "use the intensified Manchurian problem as the motor for domestic reform."[71] Army leader Suzuki Teiichi, said:

> One cannot distinguish domestic and foreign policies. The two evolve influencing each other. Without attention to the external [problem], the internal [society] will not cohere. If you ignore the external, you may think you can unify domestically, but you cannot.[72]

General Ugaki Kazunari, a relative moderate, also perceived a link between the domestic labor crisis and the need for foreign aggression, although he characterized it differently. He wrote in November, 1930:

> Industrial rationalization will only increase unemployment and lead to social tragedy unless accompanied by expanded markets as outlets for our goods. These markets will be won in economic competition over price and quality. But if foreign relations atrophy, the competition will be restricted. We greatly need renovation of foreign policy and rationalization of industry.[73]

General Ugaki "confided in his diary in December, 1931 that the major objectives of his tenure as army minister had been achieved through the Manchurian offensive: the unity of the military and the people and the 'popularization' of national defense. In 1932 the Justice Ministry's *Monthly Thought Bulletin* stressed that in a time of intense social ferment, the surge of support for foreign expansion after the Manchurian Incident was a 'divine wind.' And a May, 1932 paper of the Army Ministry titled 'Judgment of the New Situation in the Far East' could not have been clearer on this connection: 'Since the Manchurian Incident, confrontational attitudes between social classes with differing economic interests appear to have gradually subsided... [The incident] seems to have bred a spirit of solidarity.' "[74]

As intended, the Manchurian Incident put the working class on the defensive by whipping up nationalism. The state and the Fascist organizations declared class struggle to be unpatriotic. Between 1930 and 1935 the labor movement foundered. "In 1931 police halted over 5 percent of *all* speeches at political rallies in Tokyo, the second highest rate of suppression ever recorded."[75] The army investigated "262 antiwar incidents between September 1931 and...February 1932," and the state "intensified surveillance and repression."[76] The atmosphere of nationalism isolated and pressured the labor and working class party movements, who felt it necessary to retreat. "In the winter of 1933, an estimated 80,000 union workers and 20,000 non-union employees agreed to work on a Sunday or holiday and donate that day's wages to the army's National Defense Fund Drive."[77] At this time most Sodomei union contracts now included a new element of patriotism—a promise of "industrial service to the nation."[78]

Still, in 1933 Japan's rulers remained frightened of losing control of the working class. This is the period during which Lieutenant General Suzuki Teiichi's diary, referred to in the quotation at the beginning of this section, describes the obsession of Prime Minister Saito and his cabinet with "domestic unrest" and Suzuki's call for "a great war" to solve the problem.

By 1935 the nationalist upsurge from the Manchurian Incident had worn thin and the labor movement revived. "The number of organized workers rose 25 percent from a 1934 low to a peak of 81,500 in 1936," and the national proportion of organized workers increased from 1934 to 1935. The number of workers joining strikes or slowdowns "jumped from 31,000 in 1936 to 124,000 the next year, exceeding even the 1930 peak of 81,000."[79] "The number of participants per strike increased substantially in 1937," and the government classified over two thirds of the strikes as "assertive," compared to less than one-fourth in 1930 and 1931, when strikes were mainly defensive efforts to get severance pay for laid off workers.[80] Not only were the strikes now larger and more assertive, but they were also frequently not even under the control of a moderate union or indeed of any union. In 1937 only 38 percent of all disputes were led by unions, down from 70 percent during the depression. In the late spring of 1937 "a contributor to *Chuo Koron* warned that the pace of labor unrest was far ahead of the most turbulent year of the depression. Disputes were more intense, more politicized, and not often led by unions."[81]

Once more, Japan's rulers used foreign aggression to put workers on the defensive. In July 1937 the Japanese government went to war in China again, and demanded that Japanese workers restrain themselves in support of the "holy war." The effect was dramatic: of all the strikes in 1937, 89 percent occurred in the first six months before the July war in China was launched.[82] As before, however, the government remained exceedingly fearful of the working class. In July 1940 the Konoe cabinet inaugurated its "New Order," which was a sweeping implementation of an essentially Fascist reorganization of society. As part of the "New Order," the government forced all of Japan's unions to dissolve "voluntarily."[83]

The official explanation for Japan's military aggression in Asia and against the United States base at Pearl Harbor is that Japanese rulers wanted to control Asia's resources and markets and they viewed the United States as an obstacle to achieving that goal. What this explanation leaves out, however, is the *reason* why Japan's rulers felt they needed Asian markets and " holy wars" of aggression to acquire them. They needed these things as a means of controlling their own domestic working class. Some of the rulers, like General Suzuki, focused on the need for a war-induced nationalism to put workers on the defensive ideologically. Others, like General Kazunari, focused on the need for foreign markets to prevent unemployment (caused by the "rationalization of industry") from reaching levels so high (as it did during the Depression) that it generates dangerous social upheavals that threaten elite rule ("lead to a social tragedy"). In a truly democratic and equal society, of course, the rationalization of industry would not lead to unemployment or threaten anybody; it would simply enable workers to enjoy the fruits of their greater productivity by having more leisure time and a better standard of living. Obviously, Japan's rulers never considered solving the problem of unemployment by making Japan a genuine democracy; their goal was to preserve undemocratic elite rule and somehow prevent the resulting anger of workers from leading to revolution. Pearl Harbor was their solution, the "great war" that the Army's Teiichi Suzuki said "would fundamentally strengthen the people and their nationalism." When the Japanese elite attacked U.S. ships at Pearl Harbor, they were doing what they believed was necessary to win the war against their own working class. This is why they felt compelled to attack the United States despite warnings from their Navy commanders that the U.S. was materially too powerful to defeat except in the unlikely event that it surrendered before gearing up for protracted war.

SOVIET UNION

More than 20 million people in the Soviet Union, a number far surpassing that of any other country, died in the fight against the Nazis. The Soviet Union's defeat of German forces in the greatest confrontation of armies the world had ever seen determined, above everything else, the outcome of the war. Based on this, and also based on the perception by many that the Soviet Union was the only country in the world in which working people held power and the leaders were revolutionaries, many people around the world during World War Two stood in awe of the Soviet Union and in particular of Stalin, a man who used every means to magnify his image as the greatest living revolutionary. Stalin used his power and reputation to wield enormous influence over the foreign Communist parties that led the anti-Fascist resistance movements in European and Asian nations that German or Japanese Fascists had occupied.

We are going to look closely at the origins of Communist power in the Soviet Union in order to explain what would otherwise be paradoxical—the fact that Stalin played an extremely counter-revolutionary role during the war, ordering Communist parties, in the name of ensuring an Allied victory over Fascism, *not* to pursue revolutionary anti-capitalist goals. This is an important question to resolve, because the standard story of World War Two derives much of its credibility from a false explanation of the paradox. In the standard story Stalin was the world's foremost revolutionary opponent of capitalism, and his wartime alliance with the capitalist elites of Great Britain and the United States demonstrates that the war was a conflict between all decent people—no matter what they thought about capitalism pro or con—and Fascists, whose evil was unrelated to the fact that they happened to be pro-capitalist. In this view, in other words, the central conflict in the world was between decency, led by the leaders of the Western capitalist nations, and Fascist evil; it had nothing to do with capitalism. To appreciate how false this story is, one must step back and look at Russian history; it reveals that neither Stalin, nor the Soviet Union's Communist ("Bolshevik") Party going back to its origins with Lenin and the 1917 Russian Revolution, were ever revolutionary in the sense of wanting ordinary working people to hold power in society. Contrary to the standard story, Stalin's alliance with western capitalist leaders was not an alliance between all the decent people in the world against evil; it was an alliance of the world's counter-revolutionary elites (both capitalist and Communist) against the revolutionary working class.

The historian, Gabriel Kolko, characterizes Stalin's role at this time. "The decision of much of Europe's middle and traditional ruling classes to compromise with Nazi Germany, or actively to support it in the case of Italy and France" led to millions of people, for the first time, perceiving the Left as the only legitimate moral and political force that could fill the vacuum created by the elites' collaboration. After 1943 the armies and police forces which the old rulers had relied upon to protect them were so compromised that they were "immeasurably weakened." In large parts of Europe, during crucial weeks and months, no armed force existed that could have prevented the Resistance movements of workers and peasants, many of them armed, from taking political and administrative power. Kolko writes:

> Europe's oppressed seemed highly likely to triumph in all or at least major portions of three nations...[T]he men and groups that chose to collaborate [with the Fascists] after 1939...could not even begin to imagine beforehand...that the very existence of traditional capitalist social systems might...gain profoundly from the stabilizing role that Bolshevik Russia could play...The Russians repeatedly assured their allies that they would oppose revolutions in those places most vital to Anglo-American interests.[84]

Although he used the rhetoric of revolution against capitalism to appeal to the masses, and to justify every twist and turn of Soviet foreign and domestic policy,[85] Stalin never wanted, neither at home nor abroad, what most people meant by "revolution"—ordinary working people taking power over their lives and society. Stalin wanted to emerge from the war with his Communist party ruling an enlarged Russian empire that would include eastern Europe, and he hoped to make this empire secure by establishing an agreement with the

United States and Great Britain to divide the world up between them and to help each other prevent working class revolutions from succeeding anywhere. Stalin viewed the wartime alliance not just as a temporary alliance with capitalist nations to defeat Fascists, but as a permanent alliance against the working class.

After failing to establish a lasting alliance with Hitler at the outbreak of the war, Stalin used his influence on Communist parties around the world to strengthen his alliance with Great Britain and the United States. He ordered Communists to go back to the strategy of a "United Front Against Fascism" (embraced originally at the 1935 7th Congress of the Communist International and abandoned by Stalin when he signed the Nazi-Soviet Non-Aggression Treaty in 1939), supporting British and American capitalist leaders, dropping all anti-capitalist goals, and only fighting Fascists. Why did Stalin play such a role when he was supposedly the leading advocate of Communist revolution and workers' power? The answer becomes clear when we look closely at the Russian Revolution of 1917 and subsequent years to see how the "science of revolution" developed by Karl Marx provided Communist leaders like Lenin and Trotsky and Stalin a theory that led sincere revolutionaries to be brutal oppressors of working people and staunch allies of Western capitalism, all in the name of working class revolution.

The Communist Revolution In Russia

At the close of World War I people in every warring nation were furious at their leaders for inflicting heretofore unimaginable hardships on them. The war rhetoric which had seemed so persuasive at the beginning of the war came to be totally unconvincing three years later. Nowhere was this more true than in the Russian Empire of Tsar Nicholas II. Amidst mass desertions of peasant-soldiers who left the front line but kept their rifles as they headed home, and following a general strike by workers in the capital city of Petrograd, the Tsar abdicated on March 2, 1917.[86] The power vacuum was filled by a succession of self-appointed governments formed from members of political parties that had won elections to a powerless parliament, or "Duma," which the Tsar had permitted to exist in an earlier effort to head off revolution. At the same time, there were workers' councils, called soviets, in many cities elected by local factory workers. A number of different revolutionary parties had members elected to both the Duma and the soviets, including Lenin's Bolshevik Party, one of the smallest of the parties, which later called itself the Communist

Party. The soviets were the most representative bodies and they acted like a government also. The day before the Tsar abdicated, the largest soviet, in Petrograd, issued Order No. 1 which "abolished the code of military discipline" and called on the troops in the city to "subject themselves to the authority of the [Petrograd] Soviet."[87] The soviet then ordered an eight hour day. Workers in some factories tied up unpopular foremen "in sacks and paraded them around their works in wheelbarrows"; in the Baltic fleet sailors lynched several unpopular officers, tore off epaulettes and stopped saluting. The lower ranks made it clear they would "scrutinize and discuss instructions from above" before deciding whether to carry them out. Workers set up factory-workshop committees and sailors and soldiers did the same kind of thing in military units. "The committees were at first held regularly accountable to open mass meetings....If a committee failed to respond to its electors' requests, an open meeting could be held and the committee membership could straightaway be changed."[88] People called this "Workers' Control" and this democracy in action spread rapidly. Soon even passengers on trains were doing it, to decide things like how to pick up and distribute food along the journey. Peasants had similar soviets based on centuries-old traditions of communal self-government, and they seized huge tracts of land owned by the aristocrat landlords and decided in their communal organizations how to divide the land up amongst themselves.[89]

In June soviets from all over the country sent representatives to Petrograd for the first All-Russia Congress of Workers' and Soldiers' Deputies. Lenin called on his small party, which numbered only about two thousand members at the beginning of October 1917,[90] to win a majority in elections to the soviets, and then to fight for All Power to the Soviets.[91] The Duma government, headed by Aleksander Kerenski, was growing increasingly unpopular because it continued to fight the war, and people suspected that it "might still be pursuing expansionist aims."[92] "The political and administrative system was in an advanced condition of disintegration. Peasants in most villages across the former Russian Empire governed themselves. The military conscripts intimidated their officers. The workers...wished to impose their control over the factories and mines. Kerenski had lost authority over all these great social groups."[93]

On the basis of its slogans for "All Power to the Soviets," "Workers' Control," "Peace, Bread, and Land to the Peasants," the Bolsheviks gained members and won elections in the soviets which enabled them to lead a unit of soldiers in Petrograd to take over key buildings in the city and declare themselves the new government on October 25, 1917.[94] The next day Lenin issued a Decree on Peace calling on 'all the warring peoples' to bring about a 'just, democratic peace' and a Decree on Land calling on the peasants to expropriate the land from the nobility without paying compensation. He also formed the infamous *Cheka*, a police force to eliminate opposition to the October Revolution.[95]

Elections, previously called by the Duma for a Constituent Assembly, were held all over Russia during November and December 1917, and the elected delegates assembled in Petrograd January 5, 1918. The Bolsheviks had expected to win a majority, but they won only 175 out of 707 seats,[96] and in response the Bolsheviks broke up the meeting of the Constituent Assembly on its first day. Twenty people died when Bolshevik troops broke up a small demonstration against the dissolution of the Assembly.[97] From this day on, the Bolsheviks began strengthening a dictatorship of their Communist Party over the entire population.

How could this have happened in a revolution that began with the overthrow of a despotic tsar and the slogans "All Power to the Soviets" and "Workers Control?" This question is the key to understanding the influence that Stalin would later hold over workers and peasants throughout the world during World War Two, through his control of numerous foreign Communist parties. The answer can be found by looking at the role of Marxism, and Lenin's contribution to it, in the shaping of events immediately following the October revolution. The reason people permitted the small Bolshevik Party to acquire dictatorial power in the early years of the revolution is the same reason that so many people on the Left followed Stalin's lead even when he instigated the Great Terror against workers and peasants in 1936-7, flip flopped on whether to oppose Hitler between 1939 and 1941, and ordered Communist parties in other nations not to make revolutions against capitalism.

The Tragedy Of Marxism

Lenin's Communist Party's membership grew from only two thousand shortly before the October revolution to 300,000 members by the end of that same year.[98] Many people joined the Party not only because it claimed to be for workers and peasants taking power, but also because it claimed to possess a science—Marxism—for understanding how to achieve a more humane society called "communism." Marx described communism as a classless society without exploitation, inequality or economic scarcity, in which people might work according to their ability and receive according to their need. Although there is, as we shall see, something about Marxism that leads its practitioners to be anti-democratic, Marxism nonetheless appeals to people's desire for a real democracy. In the Communist Manifesto Marx and Engels asserted that, "the first step in the revolution by the working class is to raise the proletariat to the position of ruling class to win the battle of democracy."[99] Marxism held an enormous appeal for many people in Russia and throughout the world who wanted a better world. To understand events in the Soviet Union, we need to understand why Marxism fails to make the kind of world most of it's followers wanted.

Many people before Marx had expressed revolutionary aspirations for egalitarian societies without class exploitation. What distinguished Marxism was that it claimed to be a science which proved that this goal was the inevitable outcome of impersonal historical and economic forces. The tragedy of Marxism is that, on the one hand this "science" has inspired millions of people to revolution by giving them hope in its inevitability, but on the other hand it embodies a view of ordinary people the logic of which requires the revolution to be anti-democratic. To see how this played out in practice, we need first to look at the "science" that Marx invented.

Marx stood on the shoulders of Adam Smith, the 18th century founder of modern economics, who, in perhaps the most infamous apology for capitalism ever penned—the famous "invisible hand" statement—said of British capitalists:

> By preferring the support of domestic to that of foreign industry, he intends only his own security; and by directing that industry in such a manner as its produce may be of the greatest value, he intends only his own gain, and he is in this, as in many other cases, led by an invisible hand to promote an end which was no part of his intention. Nor is it always the worse for the society that it was no part of it. By pursuing his own interest he frequently promotes that of the society more effectually than when he really intends to promote it.[100]

Marx gave the "invisible hand"—i.e., the idea that the result of individuals acting on selfish motives has consequences for society as a whole that were never intended by the individuals—a twist. Instead of self-interest in the capitalist framework serving the needs of society and thereby securing permanence for capitalism, the invisible hand in Marx's scheme acted as a dynamic historical force. First it promoted capitalism as a mode of economic production superior to feudalism; but next, according to Marx, the invisible hand would lead the capitalist class to create a fatal crisis for the capitalist system which would force the working class to overthrow the capitalist class and usher in a new phase of history that would culminate in communism. That workers as well as capitalists, in fact everybody, acted in their self-interest, Marx did not deny, and he even quotes Adam Smith to that effect: "individuals seek *only* their particular interest." (Marx's emphasis)[101]

Much of Marxism's appeal to the revolutionaries it attracted was precisely that it posited neither the existence nor the need for a working class with anti-capitalist values and goals. The "invisible hand" core of Marx's science explains why there was nothing contradictory about Marx painting workers in a very bad light as individuals, and at the same time declaring that as a group they would usher in a communist society. For example, again quoting Adam Smith, Marx wrote that capitalism made the worker "as stupid and ignorant as it is possible for a human creature to become."[102] The Communist Manifesto makes the same point about the rural peasant, noting that the bourgeoisie "has created enormous cities, has greatly increased the urban population as compared with the rural, and has thus rescued a considerable part of the population from the idiocy of rural life."[103] No matter how stupid, ignorant, self-serving and idiotic the worker was, however, the invisible hand would "promote an end which was no part of his intention."

Workers would not make a revolution because they had revolutionary values opposite to those of capitalism, but because the worker "becomes a pauper, and pauperism develops more rapidly than population and wealth" and "it becomes evident that the bourgeoisie...is unfit to rule because it is incompetent to assure an existence to its slave within his slavery, because it cannot help letting him sink into such a state, that it has to feed him, instead of being fed by him."[104] In the Marxist framework material self-interest drives history and motivates capitalists and workers alike. The conflicting values of working people and capitalists, values expressed by the kinds of relationships people form with others—either mutually supportive ones or exploitive ones, based on equality or inequality—play no important role in the Marxist "science." Class struggle in the Marxist view stems from conflicting material interests of workers and capitalists, not from conflicting values.

Although values, which are often held only implicitly and not articulated explicitly in words, are not important in Marxism, the ideas held by intellectuals do receive attention by Marx, but he says they reflect rather than cause changes in the world: "When people speak of ideas that revolutionize society, they do but express the fact that within the old society the elements of a new one have been created, and that the dissolution of the old ideas keeps even pace with the dissolution of the old conditions of existence."[105]

The anti-democratic nature of Marxism enters the theory right at this point. Marxism is built on a view of ordinary people that is wrong, and the logic of this view requires anti-democratic methods by revolutionaries. Contrary to what Marx believed, self-interest is not what motivates most working people. It may motivate scabs, but most workers don't scab. Throughout history working people have developed a culture that respects solidarity and treating others as equals, and that holds in contempt those who set themselves up as better and more deserving than others. Workers routinely buck the pressure of capitalism to put self-interest first; they do this by supporting each other in acts of solidarity ranging from everyday kindness and help for those in hard times to more organized and collective actions like slowdowns and strikes. People try, without giving it a second thought, to create relations based on commitment to each other, trust and equality—sometimes with more and sometimes with less success in a world where capitalist power creates a hostile environment for such efforts. The values and aspirations of ordinary people are for a more equal and democratic world based on solidarity, the opposite of the capitalist goal of a world of winners and losers—haves and have-nots—controlled from the top down, in which everybody is in dog-eat-dog competition with everybody else. Democratic revolutions occur when ordinary people see clearly and explicitly the enormous contradiction between their goals and values and capitalist goals and values, see themselves as the source of what is good in the world, and aim to succeed on a large scale in the efforts and struggles that they engage in everyday. Marxism, on the contrary, views the goal of the revolution as something that will be achieved in spite of, not because of, working people's own goals and values. Marxist "science" is an elaboration of this basic anti-democratic notion.[106]

By making the invisible hand a dynamic force that drives history towards a goal, Marx created a coherent view of the world that assigned to every human activity the character of being either "progressive" or "reactionary," i.e., hastening the process or slowing it down. But what determined if something was progressive or not did not necessarily follow from the stated values or intentions of the people involved. For example, during the great Russian famine of 1891, the young Lenin, then a lawyer named Vladimir Ilych Ulyanov, lived in Samara, the regional capital of one of the hardest hit areas of the famine" "He was the only member of the local intelligentsia who not only refused to participate in the aid for the hungry, but publicly opposed it. As one of his friends later recalled, 'Vladimir Ilich Ulyanov had the courage to come out and say openly that famine would have numerous positive results, particularly in the appearance of a new industrial proletariat, which would take over from the bourgeoisie...Famine, he explained, in destroying the outdated peasant economy, would bring about the next stage more rapidly, and usher in socialism, the stage that necessarily followed capitalism.' "[107]

Marx believed that a communist society would emerge, and could only emerge, after the working class increased the level of economic production sufficiently to eliminate all economic scarcity. Only in such a society, he said, would the material conditions exist that would foster the development of egalitarian ideas among the masses. Therefore, the revolution's purpose, in the logic of the Marxist framework, is to free the economy from the fetters of the private property and profit system, and "to increase the total of productive forces as rapidly as possible."[108] On this basis Communists like Lenin and Stalin believed that they needed to use whatever coercion was necessary to make working people, presumed to be motivated only by self-interest, produce as much as possible. Inequality was maintained on the grounds that greater pay and privileges gave workers an incentive to work more diligently. Rumblings for democracy and equality were viewed as "reactionary" because they threatened the discipline that the Communists felt was required for economic productivity.

Marxist-Leninist revolutionaries had a theoretical framework within which their violent suppression of workers and peasants was absolutely necessary to achieve a better world. The anti-democratic essence of Leninism, however, was hardly ever acknowledged openly and explicitly. Critics of the Bolshevik's dictatorial methods often point to Lenin's famous book, *State and Revolution*, and cite it as proof that Lenin openly advocated a dictatorship because the book does indeed call for the "dictatorship of the proletariat." But it's not that simple. Lenin used this famous phrase to mean that working people as a class had to forcibly prevent capitalists and big landlords from regaining power. The book emphasized that such a force was, from the point of view of the exploiting class, a dictatorship, and that workers should not hesitate to exercise such a dictatorship. But the book never suggested that workers themselves should be subjected to a dictatorship, and on the contrary argues that Bolshevik power makes the workers the ruling class.

In practice, the party's dictatorship over the workers and peasants was disguised as best it could as the dictatorship of the working class over the exploiting classes. When this deceit was too transparent, Bolsheviks played their trump card: the need to subject all other considerations to the requirements of increasing economic production which was in turn justified by the grand Marxist science that made this the key condition for achieving communism in the distant future. Whether top communists like Lenin and Stalin were really motivated by the dream of a communist society or whether they just sought personal power is less important than the fact that their actions flowed directly from the logic of Marxism. Millions of people either served the communist dictatorship actively or consented to it, or at least did not oppose it as much as they might otherwise have done so, because they sincerely dreamed of and hoped for the new society that Marxism promised and, to some extent, they accepted the Marxist logic about what was required to achieve it. This is the tragedy of Marxism.

Marxist Ideology In Practice

The October 1917 revolution faced extremely challenging problems, especially providing city dwellers with food during a time of scarcity, and defending the revolution against real enemies including big capitalists, Tsarist military officers and foreign military forces aiming to overthrow working class power. But, as events would demonstrate, the Bolsheviks—in accordance with the Marxist view of working people—did not trust ordinary people to solve these problems democratically. Instead, the Communists feared that democracy would be the undoing of the revolution, whose goal, as they saw it, was to secure the rule of the party and to increase economic production. Democracy and equality were the goals of ordinary workers and peasants, but these were not the goals of the Communists. Instead of relying on truly representative bodies of workers and peasants to come up with solutions to problems like providing people in the cities with food—solutions that may very well have involved sacrifices, but which would have been democratically self-imposed sacrifices for agreed upon goals—Lenin assumed that only the Communists truly cared about solving such problems, that only they knew how, and that whoever didn't do exactly as the Communists ordered were counterrevolutionary enemies of the people who had to be shot or imprisoned. The Communists used every problem as an excuse for strengthening the party's power over working people and attacking all of their efforts to create more democratic and equal social relations.

Communists were able to exercise power way out of proportion to their relatively small numbers for two key reasons: 1) They had enormous self-confidence which derived from possessing a very coherent "science" in Marxism which purported to explain everything including most importantly how to change the world. Based on this confidence they, unlike ordinary people or even other revolutionaries, were able to act and command others with supreme authority, and in the name of revolutionary aspirations that huge numbers of people shared. 2) They did not hesitate to use violence ruthlessly to intimidate or even eliminate their working class and peasant opponents, most of whom were not prepared psychologically, organizationally or materially to defend themselves.

On April 29, 1918 Lenin essentially declared war on the peasants in the name of the proletariat. Speaking before the Central Executive Committee of the Soviets on April 29, 1918 he said, "The smallholders, the people who owned only a parcel of land, fought side by side with the proletariat when the time came to overthrow the capitalists and the major landowners. But now our paths have diverged. Smallholders have always been afraid of discipline and organization. The time has come for us to have no mercy, and to turn against them." A few days later the people's commissar of food told the same group, "I say it quite openly; we are now at war, and it is only with guns that we will get the grain we need."[109] By July the Communists had recruited 12,000 people to a "food army" that went into the countryside to forcibly requisition food.[110] Ninety-six percent of Russia's peasants, including most of the so-called kulaks—peasants who owned more land than most and were typically respected for their farming skills—belonged to peasant communes that exercised self-government and decided how to distribute the land taken from the large landowners. Even before the October revolution, many of the kulaks had already been required by their communes to return most of their livestock, machinery and land to the commune for redistribution according to the ancient principle based on the number of mouths to be fed in a family.[111] Peasants wanted to arrange life without outside interference. The Communists on the contrary, wanted to nationalize the land and turn the peasants into rural workers in large state-controlled farm collectives.

The Communists confiscated so much grain that "peasant households were often left starving."[112] Antonov-Ovseenko, a Bolshevik leader who led the repressions of peasants in Tambov, later admitted "that the requisitioning plans of 1920 and 1921, if carried out as instructed, would have meant the certain death of the peasants. On average, they were left with 1 *pud* (35 pounds) of grain and 1.5 *pudy* (about 55 pounds) of potatoes per person each year—approximately one-tenth of the minimum requirements for life."[113] One historian writes of the peasants' reaction to the Bolsheviks at this time, "All the trust that the Bolsheviks had gained by not opposing the seizure of land in 1917 evaporated in a matter of weeks, and for more than three years the policy of requisitioning food was to provoke thousands of riots and uprisings, which were to degenerate into real peasant wars that were quelled with terrible violence."[114] In the first twenty days of 1919 alone, the Cheka reported, "210 revolts, involving more than 100,000 armed combatants and several hundred thousand peasants."[115] These peasant armies fought not only the Communists, but the "White" counter-revolutionary armies as well.[116] The most famous such peasant army was led by Nestor Makhno, a Ukrainian anarchist (who, contrary to the common stereotype of peasants, was extremely opposed to any form of anti-Semitism.)[117] Lenin decreed the establishment of 'committees of the village poor' to report hoarding by the wealthier peasant families—the so called kulaks—but the peasants resented the entire scheme. The atmosphere is captured by Lenin's confidential telegram sent on August 10, 1918, to the Central Executive Committee of the Penza soviet: "Hang no fewer than a hundred well-known kulaks, rich-bags and blood-suckers (and make sure that the hanging takes place in full view of people)...Do all this so that for miles around people see it all, understand it, tremble, and tell themselves that we are killing the bloodthirsty kulaks and that we will continue to do so."[118] (After failing to turn the poorer peasants against the wealthier ones, Lenin stopped slandering the kulaks and in December 1920, at the Eighth Congress of Soviets, he even "urged...that richer peasant households should be materially rewarded for any additional gains in agricultural productivity rather than be persecuted as kulaks."[119]) The Marxist view of people that led the Communists to wage war against the peasants was expressed quite succinctly by the head of the Cheka,

Feliks Dzerzhinsky, when he said of the peasants, "They are so ignorant, that they have no idea what is really in their own interest."[120]

The Communists even turned against workers in the cities. They dissolved soviets and workers' committees that did not have Bolshevik majorities on June 14, 1918.[121] There were protests and strikes in working class towns. In one day the Cheka opened fire on a hunger march organized by workers in Kolpino, near Petrograd, and a detachment of Red Guards killed fifteen people in a factory in Ekaterinburg who protested the corruption of some Bolshevik commissars.[122] In May and June 1918 there were more working class demonstrations that were put down violently,[123] and the Bolsheviks responded to strikes in state-owned factories by locking the workers out.[124] During this period the "Cheka recorded seventy 'incidents'—strikes, anti-Bolshevik meetings, demonstrations—led principally by metalworkers from labor strongholds, who had been the most ardent supporters of the Bolsheviks in the period leading up to the events of 1917."[125] In Petrograd the Bolsheviks dissolved the Assembly of Workers' Representatives and arrested more than 800 of its leaders after a Bolshevik leader was assassinated. In response, workers called a general strike on July 21,1918. On March 10, 1919, a meeting of more than 10,000 workers in the Putilov factories in Petrograd adopted a resolution that read: "This government is nothing less than the dictatorship of the Central Committee of the Communist Party, kept in place thanks to the Cheka and the revolutionary courts."[126] The resolution also called for power to be handed over to the soviets, free elections for the soviets and factory committees, an end to the limitations on the quantity of food workers could bring into the city from the countryside, and the release of political prisoners from "authentic revolutionary parties." Lenin came to Petrograd from Moscow (the new capital) to personally address the workers who were striking in the factories but was booed off the stage.[127] On March 16, Cheka detachments stormed the Putilov factory which was defended by armed workers; they arrested 900 workers and executed 200 strikers without a trial. The remaining workers had to sign a declaration that they had been "led into crime" by counterrevolutionary leaders before they were rehired.[128] Events such as this occurred in the spring of 1919 in many of the largest working class centers in Russia including Tula, Sormovo, Orel, Bryansk, Tver, Ivanovo Voznesensk, and Astrakhan, always with the same grievances: "the elimination of special privileges for Communists, the release of political prisoners, free elections for soviets and factory committees, the end of conscription into the Red Army, freedom of association, freedom of expression, freedom of the press."[129]

In March 1919 in the city of Astrakhan, workers went on strike for better food rations and against the arrest of non-Bolshevik activists. On March 10 "the 45th Infantry Regiment refused [Communist orders] to open fire on workers marching through the city. Joining forces with the strikers, the soldiers stormed the Bolshevik Party headquarters and killed several members of the staff."[130] Soldiers who remained loyal to the Bolsheviks captured the town and from March 12 to 14 they shot or drowned between 2,000 and 4,000 striking workers.[131]

Late in 1919 the Communists implemented the "militarization" of work in more than 2000 businesses. Leon Trotsky led this effort, arguing that workers were naturally lazy and that, in the absence of a capitalist market that fired people if they didn't work, the state had to subject workers to military style discipline so they would obey orders as soldiers obey orders in the army. Workers, of course, hated being militarized at work, especially when they were punished for leaving work to search for food. Communist militarization led to even more work stoppages, strikes, and riots, all of which the Cheka attacked ruthlessly. The Communist Party paper, *Pravda*, wrote February 12, 1920, "The best place for strikers, those noxious yellow parasites, is the concentration camp!"[132] In the Tula arms factory on Sunday June 6, 1920, metallurgy workers refused to work new mandatory extra hours; then women workers refused to work on that Sunday or any others, explaining that was the only day they had to go out looking for food. The Cheka came and arrested the strikers and the Communists declared martial law, announcing that there was a "counterrevolutionary conspiracy fomented by Polish spies." The strike spread and more "leaders" were arrested, and then thousands of women workers and housewives presented themselves to the Cheka and asked to be arrested too. Then men did the same thing, *en masse*. In four days, more than 10,000 people were detained in an open-air space guarded by the Cheka. Finally, the Communists realized they needed these skilled armaments workers back on the job, and so they freed workers who would sign a confession that they were "a filthy criminal dog."[133]

By 1921 Communists faced full scale revolts by the working class in both Moscow and Petrograd. A Cheka report from January 16 stated, "The workers are predicting the imminent demise of the regime. No one works any more because they are all too hungry. Strikes on a huge scale are bound to start any day now. The garrisons in Moscow are less and less trustworthy and could become uncontrollable at any moment. Preventive measures are required."[134] On February 26, Grigory Zinoviev, the head of the Communist Party in Petrograd sent a telegram to Lenin which read, "The workers have joined up with the soldiers in the barracks...We are still waiting for the reinforcements we demanded from Novgorod. If they don't arrive in the next few hours, we are going to be overrun."[135]

Two days later sailors on two warships in the Kronstadt base near Petrograd mutinied, and issued a 24 hour ultimatum to the Communist government, demanding "free and secret elections, freedom of speech and freedom of the press—at least for 'workers, peasants, anarchists, and left-wing socialist parties,'... equal rations for all, the freeing of political prisoners, the convocation of a special commission to reexamine the cases of those imprisoned in concentration camps, an end to [food] requisitioning, the abolition of the special Cheka detachments, and freedom for the peasants 'to do whatever they want with their land, and to raise their own livestock, provided they do it using their own resources.' "[136] On March 1 a huge meeting of more than 15,000 people—a quarter of the entire civil and military population of the naval base—gathered in Kronstadt. The local high ranking Communist, Mikhail Kalinin, tried to address the crowd but was booed off. Two thousand rank and file Communists joined the rebels and formed a provisional revolutionary committee that tried to link up with the strikers and soldiers from Petrograd. On March 7, the Cheka attacked the Petrograd workers, and arrested more than 2,000 of them. From March 8-18, General Mikhail Tukhachevsky used special Cheka detachments and young soldiers fresh out of military school with little revolutionary tradition to re-capture Kronstadt. Between April and June 1921 2,103 Kronstadt workers were sentenced to death and 6,459 were sent to prison or concentration camps.[137]

Stalin's Alliance With Western Capitalism

By the time Stalin came to power after Lenin's death in 1924, the Communist Party was firmly entrenched as the ruling class of the Soviet Union. Stalin's priorities were the same as Lenin's: first hold onto power and second increase economic production. As we shall see next, Stalin's fear of the working class and eagerness to ally with Western capitalist elites stemmed from his making economic production rather than democracy and equality the goal of the Communist Party.

From 1921 to 1928 the Party had implemented a New Economic Policy (NEP) as an attempt to calm down the extreme opposition to the government's forced requisition of food from starving peasants. Kulaks were no longer demonized and peasants were allowed to have their own land and sell to whomever they wished within limits. Also, foreign investors were encouraged to invest in the Soviet Union in "concessions."[138] By 1928 Stalin felt that it was again possible to be more aggressive against peasants and workers and to increase production faster than had occurred under the NEP. He implemented a Five-Year Plan (1928-32) which called once again for requisitioning stocks of grain from the peasants and forcing them into large state-owned collective farms, and imposing increased production quotas on the workers in state-owned industries.[139] As before, the government acted tyrannically and people resisted as best they could. Every act of resistance, no matter how minor, was condemned by the Communist leaders and especially by Stalin as a counter-revolutionary act of deliberate sabotage, requiring harsh repression: "kulaks were repressed, managers were persecuted, and wages were lowered"[140] in addition to wage differentials being sharply widened.[141] The repression led to more resistance, either openly or by subterfuge, and thus a vicious cycle was created which ended up with the government using punitive food requisitioning that produced the worst famine in Russia's history in 1932-3, followed by repression on a scale never before seen—the "Great Terror" of 1937-8—four years before Hitler's invasion of the Soviet Union.

During the renewed effort to collectivize the peasants' farms against their will in 1930, the Communists identified three categories of kulaks in terms of their attitudes towards the regime, and gave local authorities quotas for the numbers in each category to punish by 1) either arrest and transfer to GPU (the new name for the Cheka) work camps or executed, with their families deported and all property confiscated, 2) arrest and deportation to distant regions of the country, or 3) (for those "loyal to the regime") transfer to peripheral regions of the districts in which they lived on land requiring improvement.[142] Because of the quotas, peasants with relatively little wealth were often labeled kulaks. A GPU report from Smolensk read, "the brigades took from the wealthy peasants their winter clothes, their warm underclothes, and above all their shoes. They left the kulaks standing in their underwear and took everything, even old rubber socks, women's clothes, tea worth no more than fifty kopeks, water pitchers, and pokers...The brigades confiscated everything, even the pillows from under the heads of babies, and stew from the family pot, which they smeared on the icons they had smashed."[143] Peasants were arrested for crimes such as having killed a pig "with the intention of consuming it themselves and thus keeping it from socialist appropriation" and for "taking part in commerce" when they sold something of their own making. Peasants were deported for "excessive visits to the church" or having an uncle who was an officer under the Tsar.[144] In 1930 "nearly 2.5 million peasants took part in approximately 14,000 revolts, riots, and mass demonstrations against the regime."[145] Circulars were sent to local authorities calling for a slowdown in collectivization because there was a genuine danger of "a veritable tidal wave of peasant wars" and of "the death of at least half of all local Soviet civil servants."[146] In March, 1930, more than 1500 civil servants already had been killed, wounded or badly beaten by peasants armed with axes and pitchforks.[147] The number of people officially deported in 1930 and 1931 was 1,803,392, many of whom, without clothes and other necessities, died of cold and hunger.[148]

Forced collectivization of the peasants was intended to deliver pre-determined quantities of agricultural products to the state, which took increasingly larger shares of the collective harvest. The requisitioning grew to such a large proportion of the harvest that the peasants' very survival was threatened. Under the NEP peasants sold between 15 and 20 percent of the produce, and required the rest for the next year's sowing, feeding cattle, and their own consumption. In 1931 the state took between 40 and 47% of the harvest, depending on the region.[149] Removing produce on this scale required mass arrests, searches for hidden grain and the use of torture to make peasants say where they hid grain in their homes. Prisons were filled to overflowing with peasants in the fall harvest season. Many peasants realized they would starve on the collectives and requested that they be deported to the north.[150] One famous decree promulgated August 7, 1932 provided for execution or sentencing for ten years for "any theft or damage of socialist property." People called it the "ear law" because many of those condemned under it had only taken an ear of corn from the fields of the collective. From August 1932 to December 1933 more than 125,000 people were sentenced under this law and 5,400 received death sentences.[151] In November 1932 the Politburo of the Communist Party sent local authorities a letter ordering new raids on collective farms that had not met their quotas, and also ordering that the reserves kept back for sowing the next year's crop be confiscated as well.[152] This order came after a report by Molotov to the Politburo in August, stating that there was "a real risk of famine even in areas where the harvest has been exceptionally good."[153]

Famine did occur in 1932-33. Peasants without any means of obtaining food tried to leave the farms and migrate to the cities. But the government on December 27, 1932 introduced identity papers and obligatory registration for all citizens in order to prevent this internal migration. Stalin ordered the GPU to ban "by all means necessary the large-scale departure of peasants from Ukraine and the Northern Caucasus for the towns."[154] Stalin, of course, called the desperate peasants "counter-revolutionaries" and ordered that they be arrested. In March 1933 the GPU reported that in one month alone 219,460 people had been intercepted. Many peasants brought their children to cities hoping they would be cared for, and then they returned to the farms to die. Italian diplomatic bulletins from Kharkiv reported that, "Every night the bodies of more than 250 people who have died from hunger or typhus are collected."[155] The government denied there was a famine and turned down foreign offers of assistance, and even shipped 1.8 million tons of grain abroad "in the interests of industrialization."[156] In 1933 for the whole country, there were 6 million deaths attributable to the famine[157] which in turn was caused by the forced requisitions of grain from the collective farms. In addition there were nearly one million people in forced-labor camps and colonies operated by the OGPU (another successor of the Cheka).[158] An historian writes of Stalin and his associates at this time, "They knew that resentment of their rule in the rest of society was deep and wide."[159]

On July 2, 1937 the Politburo sent a telegram to local authorities ordering that "all kulaks and criminals must be immediately arrested...and after a trial before a troika the most hostile are to be shot, and the less active but still hostile elements deported."[160] This order resulted in 259,450 people being arrested and 72,950 shot, according to official records.[161] Local authorities were given quotas, and often they asked for the quotas to be raised in order to prove their zeal and loyalty and thereby avoid punishment to themselves. The arrests and executions continued for over a year. "Spies and subversives"[162] were added to criminals and kulaks as categories of people to round up and execute, and many such "spies" turned out to be Stalin's enemies in top levels of the Communist Party and in the military leadership, some of whom were given elaborate show trials in which they were made to confess to diabolical schemes. In what came be known as the Great Terror, 1,575,000 people were arrested between 1937-8, of whom 85.4% were sentenced, of whom 51%—681,692 people—were executed.[163]

Harsh repression of workers and peasants in order to increase economic production, however, was only one side of Stalin's Five-Year [1928-32] Plan coin. The other equally important side concerned the regime's relationship with foreign capitalist powers. As one historian puts it: "The economic transformation, in Stalin's opinion, could not be accomplished unless the USSR stayed clear of military entanglements abroad. His Five-Year Plan was premised on the Kremlin's need to purchase up-to-date machinery from these powers. It would obviously be difficult to induce foreign governments and business companies to enter into commercial deals if there remained any suspicion that the Red Army might be about to try again to spread revolution on the points of its bayonets."[164] Businesses in the United States and Germany were especially eager to invest in the Soviet Union, and sell modern machinery to the Bolsheviks. Ford Motor Co. actually "signed a deal to build a gigantic automotive works in Nizhni Novgorod [in 1928]."[165] This is the origin of Stalin's alliance with the world's leading capitalists against "his own" workers. The ideological basis for it was the elitist Marxist idea that ordinary people won't work for an egalitarian society until there is economic abundance. The pattern for Stalin's alliance with capitalists was set long before the Nazis attacked the Soviet Union, demonstrating that the alliance between Stalin and the Allied governments during the war was rooted in a shared elitist view of the working class and was not merely the accidental result of their having a common enemy in the Nazis.

When Hitler occupied all of Czechoslovakia in March, 1939, his troops for the first time were on the border of the Soviet Union. Stalin had no particular preference for either the parliamentary-style capitalist governments of Britain and France or the Fascist government in Germany. But Stalin did want to do whatever was necessary to prevent any nation from successfully invading the Soviet Union, and towards this end he first tried to establish an alliance with Britain and France against Germany. On April 18, 1939 Stalin made a formal proposal to Britain and France for such an alliance. The British reaction was hostile.[166] In the summer of 1939 Moscow hosted a meeting to negotiate the alliance, and the British, instead of sending their Foreign Secretary by plane, sent a military *attaché* who had not been empowered to bargain—by boat. This sent a clear signal to Stalin that he could not rely on an alliance with the Western powers.[167]

On August 21 Hitler and Stalin exchanged messages which led to the German Foreign Minister, Ribbentrop, traveling to Moscow and agreeing to a Nazi-Soviet Non-Aggression Treaty, signed August 23, which increased trade between the two nations and, secretly, agreed on a division of territory between Germany and the Soviet Union—Finland, Estonia and Latvia would belong to Stalin and Lithuania and most of Poland would belong to Hitler.[168] (David Kaiser notes, "The Nazi-Soviet Pact included generous economic clauses that provided Germany with large immediate deliveries of food and raw materials in exchange for *future* deliveries of industrial goods and thus enabled Hitler to begin the war with some confidence."[169]) On September 1 Hitler invaded Poland, and Britain and France declared war on Germany, launching World War II. On September 17, two days after Moscow and Tokyo negotiated an end to their military hostilities in Manchuria, Stalin invaded eastern Poland, thereby depriving the Polish army of a chance to concentrate its forces against the Nazis. At this time Stalin assured Ribbentrop "on his word of honor that the Soviet Union would not betray it's partner" and they signed another agreement giving Stalin Lithuania in exchange for territory in eastern Poland.[170] On November 30, the Red Army also invaded Finland (the "Winter War") but the Finns fought back and 200,000 Soviet soldiers were killed before a settlement was reached in March 1940. Stalin also commanded the governments of Estonia, Latvia and Lithuania to join the Soviet Union and in July 1940 he annexed Bessarabia and northern Bukovina from Romania. All who resisted their nation's takeover were killed or sent to the infamous Gulag prison camps. Four thousand four hundred refugee Polish officers were secretly shot and buried in Katyn Forest.[171]

Stalin felt confident that French resistance to Hitler would tie Hitler down and guarantee that he would not consider attacking the Soviet Union. But when tensions developed between the USSR and Germany over interests in Persia, Turkey and Bulgaria, Stalin grew concerned about German intentions and tried to shore up the alliance by stepping up the shipment of Soviet raw materials, especially oil, to Germany, thus helping the Nazi military.[172] In the first half of 1941 Stalin and his Generals worried about a German invasion, but felt so confident they could defeat it that they even toyed with a project for the Red Army to wage an offensive war against Germany. As long as

Germany did not make any demands on the Soviet Union with an ultimatum, as Germany had done before its aggressions in eastern Europe, Stalin felt confident that no attack was imminent. When spies warned Stalin the attack was coming, he did not believe them. Even when the Germans attacked Soviet forces on June 22 1941 (Operation Barbarossa) Stalin denied General Pavlov permission to fight back for three hours, believing it was merely a German provocation.[173] Thus began what Stalin called the "Great Fatherland War"—a phrase he used to rally people on the basis of nationalism, not class, because Soviet citizens by this time had few illusions that their government had anything to do with democracy and working class power. In June 1943, Stalin changed the Soviet Union's state anthem from the *Internationale*, one of the greatest expressions of international working class solidarity ever composed, to a set of verses featuring "Russia the Great."[174] Soviet propagandists "who had portrayed Germans as honorary Russians during the two years of the Nazi-Soviet Non-Aggression Treaty came to treat the entire German people as the enemy," employing for example a poem by Konstantin Simonov ending with the words: "Then kill a German, kill him soon—And any time you see one, kill him."[175]

As we shall see in section III, *Allied War Objectives In Europe and Asia*, Stalin used the appeal of Marxism and the prestige of the Soviet government as the "only socialist government in the world" to command the Communist parties in Fascist-occupied countries to abandon any goals for genuine workers power and democracy, and to yield to the leaders of Great Britain and the U.S. on all matters. Stalin made a deal with British and U.S. leaders. In exchange for their help in preventing Hitler from conquering the Soviet Union, Stalin would help them conquer the working class in western Europe and Asia. To demonstrate his sincerity in this deal, Stalin dissolved the Comintern (the international organization of Communist parties) in May 1943.[176]

UNITED STATES

FDR's Class Loyalty

Understanding which side President Franklin Delano Roosevelt was really on in the struggle between American workers and big business is the first step towards understanding how and why FDR ("FDR" in this context really means not just the man, but all of his influential advisors in and out of government who, collectively, ruled the nation) led the United States into World War II.

When Franklin Roosevelt became President of the United States in 1932 during the Great Depression, he offered Americans a New Deal that, to this day, has given him a reputation as a "friend of the working man." Roosevelt often railed against America's "economic royalists," but in truth, contrary to the public image of himself that he worked so hard to maintain, FDR handed government authority to people who sought to control the working class and keep power firmly in the hands of the capitalist class in the United States. Roosevelt's "pro-working class" reputation resulted from people not understanding that the New Deal reforms during the Great Depression were the elite's way of containing and controlling a working class movement that fundamentally threatened elite power.

FDR crafted labor legislation like the Wagner Act (which legalized unions and enmeshed them in government regulations) to reverse the radical direction of labor and to restore labor peace and uninterrupted production by strengthening the control of conservative labor leaders over rank and file workers. Labor legislation sought not to destroy the unions but to turn them into "responsible" managers of the labor force by making them dependent upon government and corporate support rather than their own rank and file members, even, during the war, forcing members to remain in the union for the length of the contract.

As a War Labor Board decision put it,

> If union leadership is responsible and cooperative, then irresponsible and uncooperative members cannot escape discipline by getting out of the union and thus disrupt relations and hamper production.[177]

Frances Perkins, President Roosevelt's Secretary of Labor, understood this perfectly when she related FDR's advice to a group of business leaders who were nervous about allowing the Congress of Industrial Organization (CIO) to create industry-wide unions:

You should not be afraid to have the CIO organize in your factory... they don't want to run your business. You will probably get a lot more production and a lot more peace and happiness if you have a good union organization and a good contract...[178]

Even the so-called voices for labor in Roosevelt's government were anti-working class in advocating that labor should collaborate with big business, not organize against it, a viewpoint which, in practice, served only to disarm workers ideologically and prevent them from using their strength on the shop floor to win improvements in their lives that business owners would never otherwise permit. One of the most prominent such individuals was Sidney Hillman, a Vice-President of the CIO who, together with William S. Knudsen (President of General Motors) headed the powerful Office of Production Management (OPM) formed in 1941. In 1938, Sidney Hillman summed up his "partnership between labor and capital" creed: "Certainly, I believe in collaborating with the employers! That is what unions are for. I even believe in helping an employer function more productively. For then, we will have a claim to higher wages, shorter hours, and greater participation in the benefits of running a smooth industrial machine...."[179] Sidney Hillman was in FDR's government not because he was a friend of labor, but because he was friend of capital. This is what Labor Secretary Frances Perkins wrote about him in regard to the historic sit down strikes at the General Motors plant in 1937: "I know for a fact that John Lewis and Sidney Hillman and Lee Pressman (Chief CIO lawyer) made great efforts to get the men to leave the plants."[180]

Most of the people FDR appointed to government offices were quite obviously anti-working class. In 1934 FDR's National Recovery Administration chief, General Hugh S. Johnson, went to San Francisco and declared the general strike taking place there a "menace to the government."[181] FDR's first Secretary of State was Cordell Hull, a former senator from Tennessee who represented the overtly racist and anti-working class southern wing of the Democratic party. As head of the Reconstruction Finance Corporation and later the Commerce Department, FDR appointed Jesse Jones, a conservative millionaire newspaper owner. FDR made Henry Stimson Secretary of War. Stimson, who had served as Secretary of War under President William Howard Taft and Secretary of State under Herbert Hoover, was known by these self-declared pro-capitalist Presidents to be a reliable advocate of capitalist, not working class, interests. As key ambassadors, FDR appointed multi-millionaire members of the conservative upper class, such as Joseph Kennedy Sr. to England and Averell Harriman to the Soviet Union. Joseph Kennedy, who made his wealth in prohibition era bootlegging, had well known pro-Fascist and anti-Semitic views,[182] invested secretly with the Nazis, and encouraged Great Britain to ally with Hitler against Stalin.[183] Harriman's wealth began with his railroad inheritance and expanded into banking and shipbuilding; by 1932 he was board chairman of the Union Pacific Railroad. As Under-Secretary of State FDR appointed U.S. Steel millionaire, Edward Stettinius. FDR made these appointments because they reflected his true class loyalty.

When the Japanese bombed Pearl Harbor, it seemed on the surface that FDR, like the entire country, was shocked by the attack and suddenly jolted into the realization that America's self-defense required that we enter the war on the side of Great Britain and not just help her with "Lend-Lease." But in fact, as we shall see in more detail later, FDR was not shocked by the Japanese attack on the United States, since he had been working hard to provoke it, all the while lying to the American public that he was determined to keep the U.S. out of the war. To appreciate why FDR manipulated Americans in this way, we must review just how threatening to elite power was the American working class in the decades leading up to World War II. Only based on this history of class struggle will the story of how FDR pushed Americans into war make sense.

The Problem Of Peace
In the United States the peace following the end of WWI immediately released workers from feelings of loyalty to the government and gave them a sense of freedom to challenge not only individual business owners, but the federal government itself. Less than two weeks after the WWI armistice, in January 1919, 35,000 Seattle shipyard workers went on strike against their employer—the U.S. government. The workers "appealed to the Seattle Central Labor Council to call a General Strike." The Seattle Times wrote, "A general strike directed at WHAT? The Government of the United States? Bosh! Not 15% of Seattle laborites would consider such a proposition." But "within a day, eight local unions endorsed the strike," then 110 locals within two weeks. For six days virtually nothing happened in the city except as approved by the General Strike Committee. The acting governor decided his National Guard were inadequate and phoned Secretary of War Newton Baker who then sent in 950

sailors and marines to reinforce the Mayor's specially sworn in 2,400 deputies who, together, intimidated the workers into ending the strike. Seattle Mayor Hanson declared, "The so-called sympathetic Seattle strike was an attempted revolution. That there was no violence does not alter the fact...The intent, openly and covertly announced, was for the overthrow of the industrial system; here first, then everywhere."[184]

Two months later in April a movement for an eight hour day "swept the New England textile districts," leading to a strike by 120,000 workers. A pro-company labor investigator described the upheaval as, "a strike for wages carried on in a revolutionary atmosphere. That is, there are serious questionings of the justice of the existing economic order. In addition to that there is a feeling on the part of the strikers that the government is against them. To many of them American government is personified by [the Town of] Lawrence [Massachusetts] police." The same month women telephone operators went on strike against the federal government which "retained wartime control of the telephone companies." The men struck in support, and an observer wrote, "I do not believe that an industrial issue has ever before penetrated every village, hamlet or town of New England as has this strike of telephone girls." In September, Boston policemen voted 1,134 to 2 to strike after 19 policemen were fired in retaliation for the policemen's association affiliating with the AFL (American Federation of Labor). The National Guard was called in and the entire police force was fired. *The Wall Street Journal* wrote, "Lenin and Trotsky are on their way."[185]

The strike wave spread to many cities including Chicago and New York City. Then, on September 22, 1919, 350,000 steelworkers went on strike. The Sheriff of Allegheny County in Pennsylvania, the heart of the industry, "issued a proclamation forbidding outdoor meetings anywhere in the county" and in most steel centers local authorities forbade even indoor meetings. "In Gary, Indiana the National Guard occupied the city and forbade parades." Attorney General A. Mitchell Palmer "warned publicly that the strike harbored the threat of Bolshevism."[186]

On a Sunday night in the week of July 4, in the Belleville sub-district of Illinois, 2,000 coal miners adopted a resolution that read: "In view of the fact that the present-day system of Society, known as the capitalist system, has completely broken down, and is no longer able to supply the material and spiritual needs of the workers of the land, and in further view of the fact that the apologists for and the beneficiaries of that system now try to placate the suffering masses by promises of reforms such as a shorter workday and increases in wages...therefore be it resolved, that the next National Convention of the U.M.W.A. [United Mine Workers of America] issue a call to the workers of all industries to elect delegates to an industrial congress, there to demand of the capitalist class that all instruments of industries be turned over to the working class to guarantee that necessities, comforts and luxuries be produced for the use of humanity instead of a parasitical class of stockholders..."[187] Four months later, on November 1, 425,000 coal miners went on strike for a 30 hour week and a 60 percent wage increase. President Wilson sent federal troops into the "coal fields of Utah, Washington, New Mexico, Oklahoma, and Pennsylvania." When United Mine Workers President John L. Lewis ordered the miners back to work, declaring "We are Americans, we cannot fight our Government," the coal miners ignored him and stayed out for nearly a month.[188]

In May 1920 a coal strike in Matewan, West Virginia spread throughout the state leading to a three hour gun battle between strikers and guards brought in "to prevent infiltration of union men." The strike continued to August 1921 when the workers decided to use force to get through the guards, deputies and troopers who were preventing them from entering and spreading the strike to other counties. The workers formed a "citizens army" march of 4,000 led by war veterans, accompanied by nurses in uniform, and armed with every weapon they could obtain, and they battled deputies defending the non-union counties. President Warren G. Harding sent "2,100 troops of the 19th Infantry, together with machine guns and airplanes," to defeat the "citizens army."[189] The airplanes were armed with gas bombs and machine guns,[190] and although the strikers backed down before the planes were used, the federal government was forced to reveal to these West Virginia coal miners that, if necessary for the protection of capitalist power, it would bomb American citizens just as it had bombed foreigners in the First World War (and as it would bomb civilians on an unimaginable scale in a future World War.)

Enormous revolutionary impulses were released by the restoration of peace immediately following the conclusion of WWI. The American ruling elite was frightened; so frightened that it resorted to the kind of actions that were dangerous because they risked revealing to the general public how undemocratic was the real exercise of governmental power in the country. Not only were government military forces ordered to attack Americans, and the right to assemble revoked, but other laws that made the country appear to be a democracy were flagrantly ignored. U.S. Attorney General A. Mitchell Palmer conducted the infamous "Palmer Raids" against radicals and leftists in 1919. He struck without warning and without warrants, smashed union offices and the headquarters of Communist, Socialist, and other radical organizations, and arrested over five thousand people, deporting two hundred and forty nine. Also revealing, Congress refused to seat the duly elected socialist from Wisconsin, Victor Berger. Such heavy-handed actions were not necessary during the just concluded war. For America's ruling elite, war was not the problem; peace was.

When the peacetime economy led to the Great Depression in the 1930s, revolutionary impulses among American working people grew even stronger. Organizations of the unemployed formed in cities across the country. In Chicago alone the Unemployed Council had 22,000 members. The Unemployed Councils implicitly rejected the rights of private property. When landlords tried to evict tenants who couldn't pay the rent, the Councils used mass direct action to stop the evictions.[191]

General MacArthur, Officers Eisenhower And Patton, And The National Guard Attack The Enemy—Americans

The biggest fight against an eviction, however, was probably one that occurred July 28, 1932 in the nation's capital. Twenty thousand veterans of WWI, many unemployed and homeless, camped out in the Capital to demand payment of bonuses they had been promised. On that day, the future military "heroes" of WWII made their debut in history. Gen. Douglas MacArthur, with Maj. Dwight D. Eisenhower and one of his officers, George S. Patton Jr., following orders from Secretary of War Patrick J. Hurley, led four troops of cavalry, four companies of infantry, a mounted machine gun squadron and six whippet tanks, lined up on Pennsylvania Avenue near 12th Street in Washington DC, in an attack on thousands of Americans who had become known as "Bonus Marchers." Veterans who raised their arms against soldiers on horseback had their arms cut by sabers. Others were hit by the flat of the sword. In some instances ears were cut off.

Two were killed and many wounded.[192] As horses pounded toward the veterans, reporters at the White House were told the Secret Service had learned that those resisting eviction were "entirely of the Communist element." "Thank God," said President Herbert Hoover, "we still have a government that knows how to deal with a mob."[193]

In Pennsylvania, unemployed coal miners ignored the private property rights of the mine owners and dug small "bootleg" coal mines on company property, producing in this fashion in 1934 "some five million tons of coal and employing 20,000 men." The coal companies fought the "bootleggers" with company police but the miners fought back. The companies had no public support, and couldn't even convince juries to convict the "bootleggers."[194]

Seeing working people taking matters into their own hands and ignoring the rights of private property, President Franklin Delano Roosevelt crafted the "New Deal" to convince them that their problems would be solved by corporate and government leaders. But not all workers were convinced. On May 9, 1934 longshoremen on the West Coast went on strike, "cutting off nearly 2,000 miles of coast land." The strike spread to teamsters, sailors, marine firemen, water tenders, cooks, stewards, and licensed officers. On the forty-fifth day of the strike the San Francisco Chief of Police sent 700 policemen to the docks with tear gas and riot guns to break the picket lines of 5,000 strikers. A reporter wrote, "It was as close to actual war as anything but war itself could be." Two strikers were killed and 115 hospitalized. That night the governor of California ordered in 1,700 National Guard soldiers with armored cars and machine gun nests and ordered them to shoot to kill. By July 16 there was a general strike in San Francisco of 130,000 workers which spread to Oakland and then up the Pacific Coast. Authorities brought in 4,500 National Guard troops including infantry, machine guns, tank, and artillery units.

The *Los Angeles Times* wrote: "The situation in San Francisco is not correctly described by the phrase 'general strike.' What is actually in progress there is an insurrection, a Communist-inspired and led revolt against organized government. There is but one thing to be done—put down the revolt with any force necessary." FDR's National Recovery Administration chief, General Hugh S. Johnson, went to San Francisco and declared the general strike a "menace to the government" and a "civil war."[195]

On May 23, 1934, nine hundred National Guard troops with machine gun units were required to suppress a strike in Toledo, Ohio during which two workers were killed and fifteen wounded.[196] On May 22 a Teamsters strike in Minneapolis developed into a violent confrontation between most of the city's working class against the entire police force supplemented by an extra 500 men sworn in for the occasion. Twenty to thirty thousand people showed up at the market, many armed with lead pipes and clubs, and they drove the police out of the market and continued to battle them all over the city. By nightfall there were no police to be seen in Minneapolis, and strikers were directing downtown traffic. On July 20 police attacked the strikers, wounding sixty-seven people including thirteen bystanders, two fatally. That night an enormous protest meeting ended in a march on City Hall to lynch the mayor and police chief, but was stopped by National Guard troops. A mass funeral for one of the pickets drew between fifty thousand and one hundred thousand workers, and this convinced the governor, who claimed to support the strike and to be a "radical," to declare martial law. The governor arrested all the strike leaders, which led to more leaders emerging from the rank-and-file to continue the strike with even greater determination. The governor was forced to back down and release the strike leaders, and a month later the employers capitulated to the strike demands.[197]

Meanwhile, on July 16, 1934, twenty thousand textile workers in Alabama began a strike that spread throughout the South and East Coast until by September 5 325,000 textile workers, many of them women, were on strike and using "flying squadrons" to spread the strike from mill to mill, often battling guards, entering the mills, unbelting machinery and fighting non-strikers. *The New York Times* warned, "The grave danger of the situation is that it will get completely out of the hands of the leaders...The growing mass character of the picketing operations is rapidly assuming the appearance of military efficiency and precision and is something entirely new in the history of American labor struggles. Observers...declared that if the mass drive continued to gain momentum at the speed at which it was moving today, it will be well nigh impossible to stop it without a similarly organized opposition with all the implications such an attempt would entail."

The governor of South Carolina declared martial law on September 9, announcing that a "state of insurrection" existed. Fifty strike squadrons of 200 to 650 strikers moved south in the Carolinas on a 110-mile front, undeterred by National Guardsmen with orders to "shoot to kill." On September 5 a striker and a special deputy were killed in a two-hour battle at a mill in Trion, Georgia, and three pickets were shot, one fatally, in Augusta.[198] The violence spread to New England, and by September 12 National Guard troops were on duty in every New England state except Vermont and New Hampshire. That evening a crowd of 2,000 was fighting National Guardsmen in Woonsocket, Rhode Island. Guardsmen fired 30 shots into the crowd, hitting four, one fatally. The crowd was outraged, grew to 8,000, and was only quelled by two more companies of National Guardsmen who put the city under military rule. Governor Green of Rhode Island declared that "there is a Communist uprising and not a textile strike in Rhode Island," and then declared a state of insurrection. At the same time, Washington mobilized detachments of regular Army troops prepared to leave for Rhode Island "at a moment's notice."[199]

On September 17 an "army of 10,000 National Guardsmen was mobilized in Georgia, South Carolina, North Carolina, Alabama, and Mississippi, supplemented by 15,000 armed deputies" for the purpose of breaking the textile strike. But the strikers didn't back down and their numbers grew to 421,000 by September 18. Georgia Governor Eugene Talmadge declared martial law. National Guardsmen began mass arrests of flying squadrons and held them without charge in a concentration camp where Germans had been held during WWI. "By September 19 the death toll in the South had reached thirteen." On the 22nd the conservative leaders of the United Textile Workers union called off the strike with the excuse that a government Board would investigate conditions in the mills.[200]

No doubt all of these events of 1934 weighed heavily on FDR's mind when, in May 1935, he told an emissary of William Randolph Hearst, "I want to save our system, the capitalistic system; to save it is to give some heed to world thought of today. I want to equalize the distribution of wealth."[201]

Faced with a working class insurrection, Roosevelt pushed Congress to enact the National Labor Relations Act to channel labor militancy into safe orderly collective bargaining. But his strategy was not completely successful. Rubber workers in Akron, Ohio had become disgusted with their sellout union and the National Labor Relations Board, and developed the tactic of the sit-down strike to guarantee that rank-and-file workers and not union leaders would be in control. By 1936 "a week seldom passed without one or more sit-down" strikes in the Goodyear rubber plant, and workers had as much power in the plant as the company.[202] Then auto workers began using the sit-down strike at General Motors plants on such a large scale that in the first 10 days of February 1937 GM produced only 151 cars in the entire country.[203] The largest sit-down occurred at the plant in Flint, Michigan where Governor Frank Murphy called out the National Guard. Thousands of workers traveled hundreds of miles to join and support the Flint sit-down, and auto plants in Detroit and Toledo where shut down just due to the exodus. A crowd of 10,000 workers occupied Flint, and surrounded the plant armed with 30-inch wooden braces from the factory. Fearing an armed assault by police, union war veterans had a plan to "muster an armed force among their own number" to "take over the city hall, the courthouse and police headquarters, capture and imprison all officials and release union men." On February 11 General Motors agreed to recognize the United Auto Workers union, whose leadership then called off the strike.[204] But in the next four months there were 170 sit-downs in GM plants because the sit-downs were really not mainly about union recognition; they were a struggle over whether workers or capitalists were going to have actual power in the plants over issues from the speed of the line, to safety and hiring and firing.[205] Following the GM sit down, workers sat down at Chrysler. Chrysler Corporation "secured an injunction ordering the 6,000 sit-downers to leave, but as the evacuation hour came near, a huge crowd of pickets gathered—10,000 at the main Dodge plant in Hamtramck; 10,000 at the Chrysler Jefferson plant; smaller numbers at other Chrysler, Dodge, Plymouth, and DeSoto plants; 30,000 to 50,000 in all—demonstrating the consequences of an attempted eviction." The New York Times underscored what was at stake, writing, "It is generally feared that an attempt to evict the strikers with special deputies would lead to an inevitable large amount of bloodshed and the state of armed insurrection."[206]

> When they tie the can to a union man,
> Sit Down! Sit Down!
> When they give him the sack they'll take him back,
> Sit Down! Sit Down!
> When the speed-up comes, just twiddle your thumbs,
> Sit Down!, Sit Down!
> When the boss wont talk don't take a walk,
> Sit Down! Sit Down!
>
> —Maurice Sugar

In 1937 400,000 workers engaged in sit-down strikes all over the country and in all sorts of jobs from municipal trash collectors to retail store clerks to grave diggers and even blind workers at the New York Association for the Blind.

Michigan's Governor Murphy warned the state might have to use force to restore respect for the courts and other public authority, to protect personal and property rights, and to uphold the "structure of organized society."[207]

The New Deal was meant to control and contain working class struggles that challenged capitalist power and social relations. But it was failing. The Wagner Act of 1935 was supposed to channel labor militancy into legalistic procedures, not sit-down strikes that conservative labor leaders found difficult to control. The Social Security Act of 1935 and similar legislation was meant to convince Americans that the government would make sure that capitalism worked for ordinary people and not just the wealthy. But many people weren't buying it. The populist U.S. Senator from Louisiana, Huey Long, may have been a charlatan, but his "Share the Wealth" Clubs claimed seven million members; they backed a radical plan to guarantee an annual income for every American, and they thought FDR's reforms did not go nearly far enough. In fact FDR was frightened by "Democratic polls that suggested that Long's threat to run as an independent in the 1936 presidential race could jeopardize Roosevelt's reelection prospects."[208] (Long was assassinated before this could happen.)

FDR and his fellow elite knew that nothing could be taken for granted. For example, in 1934 the race for Governor of California was supposed to have been between the Democratic Party's George Creel—formerly the head of President Woodrow Wilson's Committee on Public Information during World War I and more recently FDR's West Coast chief for the National Recovery Administration—and the Republican incumbent Governor, Frank Merriam. What actually happened shocked the entire political establishment. The author and long-time socialist, Upton Sinclair, sparked an immensely popular movement called EPIC—End Poverty In California—which called for the State of California to "use its powers of eminent domain or confiscatory taxes to seize idle factories and vacant farmland" (of which there were plenty because of the Depression) to establish a "network of cooperative agricultural and manufacturing colonies" in which the state's 700,000 unemployed workers would "produce and exchange their products in a giant cash-free network." Eight hundred EPIC clubs sprouted up across the state in working class neighborhoods. They operated a weekly newspaper "which was distributed by the hundreds of thousands in local editions" and they "operated speakers' bureaus, research units, women's clubs, youth clubs, and drama groups" as well as "radio broadcasts, plays, and rodeos," and they "drew big crowds to a lavishly staged EPIC pageant that depicted the lessons of production for use." On August 28, in the primary election results, Upton Sinclair "captured the Democratic nomination with more than 436,000 votes, more than any primary election candidate in California history, more than all his Democratic opponents combined, and more than the Republican he would face in November." The voters had "turned the Democratic Party over to a former Socialist." Only an extraordinary and unprecedented attack on Sinclair by both the traditionally pro-Democratic Party newspapers owned by William Randolph Hearst as well as the "progressive" McClatchy *BEE* newspapers and the *Los Angeles Times* owned by the conservative Harry Chandler, joined by Hollywood moguls like MGM's Louis B. Mayer, in an orchestrated smear campaign, prevented Sinclair from winning the governorship. Sinclair's vote doubled to 879,537 versus 1,138,620 for the incumbent and 302,519 for a third party candidate. Twenty-four of the EPIC candidates did however win seats to California's 80 seat assembly.[209]

The ruling elite had a working class insurrection on its hands, and they needed some way to decisively contain it. If ever the ruling class in the United States had a strong motivation to restore the "good old days" of a nation-versus-nation war, when the government could convince workers that national unity trumped issues of class and that strikes and radical demands "undermined national security," it was now.

War To The Rescue

From the time Germany initiated WWII with its invasion of Poland on September 1, 1939, FDR worked to get the U.S. into the war; he had two goals: The first and most crucial was to control the increasingly revolutionary U.S. working class by using the excuse of "national defense" to demand that workers put their class demands on hold. Only a nationalistic war could rally working people behind the nation's capitalist leaders. The second goal was to defend and expand U.S. capitalist control of workers and resources in Europe, the Middle East and Asia. Ordinary Americans overwhelmingly viewed the Nazis as thugs trampling democratic values, which meant that if FDR was going to convince Americans to enter the war, it would have to be on the side of Great Britain.

However, a number of powerful American corporate leaders (with counterparts in Great Britain) thought the best way to achieve the same two goals that FDR wanted would be for the United States to work for a peace settlement in Europe on pro-Nazi terms, and to use Fascist rather than liberal (New Deal) methods of social control in the United States. Many of these individuals (including Henry Ford, owner of the Ford Motor Co.; Irénéé du Pont and other members of the du Pont family which controlled General Motors Co.; William S. Knudsen, President of General Motors; Sothenes Behn, Chief of ITT Corp. in the U.S., and Joseph Kennedy whose fortune came from bootlegging during Prohibition) admired Hitler, shared his anti-Semitism and in some cases emulated his Gestapo methods of subjugating workers in their own factories.[210] Some of these people even took preliminary steps towards organizing a coup d'etat (using weapons supplied by Remington, a Du Pont subsidiary) to depose Roosevelt and install an American "Führer"[211] in 1934, a fact known to FDR at the time.[212] Yet despite their disagreement with FDR on what might seem to be fundamental questions—like whether to use Gestapo goons to attack union organizers, or legalize unions; support Hitler or fight him—FDR included some of these individuals in important positions in his administration prior to and during the war. For example, he appointed Kennedy as Ambassador to England in 1938, and he appointed Knudsen to head the Office of Production Management in 1941. The government allowed pro-Nazi American corporate leaders to maintain their profitable wartime financial relations with the Nazis, and even allowed them to produce military equipment for Germany in overseas factories *after* the U.S. was at war with Germany.[213] The government ignored the fact that these businessmen were committing crimes that were in clear violation of "trading with the enemy" statutes.[214] (This topic is taken up in greater detail in the section *Was The War Caused By Economic Competition Between Nations?* below.) The explanation of this paradox is that, from the standpoint of the corporate elite, the disagreement between FDR and the pro-Nazi Americans was only about tactics, not about the shared goal of strengthening American elite power over working people.

Before Pearl Harbor, Americans opposed U.S. involvement in the European war and they were not very enthusiastic about going to war in Asia just to protect British and French colonies from being taken by Japan. World War I had convinced most Americans that wars were something to stay out of at all costs. Many concluded that WWI benefitted only war profiteers and people with ulterior motives. Antiwar sentiment was strong not only among right-wingers like the anti-Semite Henry Ford and Charles Lindbergh, but also in the working class, one of whose most influential labor leaders, John L. Lewis of the United Mine Workers, told workers to vote against Roosevelt lest he "make cannon fodder of your sons." Even Pete Seeger and Woody Guthrie initially opposed entering the war. Americans were very sympathetic to the victims of fascism, but at the same time very suspicious of the motives of politicians and corporate leaders who advocated war. If FDR's goal had been to rally Americans to provide economic and even military support for ordinary people in Europe and Asia in their struggle against Fascist oppression, he could have succeeded by doing two things: 1) make this goal clear, and 2) instill confidence that he had no ulterior purpose by consistently taking the side of working people in the United States itself against the capitalists who exploited them. Of course FDR did neither of these things because his goal had nothing to do with helping working people win their struggles anywhere.

Allies' Spanish Civil War Policy: "Goodness Had Nothing To Do With It"

Perhaps the clearest example of the fact that the goals of the Allied elites in World War II had nothing to do with helping working people defeat Fascism is their refusal to support the Spanish working class against the Spanish Fascists. On July 17, 1936 Spanish generals, led by General Francisco Franco and backed by Hitler and Mussolini, led a pro-Fascist revolt against the government of Spain. The Spanish government (the Republic of Spain) was democratic in form like the U.S. government and was composed of people on the left-liberal side of the political spectrum. To the surprise of the generals, militant revolutionary working class organizations, including anarchists with a strong popular following, rallied to the support of the besieged government with armed militias, turning the attempted coup d'etat into a full scale class war known as the Spanish Civil War.

Inside wide swaths of Spain, where they were strongest, workers and peasants fought not only to defeat the Fascists, but to make a fundamental social revolution against capitalism. In Barcelona in July, 1936 "hotels, stores, banks, factories were either requisitioned or closed. Those that were requisitioned were run by managing committees of former technicians and workers...And then (as a workers' committee on the Barcelona *metro* remarked) 'we set out on the great adventure.' " In the Catalonian village of Seriñena peasants destroyed all of the documents relating to rural property. "A huge bonfire was set ablaze in the middle of the main square, the flames rising higher than the roof of the church, young Anarchists throwing on new material with triumphant gestures." In several places in Andalusia, "private property was entirely abolished, along with the payment of debts to shop-keepers. Often money itself was declared illegal. In Castro del Rio, near Córdoba, a *régime* was set up comparable to that of the Baptists of Munster of 1530,[215] all private exchange of goods being banned...The great estates in this region were still worked by their former laborers, who received no pay at all but were fed from the village store according to their needs."[216] Vernon Richards, in his Forward to Gaston Laval's extensive study of the rural collective system created by peasants during the Spanish Civil War, writes: "According to Laval, in Aragon, the Levante, and Castile there was a total of 1,600 agricultural Collectives. In Catalonia all industry and public services were collectivized, in the Levante 70% of industry, and in Castile only a part of industry. In his introduction to the French edition [Laval] suggests that between 5 and 7 million people were directly or indirectly involved."[217]

Forty thousand foreigners volunteered as soldiers on the side of the Republic, including 2800 from the United States, but only 557 from the Soviet Union. Stalin was determined to prevent the Republican forces from making an anti-capitalist revolution that would jeopardize his alliance with France and Great Britain, and to secure control over events in Spain he sold arms to the Republic (at full market price, according to the Republic's War Minister) and sent nearly 2000 NKVD members to Spain to control the Spanish Communist Party and attack Republican forces who were fighting for a social revolution. Stalin's Spanish agenda was revealed, for example, by the Soviet Union's Communist Party paper, *Pravda*, which declared on December 17, 1936, "So far as Catalonia is concerned, the cleaning up of Trotskyists and Anarchists has begun and it will be carried out with the same energy as in the USSR,"[218] referring to the Soviet dictator's purge of his enemies in the Communist Party that would reach a climax in the famous staged trials of 1937.

One unusual aspect of this civil war was that the government of Spain, which the working class was defending, had all of the legal trappings of "legitimacy" by the rules of the capitalist "democracies." This proved to be a terrible embarrassment to the "democratic" governments of the U.S., Great Britain and France. On July 25 Leon Blum, the socialist leader of the "Popular Front" (the Front was supposedly against Fascism) government of France announced that France would send no arms to the Spanish Republican government! The British government too was determined not to send arms to help the Republic, claiming they did not want to antagonize Germany or Italy. Roosevelt used the Neutrality Act of 1936 as his excuse for not sending arms to the Spanish Republic. But he had a problem: the law only applied to "war between or among nations," not civil war. Nonetheless, on August 14 FDR announced that the U.S. government would "scrupulously refrain from any interference whatsoever in the unfortunate Spanish situation"[219] and he declared a "moral embargo" on any American citizen sending arms to help the Republic. In October, Secretary of State Hull "informed the Spanish ambassador in Washington, Fernando de los Rios, that despite America's traditional attitude of favoring legal governments the United States would not aid the legal Spanish Republican regime."[220] Although not able legally to prohibit exports of arms to Spain from the U.S., the government did everything it could to prevent it. The State Department "publicized each license granted for arms export in order to embarrass the shippers...Roosevelt said shipping arms was legal but 'unpatriotic.'" By January 8, Roosevelt managed to secure legislation making it illegal to ship arms to Spain. (The Senate passed the bill unanimously, but Senator Nye observed that "strictly speaking, neutrality it is not.") The Germans announced they were pleased, and General Franco "remarked that Roosevelt had behaved like a 'true gentleman' and that the rapid passage of the new neutrality law was 'a gesture we Nationalists shall never forget.' "[221] Despite mounting public opposition to the embargo on arms to Spain, the "embargo remained in effect until April 1, 1939, when, following the fall of Madrid and Valencia [to Franco's Fascists], the United States recognized the Franco regime as the legal government of Spain and, two days later, established diplomatic relations."[222]

FDR Secretly Provoked Japan To Attack The U.S.

Franklin Roosevelt may not have wanted to help revolutionary workers fight Fascists, but he did want to get the U.S. into war.

As early as 1933 Roosevelt, as President-elect, demonstrated his desire to get the U.S. into a war in the Far East. On January 9, 1933 FDR told his future Secretary of War, Henry L. Stimson, that he was committed to the "Stimson doctrine"—the idea advanced by Stimson, when he was Secretary of State under Herbert Hoover, that the U.S. should break the Anglo-Japanese alliance dating from 1902 and "draw Great Britain into the American line of policy against Japan." Raymond Mosley, who would later serve as FDR's Assistant Secretary of State and who was a close personal advisor, warned FDR at the time of the "peril involved in his commitment to Mr. Stimson's doctrine" and later wrote: "It endorsed a policy that invited a major war in the Far East—a war which the United States and England might have had to wage against Japan had England not refused to go along with Stimson."[223]

Because he wanted Americans to enter a war defined as nation versus nation and not class versus class, FDR could not make arguments for entering the war against Fascism based on class solidarity, even though these would have been the most powerful and convincing arguments for most Americans. Were it not for FDR's elitist goals, he could have exposed the Nazis' attacks on Jews and labor leaders as attempts to subjugate German and other European workers, he could have blasted the Japanese rulers for their fascist attacks on Japanese, Chinese and Korean working people, and he could have called for American solidarity with European and Asian workers against the Fascists. For a politician like Roosevelt, whose great public support derived from his claim to be a champion of working people against the "economic royalists," such an internationalization of his "friend of the working man" appeal would only have bolstered FDR's standing among working class Americans and, if anything, strengthened his electoral standing. Instead, FDR publicly denied that he wanted the U.S. to go to war, while behind the scenes he did everything he could to provoke Germany and Japan to attack the U.S. so that he could use the attack to get support for a purely nationalistic war.

"Your President says this country is not going to war." Speaking with specific reference to Japan, this is what Roosevelt declared from Buffalo, NY, while campaigning for President in 1940. Nearly a month before making this promise, on October 8, 1940, Roosevelt had a long conversation with Admiral James O. Richardson, Commander in Chief of the Pacific Fleet at the time. The Admiral, according to his testimony to the Congressional Committee on Pearl Harbor in November, 1945, "asked the President if we were going to enter the war." Richardson testified that "He [the President] replied that if the Japanese attacked Thailand, or the Kra Peninsula, or the Dutch East Indies, we would not enter the war, that if they even attacked the Philippines he doubted whether we would enter the war, but that they could not always avoid making mistakes and that as the war continued and the area of operations expanded sooner or later they would make a mistake and we would enter the war."[224]

In the 1940 presidential campaign, the Republican candidate, Wendell Willkie, charged that Roosevelt planned to send American soldiers overseas. To refute this true statement, FDR made a deal with Joseph Kennedy Sr., who had spoken against U.S. involvement in the war and was trusted by many in the anti-war camp: FDR would support Kennedy's son, Joseph Jr.'s, future bid for governor of Massachusetts, if Joseph Kennedy Sr. would make a nationwide radio speech and say what both men knew was false—that FDR had no plans to involve the U.S. in a world war. In fact FDR had exactly such plans. Kennedy made the speech, decisively helping FDR win re-election.[225]

Shortly after the election FDR set in motion a series of secret steps to provoke the Japanese to attack the U.S. Japan had to import 90% of her oil, and half of this came from the United States.[226] FDR and his advisors knew that depriving Japan access to U.S. oil would very likely induce Japan to take actions that would lead to war between the U.S. and Japan. That war was precisely the object, and not merely a necessary risk that had to be taken in the pursuit of other aims, is indicated by a letter Secretary of the Interior Harold Ickes wrote to Roosevelt in the spring of 1941: "To embargo oil to Japan would be as popular a move in all parts of the country as you could make. There might develop...a situation as would make it not only possible but easy to get into the war in an effective way."[227] It is clear that Roosevelt appreciated the connection between U.S. oil and war with Japan. On July 24, 1941, FDR addressed the Volunteer Participation Committee and led them to believe that he was trying to avoid war with Japan, saying, "And now here is a nation called Japan...If we had cut the oil off they probably would have gone down to the Dutch East Indies a year ago, and you would have had war."[228] FDR's basis for this statement was most likely the report on the effect of a U.S. oil embargo on Japan, issued the previous week (July 19) by Admiral Richmond Turner (Director of the War Plans Division of the Navy Department), that stated: "It is generally believed that shutting off the American supply petroleum [to Japan] will lead promptly to an invasion [by Japan] of the Netherlands East Indies."[229]

At the August, 1941 Atlantic Conference FDR and Churchill discussed the need for joint U.S. and British action against Japan in the event Japan attacked British or Dutch interests in the Netherlands East Indies, and in consequence of that agreement FDR issued a statement to the Japanese Ambassador on August 17, 1941 that read: "...this Government now finds it necessary to say to the Government of Japan that if the Japanese Government takes any further steps in pursuance of a policy or program of military domination by force or threat of force of neighboring countries, the Government of the United States will be compelled to take immediately any and all steps which it may deem necessary toward safeguarding the legitimate rights and interests of the Unites States and American nationals and toward insuring the safety and security of the United States." Based on a detailed examination of the drafting of this statement, historian Charles Beard writes, "...it is patent that the notice given by President Roosevelt to the Japanese Ambassador on August 17, 1941, was intended to be in the nature of a war warning" and Beard adds, "To the Japanese Ambassador, familiar with the language of diplomacy, the statement could have had only one meaning."[230] With this clear warning that the U.S. would resort to war to stop Japan from seizing oil from neighboring countries, the U.S. made it equally clear to Japan's rulers that if they were deprived of oil from the United States they would have to first destroy the U.S. military presence in the Pacific before they could expect to succeed in capturing the oil of neighboring countries.

Knowing full well that it would result in Japan attacking oil-producing British or Dutch interests in Asia, and knowing that this in turn would lead to war between the U.S. and Japan, and despite the U.S. having had no moral qualms about supplying oil to Japan after its invasion of China in 1937, suddenly in August 1941 Roosevelt froze all of Tokyo's assets in the U.S. and ordered government officials to tie up in red tape all of Japan's efforts to buy U.S. oil. At the same time FDR sent B-17 Flying Fortress bombers, which had the range required to attack Japan, to the Philippines.[231] Following the cutoff of oil to Japan, *Time* magazine reported that Japanese Ambassador Admiral Kichisaburo Nomura (who had only one eye) complained: "All over Tokyo, no taxicab." *Time* editorialized that when Normura uttered his complaint, "the sparkle goes out of his one good eye. It means Japan is desperately hard up for oil and gasoline, which means Japan must say uncle to Uncle Sam or else fight for oil."[232] An indication of the mood and intentions, at this time, of FDR and his highest level advisors is available to us in the form of diary entries by Secretary of War Stimson regarding Cabinet meetings in the month of November, 1941. On November 7, "President Roosevelt took a vote of his full Cabinet on the proposition whether the country would back up the Administration if it struck at the Japanese in the south-eastern Pacific area; and the Cabinet was 'unanimous in feeling the country would support us.'" On November 21, "Mr. Stimson had a talk with President Roosevelt about preparations to use poison gas in the Philippines in case the Japanese began to use it."[233]

In November Americans had broken the Japanese "Purple" code for sending secret messages and, from intercepts code named "Magic," knew that Japan's military had decided to go to war against the U.S. unless an agreement on purchasing oil was reached by November 29.[234] "After that, things are automatically going to happen," Roosevelt told Churchill on November 24.[235] Secretary of War Stimson's diary report of a meeting in the Oval Office November 25 with FDR and other military leaders reads, "There the President, instead of bringing up the Victory Parade [an office nickname for a plan of action in case of war in Europe], brought up entirely the relations with the Japanese. He brought up the event that we were likely to be attacked perhaps (as soon as) next Monday, for the Japanese are notorious for making an attack without warning, and the question was what we should do. The question was how we should maneuver them into the position of firing the first shot without allowing too much danger to ourselves.' "[236] On November 26 Secretary of State Hull delivered an absurdly unrealistic ultimatum to the Japanese demanding that they withdraw from China and repudiate their Tripartite Pact agreement with Germany, or else no oil would be forthcoming.[237] By this date, American leaders knew Japan would attack imminently, they just didn't know it would be Pearl Harbor;[238] they expected to be hit in the Philippines or Southeast Asia. On December 1 Roosevelt summoned the British ambassador, Lord Halifax, and urged the British navy to take preventive steps to thwart a possible attack on Thailand by Japanese troopships reportedly in the South China Sea, and "assured Halifax of American backing. As for a Japanese attack on British or Dutch Far East possessions, 'we should obviously all be together.' Those last words make it clear that Roosevelt now saw Japan as, in Harold Ickes's words, a way to get into the global war in an 'effective' way."[239] Far from being a shocking surprise and a terrible calamity for President Roosevelt and his close advisors, Pearl Harbor was the much sought-after solution to their great problem of getting a reluctant American population fired up for a nationalistic war. Secretary of War Stimson's diary entry at 2pm December 7, written after learning from the President about the attack on Pearl Harbor, says it all: "Now the Japs have solved the whole thing by attacking us directly in Hawaii...My first feeling was of relief that the indecision was over and that a crisis had come in a way which would unite all our people."[240]

FDR Provoked The German Declaration Of War On The U.S.

On December 8 President Roosevelt declared the 7th "a date which will live in infamy" but did not mention Germany. On December 9 FDR asserted on national radio that "Germany and Italy consider themselves at war with the United States without even bothering about a formal declaration"[241] which was simply untrue and seems calculated either to have provoked a German declaration of war on the U.S. or else to convince Congress to declare war on Germany. The fact of the matter was that under the Tripartite Pact, Germany was not obligated to join Japan in a war Japan initiated.[242] In fact, Hitler did not want the U.S. as an enemy and for that reason had ordered his U-boats and aircraft to avoid attacks on Americans and ignore American provocations in the period before Pearl Harbor. Even after FDR ordered American warships to "shoot on sight" at German submarines, Hitler ordered Grand Admiral Alfred Erich Raeder, the German navy's commander in chief, on October 8 1941, to avoid incidents that could be used as a pretext for Americans to declare war.[243]

What finally did provoke Hitler to declare war on the U.S. was the publication on December 4, 1941 (just days before Japan attacked Pearl Harbor) in the *Chicago Tribune*, under the headline "FDR's WAR PLANS!" of a top secret document called Rainbow Five and a copy of FDR's letter ordering preparation of the document.[244] Rainbow Five was the plan, drawn up at FDR's order by the joint board of the U.S. Army and Navy, that called for the creation of a 10-million man army, including a force of 5 million men that would invade Europe in 1943 to defeat Germany.[245] The evidence that FDR himself leaked Rainbow Five is, as Thomas Fleming recounts in *The New Dealers' War*, quite convincing. The publication prompted the America First organization, the largest foe of U.S. intervention in the war, to escalate their condemnation of the President—as FDR knew it would—but then three days later Japan's attack on the United States (on Pearl Harbor, as it turned out) made them eat their words and lose all credibility—also as FDR knew it would. On December 11 Hitler did finally declare war on the United States because he and his military chiefs all considered Rainbow Five proof that the U.S. was already at war with Germany.

Why All The Deceit To Fight A "Good War?"

President Roosevelt's manipulation and deceit to get the U.S. into World War II were only necessary because he dared not call for a war of working class solidarity against the Fascists. A call to war on this basis would have resonated with most Americans and it would have required no deceit whatsoever. But the last thing FDR wanted was for ordinary people to understand the world in terms of conflicting values and goals of working people versus elites. Instead, FDR wanted to use war to line American working people up behind their corporate masters and against foreign workers, on the basis of the big lie of nationalism. To mobilize people around a lie requires deceit and manipulation of the kind for which politicians like FDR (and those who have followed him) are famous. This is why FDR secretly provoked a Japanese attack on the U.S., an attack sure to elicit a nationalistic response that would pressure workers to yield to corporate control in the name of national defense. He wanted Americans to view the entire Japanese and German populations as a united enemy nation, and (the flip side of the coin) to view all Americans, regardless of class, as united in "the good fight," in particular united around American corporate leadership and willing to make whatever sacrifices American capitalists said were required to win the war. The importance FDR placed on this anti-working class purpose of the war is, as we shall now closely examine, evident from his actions at this time, in particular: 1) he used the war to attack American workers; 2) he used the war to promote virulent racism and nationalism; 3) he insisted on "unconditional surrender" to squash any solidarity with anti-Fascists in Germany or Japan; and 4) he shamefully covered up the Nazi killing of Jews.

FDR Used The War To Fight American Workers

FDR repeatedly used the war as a pretext to put the American working class on the defensive. In early 1941, before Pearl Harbor, Roosevelt proposed, and Congress passed, a bill—HR 1776—to "lend-lease" $7 billion in weaponry to Great Britain; the new law gave the President power to ban strikes and ignore labor legislation in factories producing weapons.[246] When the United States did enter the war FDR pressured the leaders of both the American Federation of Labor and the Congress of Industrial Organizations to prove their loyalty to the government, which they did by pledging that there would be no strikes or walkouts for the duration of the war.[247] In the first week after Pearl Harbor the United Automobile Workers (UAW, CIO) International Executive Board pledged "uninterrupted production." Also in the same month the AFL Executive Council "unanimously voted a no-strike policy in war industries" and "100 leaders of AFL unions extended that policy to their entire 5 million member-ship."[248] FDR established a War Labor Board empowered to impose final settle-ments on all labor disputes, and in 1942 he requested, and Congress passed, the Economic Stabilization Act which froze wages at the September 15, 1942 level at a time when both profits and the demand for labor were high and higher wages could have been easily secured with work stoppages or even the threat of them.[249] But FDR declared striking "unpatriotic." In May 1943, the nation's coal miners walked out on strike. Roosevelt responded by ordering In-terior Secretary Harold Ickes to take over the mines and tell the miners they were now working for Uncle Sam. "About fifty percent stayed home."[250]

With help from Stalin, Roosevelt even used the war to turn the once-militant Communist controlled unions in the U.S. into abject servants of big business. Using the war as justification, Stalin ordered the U.S. Commu-nist Party to discipline American workers and force them to work hard for their corporate masters, just as he was doing the same thing to workers in the Soviet Union. As *Business Week* noted March 18, 1944, "A more conciliatory attitude toward business is apparent in unions which once pursued intransi-gent policies. On the whole, the organizations involved are those which have been identified as Communist-dominated...Since Russia's involvement in the war, the leadership in these unions has moved from the extreme left-wing to the extreme right-wing position in the American labor movement. Today they have perhaps the best no-strike record of any section of organized labor; they are the most vigorous proponents of labor-management cooperation; they are the only serious labor advocates of incentive wages...In general, employers with whom they deal now have the most peaceful labor relations in industry. Complaints to the union's national officers usually will bring all the organiza-tion's disciplinary apparatus to focus on the heads of the unruly local lead-ers."[251] No doubt this partly explains why FDR praised Stalin effusively during the war, even requesting Jack Warner, head of Warner Brothers studio, to pro-duce the film version of the pro-Soviet book, *Mission to Moscow*, which "por-trayed Stalin as a beaming pipe-smoking 'easy boss' of Russia, a kind of old-fashioned Tammany leader writ large" in "a land of happy collective farm-ers and cheerful factory workers."[252]

It is important, however, to bear in mind that notwithstanding all of these efforts by FDR to prevent workers from striking during the war, the fact is that they continued to strike anyway, only now the strikes were all wild-cats—unauthorized by the national union leadership. In fact, as one labor historian has written: "When the war came to a close on August 14, 1945, the American workers had chalked up more strikes and strikers during the period from December 7, 1941, to the day of Japanese surrender three years and eight months later, than in any similar period of time in American labor history."[253]

FDR Used The War To Promote Racism And Nationalism

FDR promoted a nationalist, racist notion that all Japanese—from the lowliest peasant to the Emperor—were the enemy. He did this most dramatically and disgustingly by interning all American Japanese and by routinely calling Japanese people "Japs" and comparing them to "monkeys, baboons and gorillas"[254] and condoning this kind of language by people in the government and the media. Time magazine, for example, responded to Pearl Harbor with "Why the little yellow bastards!" In September 1942, FDR's chief of staff, Admiral William Leahy, told Vice President Wallace that Japan was "our Carthage" and "we should go ahead and destroy her utterly." The President's son, Elliott Roosevelt, told the Vice President that Americans should kill "about half the Japanese civilian population," while Paul McNutt, chairman of the War Manpower Commission, recommended "the extermination of the Japanese in toto."[255]

Similarly, FDR labeled all Germans the enemy, declaring on August 19, 1944 that, "We have got to be tough with Germany and I mean the German people, not just the Nazis. You either have to castrate [them] or you have got to treat them...so they can't just go on reproducing people who want to continue the way they have in the past."[256] FDR also told Treasury Secretary Morgenthau that, "Too many people here and in England hold to the view that the German people as a whole are not responsible for what has taken place—that only a few Nazi leaders are responsible. That unfortunately is not based on fact. The German people must have it driven home to them that the whole nation has been engaged in a lawless conspiracy against the decencies of modern civilization."[257] On the following Labor Day Secretary of the Treasury Morgenthau suggested transporting most of the Germans between the ages of twenty and forty out of Germany to toil on "some big TVA project" in Central Africa for the rest of their lives. They were supposedly too tainted by Nazism to reeducate. What to do with their children, he admitted, would be "a big problem."[258] The "hate all Germans" thinking was encouraged by virtually all of FDR's top government officers. For example, top intelligence officer, Allen Dulles, future head of the CIA, in his instructions to operatives carrying out a raid behind enemy lines told them to leave a note saying "DEATH TO ALL

GERMANS."[259] (British leaders drummed up nationalist hate the same way. Churchill gave a speech to the House of Commons in 1943 announcing that Germans "combine in the most deadly manner the qualities of the warrior and the slave. They do not value freedom themselves and the spectacle of it among others is hateful to them."[260])

Why FDR Demanded "Unconditional Surrender"

To enlist public support for the war, Roosevelt needed to give it a higher moral purpose, but at the same time avoid making it a war for working class values and genuine democracy. His solution was to assert that certain foreign peoples were the enemy of all that was good, and then to make refusal to compromise—i.e., the demand for unconditional surrender—the defining feature of morality, thus shifting attention from the actual goal of the war to the secondary question of not compromising. An example of this was FDR's speech to congress on January 6, 1942 in which he declared: "There has never been—there can never be—successful compromise between good and evil. Only total victory can reward the champions of tolerance, and decency, and faith."[261]

The importance FDR placed on casting entire populations as the enemy explains two controversial strategy decisions FDR made which are otherwise difficult to understand: his insistence on unconditional surrender and his refusal to give any assistance to high ranking Germans who were trying to assassinate Hitler to make a coup d'etat and end the war. When Roosevelt made unconditional surrender Allied policy, the reaction of military leaders was universally negative because they knew it was disastrous from a military point of view. General Eisenhower thought it would do nothing but cost American lives, and said, "If you were given two choices, one to mount a scaffold, the other to charge twenty bayonets, you might as well charge twenty bayonets."[262] General Albert Wedemeyer, who had written Operation Rainbow Five, said it would "weld all Germans together." Major General Ira C. Eaker, commander of the U.S. Eighth Air Force wrote: "Everybody I knew at the time when they heard this [unconditional surrender] said: 'How stupid can you be?' All the soldiers and the airmen who were fighting this war wanted the Germans to quit tomorrow. A child knew once you said this to the Germans, they were going to fight to the last man. There wasn't a man who was actually fighting in the war whom I ever met who didn't think this was about as stupid an operation as you could find." Chief of Staff General George Marshall thought the policy was a major blunder. Dr. Joseph Goebbels, Hitler's propaganda chief, remarked, "I should never have been able to think up so rousing a slogan. If our Western enemies tell us, we won't deal with you, our only aim is to destroy you...how can any German, whether he likes it or not, do anything but fight on with all his strength?"[263] Stalin thought it would only unite the German people and preferred an explicit statement of terms and an appeal to the German people to discard Hitler.[264]

But FDR insisted on unconditional surrender and took pains to prevent Americans from even suspecting that some Germans might be anti-Nazi. When an Associated Press war correspondent in Paris, Louis Lochner, tried to file a story on German citizens in Paris who were operating an anti-Nazi movement and sending agents with money and information into the Reich, U.S. Army censors killed it and told him that it was because a regulation was in force "from the President of the United States in his capacity as commander in chief, forbidding all mention of any German resistance."[265] In keeping with this policy, the President refused to give any assistance whatsoever to the Front of Decent People, a German clandestine organization of approximately 7,000 people including high-ranking government and military officials who made numerous attempts to assassinate Hitler and a failed attempt at a coup d'etat in July 1944 (shortly after D-Day), for which many of them paid with their lives. The Front of Decent People was pro-U.S. and anti-Soviet. They had appealed for assistance from the U.S. and were turned down. The unconditional surrender policy itself made it more difficult for them to recruit support from other influential Germans. In spite of these obstacles the coup d'etat came close to succeeding. As it was in progress Germans in Stalin's Free German's Committee broadcast: "Generals, officers, soldiers! Cease fire at once and turn your arms against Hitler. Do not fail these courageous men!"[266]

The cost in the lost lives of working class soldiers exacted by the Allied leaders' insistence on unconditional surrender is staggering. In the months before the June 6, 1944 D-day Allied invasion of Europe at Normandy, Admiral Canaris, a high ranking German intelligence officer who secretly opposed Hitler, "leaked vital intelligence to the British and Americans, including the German army's order of battle, an invaluable insight into the Wehrmacht's intentions." Canaris offered "the support of General Rommel for a bloodless conquest of the western front if the Anglo-Americans would give the slightest sign of a disposition for an armistice...The British reply: there was no alternative to unconditional surrender."[267]

Because of the failure of anti-Hitler Germans to get U.S. support and topple Hitler, and because unconditional surrender convinced many German officers who might otherwise have surrendered to fight more ferociously, the Wehrmacht in November 1944 inflicted a strategic defeat on the American army trying to reach the Rhine. On November 22, General Eisenhower cabled the Joint Chiefs of Staff urging "that we should redouble our efforts to find a solution to the problem of reducing the German will to resist." But Roosevelt and Churchill held fast to unconditional surrender. On December 21 the Wehrmacht, which was believed demoralized, shocked Allied commanders by suddenly launching an offensive army of 250,000 men and 1000 tanks in a stunning attempt to capture the port of Antwerp and thereby strand the American army without food or gasoline. This was the Battle of the Bulge, in which 80,000 Americans died. By making it more difficult for the Front of Decent People to succeed in toppling Hitler and ending the war soon after D-Day, the policy of unconditional surrender resulted in enormous numbers of people dying in the subsequent fighting: 418,791 Americans and 107,000 British and Canadians were killed or wounded. The figure rises to two million if Russians and Germans (including civilians) are added; and if Jews killed in the Holocaust after D-Day are added the figure rises to at least four million people.[268]

Why FDR Didn't Tell Americans That Nazis Were Killing The Jews

Even though Roosevelt obviously wanted to convince Americans to go to war, his anti-working class goals prevented him from using the most effective means of doing it, which would have been to appeal to their desire to act in solidarity with German, Japanese, and other workers being oppressed by the Fascists. Thus FDR refused to talk to Americans about working class reasons for fighting the Fascists—such as the fact that Fascists were attacking their own as well as other workers and using anti-Semitism and racism to do it. Most Americans, to this day, do not know that the Nazis rose to power by fighting German working people and by demonstrating to the German elite how ruthlessly they would continue doing so if they had formal power. And even though Jews were staging rallies in Madison Square Garden against the Nazi Holocaust in 1943, most Americans did not believe there was a Nazi campaign to exterminate the Jews because FDR remained silent on the matter. Behind the scenes, when the Nazis were killing 6,000 Polish Jews a day, the State Department ordered the Ambassador in Switzerland to stop transmitting his messages documenting the Holocaust.[269] Randolph Paul, an aide to Treasury Secretary Morgenthau (who was Jewish and alarmed by the Holocaust) wrote a document entitled, Report to the Secretary on the Acquiescence of this Government in the Murder of the Jews, but the Secretary never showed it to the President,[270] knowing he would not wish to see it. FDR's reason for not exposing the Nazi's anti-Semitic violence was not anti-Semitism per se. The explanation was given by Assistant Secretary of State Breckinridge Long, who wrote in his diary at the time, "One danger is...their [American Jews pressing for action against the Holocaust] activities may lend color to the charges of Hitler that we are fighting this war on account of and at the instigation of and direction of our Jewish citizens."[271] The obvious solution to this problem, of course, would have been to make the purpose of the war crystal clear, and if it had been to fight in solidarity with the working class of the world against their Fascist enemies, everybody would have understood perfectly and nobody except pro-Nazis would have listened to Hitler's nonsense about it being a "Jews' war." But FDR would not avail himself of this obvious solution. Instead he wanted Americans to see the conflict purely as nation versus nation. He only had lies to offer as the reason for the war, and how did he know that Hitler's lie wouldn't be as persuasive as his own lies? So he covered up the Holocaust.

WAS THE WAR CAUSED BECAUSE NATIONAL ELITES FEARED EACH OTHER, OR FEARED THE WORKING CLASS?

The thesis of this book—the "social control" view—is that wealthy elites waged World War Two to protect their wealth and power from a working class which they perceived to be dangerously revolutionary. There is another explanation of the origins of World War Two, an explanation which sharply disagrees with the one presented here. According to this view, which I will call the "competition" view, wealthy elites in the Axis and Allied nations waged the war to protect their wealth and power from each other, not the working class. In the competition view the war may have provided an opportunity and a pretext for national rulers to suppress domestic and foreign working class movements, but this was not the reason they went to war; the real motive, according to this theory, was conflicting economic national interests, specifically over the issue of which nation's business class would control the economic resources and markets of various regions of the world. The competition theory says that the leaders of the warring nations were not worried about losing control to working people at home or abroad, but rather were driven to wage war in order to protect and expand their economic interests in the face of threats from competing foreign capitalists with the same intentions. For the competition theory to make sense, one must either reject the evidence I have presented here that inside Germany, Japan and the United States there was a raging class struggle going on in the pre-war years, or at least one must minimize the seriousness with which the elite rulers of these nations viewed these struggles. On the other hand, if one accepts that these elites feared domestic revolution, then it would seem far-fetched to deny that their decision about something as fundamental as war would be primarily driven by anything other than the objective of remaining in power. In this case the "social control" theory that the war was predominantly a method of domestic social control would make the most sense.

But choosing between the competition versus the social control theory of the motives for the war must also involve deciding which theory best explains what we know about the actions and words of powerful business and government leaders. To make the scope of this discussion manageable I will focus here only on the United States. I intend to show that, by dismissing the great difficulty elites have in controlling their populations and by ignoring, therefore, the role of war in this regard, proponents of the competition theory of the origins of World War Two see the trees but not the forest. The trees are the economic concerns, such as access to raw materials and markets, that industrialists and bankers indisputably had. The forest is the major disagreement among America's business class about how to control the working class. One camp thought Fascist methods should be embraced—meaning Gestapo-style terror employing anti-black and anti-Semitic forces inside the United States, and establishing a world order based on a peace settlement with Germany and Japan. The other camp favored the sophisticated use of undemocratic labor unions combined with nationalism generated by an anti-Fascist war. The former camp made business alliances with business leaders in Germany and Japan before and during the war and were optimistic about doing business in a world where Fascist nations controlled Europe and Asia. The latter camp wanted a war for purposes of social control, and viewed the Fascists as the natural and obvious choice of an enemy against whom to wage the war.

With the hostility to the Fascist nations as a premise, this camp considered the economic consequences of enemy nations controlling Europe and Asia and came to the unsurprising conclusion that, from a strictly economic point of view, it was preferable to win the war, not lose it. What follows is a close look at the two camps, first the pro-Fascist one which owned great wealth but clearly failed to determine the government's policy, and then the anti-Fascist one which was dominant.

As we will see, the policy dispute was real enough, but the two camps nonetheless served together in the same government, and the anti-Fascists treated the pro-Fascists with kid gloves (when they could have prosecuted them for treason), because both sides understood that their dispute was secondary to controlling the working class, and that the war was primarily an instrument for this very purpose.

Axis And Allied Businessmen: Enemies Or Partners?

The chief assumption in the competition theory is that the ruling classes of the warring nations were engaged in such intense economic competition against one another that, to prevail against their competitors, they resorted to the awful violence of a world war. The image of capitalists competing fiercely is a familiar one that capitalists themselves love to promote. But were the bankers and captains of industry in the warring nations truly at war with each other during World War Two? Was the war simply business competition carried out by other means? The historical record was examined closely by Charles Higham in his 1983 book, *Trading With the Enemy* (the source of the information and quotations about pro-Fascist American business leaders presented below), which detailed the sector of American business leaders who were pro-Fascist. While the pro-Fascists are not the whole story, their very existence as an important part of America's economic elite constitutes an unexplained anomaly for the competition theory. They deserve careful scrutiny, especially to see if they were marginal or indeed central players in America's business class.

bankers

During the war American and British capitalists conducted business as usual inside Nazi-ruled territory, in a manner that hardly suggested that the outcome of the war was of any great concern to them. Consider first banking. The Bank for International Settlements (BIS) was created by the world's central banks in 1930. The bank's charter stated that the bank was to be "immune from seizure, closure, or censure, whether or not its owners were at war." The owners included the Morgan-affiliated of New York, the Bank of England, Germany's Reichsbank, the Bank of Italy, the Bank of France, and other central banks. At the outbreak of World War II and for the duration of the war the bank's President was an American, Thomas McKittrick, and under him on the board of directors sat, in addition to representatives from other nations, the elite of Nazi banking and industry: "Hermann Schmitz, head of the colossal Nazi industrial trust I.G. Farben, Baron Kurt von Schröder, head of the J.H. Stein Bank of Cologne and a leading officer and financier of the Gestapo; Dr. Walther Funk of the Reichsbank, and...Emil Puhl. These last two figures were Hitler's personal appointees to the board."

McKittrick was a solid American member of the Wall Street establishment, educated at Harvard (editor of its student newspaper, the *Crimson*), and former chairman of the British-American Chamber of Commerce. McKittrick was appointed President of the BIS shortly after the Nazis, in March 1938, looted Austria's gold and placed it in vaults controlled by the BIS. The gold was then channeled by the BIS to the Reichsbank "under Funk, in the special charge of Reichsbank vice-president and BIS director, Emil Puhl." Shortly after this, on March 15, Nazis held the directors of the Czech National Bank at gunpoint and demanded they hand over the national treasury of $48 million in gold reserves. When the Czechs said the gold was deposited in the BIS at the Bank of England, the Nazis asked Montagu Norman, the governor of the Bank of England, to "return the gold." The gold never left London, but Norman transferred it to the Nazis' account, which amounted to the same thing as if it were physically shipped to Berlin. After Great Britain had declared war on Germany, Norman and Sir Otto Niemeyer, also of the Bank of England, remained on the BIS board, knowing full well that it was dominated by the Nazis and used by them to bank their looted gold.

On February 5, 1942, after Germany and the United States had declared war on each other, the Reichsbank and the German and Italian governments approved keeping McKittrick as President of the BIS until the end of the war, remarking in one of the authorizing documents, "McKittrick's opinions are safely known to us." At this time McKittrick arranged a loan "of several million Swiss gold francs to the Nazi government of Poland and the collaborative government of Hungary." Despite the fact that their nations were at war, "[M]ost of the board's members traveled freely across frontiers throughout the war for meetings in Paris, Berlin, Rome, or (though this was denied) Basle." The BIS remained listed as the Correspondent Bank for the Federal Reserve Bank in Washington.

One of the most gruesome activities of the BIS was to arrange for gold taken from Jewish and other concentration camp prisoners to wind up in respectable Nazi accounts in the Swiss National Bank, which was in a partnership with the BIS. At the Nuremberg Trials in May 1946 the Nazi BIS director, Funk, testified that Puhl, another Nazi BIS director, had been in charge of melting down gold from "monocles, spectacle frames, watches, cigarette cases, and gold dentures...gold teeth, wedding bands" into gold bars and shipping them to Switzerland. Puhl confirmed this.

How could the BIS have operated so smoothly and so cooperatively between bankers from warring nations if the war was driven by their extreme mutual animosity? In reality, of course, there was no such animosity. When questioned on this point by a representative from the U.S. Treasury, Orvis Schmidt, in March 1945 at a meeting in Basle, McKittrick replied, "In order to understand, one must first understand the strength of the confidence and trust that the central bankers had had in each other and the strength of their determination to play the game squarely." These men were not enemies at all. Puhl had been offered a major post at Chase in New York shortly before Pearl Harbor, and at the war's end, McKittrick—a Nazi collaborator if ever there were one—was made Vice President of the Chase National Bank. In 1950 Puhl was McKittrick's honored guest in the United States.[272]

Friendly wartime relations between American and Nazi bankers was not limited only to the central banks. The Chase National Bank (later the Chase Manhattan Bank), owned by the Rockefeller family, was the wealthiest and most powerful bank in the United States at the outbreak of World War Two. Joseph L. Larkin was the bank's Vice President in charge of European affairs during the war. Hans-Joachim Caesar was the Nazi Emil Puhl's "right hand man at the Reichsbank." According to the competition theory of the war American and Nazi bankers like these men were staunch enemies. But after Pearl Harbor Larkin and Caesar both "authorized the retention of the Chase bank in the Nazi-occupied city [of Paris] for the duration." With full knowledge of Chase's New York headquarters, Chase's Paris office financed the Nazi embassy's activities throughout the war. The Vichy branch of Chase (Vichy, France, was the location of the Nazi collaborationist government) even en-

forced restrictions against Jewish property, refusing to release funds belonging
to Jews. Throughout 1942 Larkin approved the transfer of "securities and large
sums of money from Vichy to Germany and German-occupied countries
abroad via Emil Puhl." The Chase also handled transactions for the bank in
Latin America (the Banco Aleman Transatlantico) that acted as the treasurer
of the Nazi Party in South America. In 1942 a Chase officer at the Vichy
branch (Albert Bertand) wrote to Larkin from Vichy, and said, "The present
basis of our relationship with the authorities of Germany is as satisfactory as
the modus vivendi worked out with German authorities by Morgan's. We anx-
iously sought and actually obtained substantial deposits of German funds...
which funds were invested by Chase in French treasury banks to produce additional income." During the war Caesar repeatedly told the Chase New York
office how the German authorities held the bank in high esteem. And an
American officer of the bank in Manhattan described Chase as "Caesar's be-
loved child." A U.S. Treasury report on December 20, 1944 stated that the
manager of the Chase office in Paris, Carlos Niedermann, was a Nazi collaborator, that Larkin knew it but would not remove him, and that the New York
office authorized the Paris office to maintain the account of the German embassy "as every little thing helps to maintain excellent relations between Chase
and the German authorities." Carlos Niedermann even communicated directly to Emil Puhl's office at the Reichsbank, offering to be "at your disposal to
continue to undertake the execution of banking affairs in France for your
friends as well as for yourselves." If fierce economic rivalry is the explanation of
the outbreak of World War Two, the competition theory will have to explain
why America's leading bankers and the chiefs of Nazi banking got along so
fabulously during the war.[273]

industrialists

In 1937 the ten wealthiest families in the United States and their primary
sources of wealth were as follows, in order of wealthiest first: Rockefellers
(Standard Oil), Fords (Ford Motor Co.), Harknesses (Standard Oil), Mellons
(Alcoa), Vanderbilts (New York Central Railroad), Whitneys (Standard Oil),
duPonts (General Motors and DuPont Corp.), McCormicks (International
Harvester), Bakers (First National Bank), and the Fishers (General Motors.)[274]
We have seen above that the Bakers' First National Bank was an owner of the
Nazi-friendly Bank for International Settlements. Next we will look at the role
played by the Rockefellers' and Harnesses' and Whitneys' Standard Oil, the

Fords' Ford Motor Co., the duPonts' and Fishers' General Motors and the Mellon's Alcoa. We will see that the congeniality among Allied and Axis businessmen was not a peculiarity of the banking sector. America's industrial giants also maintained friendly and cooperative "business as usual" relations with the Nazis prior to and during the war, in a manner that is inconsistent with the theory that they viewed the Axis nations as an enemy which had to be defeated in order to protect their business interests.

In 1941 the largest petroleum corporation in the world was Standard Oil of New Jersey (now Exxon), and the largest chemical manufacturing enterprise in the world was the German conglomerate, I.G. Farben. John D. Rockefeller II controlled Standard Oil and made Walter Teagle chairman and William Farish president. Hermann Schmitz founded I.G. Farben in 1925 and made it, by the outbreak of World War Two, a giant global enterprise that produced innovative products from medicines to synthetic rubber and gasoline. By 1939 I.G.Farben had 2,000 cartel agreements with foreign firms, including Standard Oil of New Jersey, DuPont, Alcoa (the prime source of wealth for America's third wealthiest family, the Mellons), Dow Chemical, and others in the United States. During the 1930s Teagle and Schmitz were close personal and business friends. Teagle was director of American I.G. Chemical Corp., a subsidiary of I.G. Farben, in which Teagle invested heavily, while American I.G. invested heavily in Standard. Teagle, along with Edsel Ford (Henry Ford's son) sat on the board of I.G. Farben. After Hitler was appointed Chancellor, Teagle and Schmitz jointly hired Ivy Lee[275] to supply the Nazi government with information regarding the American reaction to German armament, the German government's treatment of the church, and the organization of the Gestapo, and to create a positive image of the Nazis in the United States.

If Rockefeller was worried about Nazi Germany's or Japan's world aggression being a threat to his profits, his behavior certainly did not indicate it. The German and Japanese air force required an aviation gasoline additive called tetraethyl lead, to which only Standard, Du Pont, and General Motors had the rights. Yet Teagle made sure the Axis governments were supplied with the additive, organizing a sale to Schmitz in 1938 and arranging for the British subsidiary of Standard (Ethyl) to loan him 500 tons of it. In 1939 Standard sold Schmitz a further $15 million worth of the additive, and Standard also sold it to Japan.

Just after war erupted in Europe, Standard Oil sent Frank Howard, a vice-president, to meet with Fritz Ringer, a representative of I.G. Farben, at

The Hague on September 22, 1939. The two men drew up an agreement, known as the Hague Memorandum, that specified they would remain in business together "whether or not the Unites States came into the war." At the meeting, Ringer handed over to Howard "a thick bundle of German patents that were locked into Standard agreements so that they would not be seized in wartime." The Hague Memorandum guaranteed that I.G. Farben would get back its patents the moment the war ended.

On May 5, 1941, Göring, knowing that Germany was growing desperate for oil, held a meeting with the Fascist Rumanian General Ion Antonescu to ensure that if America and Germany went to war, Antonescu would allow Germany to use the oil fields in Rumania that were owned by Standard Oil. The general said he would have to confer with Schmitz and Standard Oil executives in Bucharest. These executives gave Göring use of the oil fields "whether or not America came into the war" in exchange for $11 million in bonds.

When the British ran a naval blockade the length of the Americas on the Atlantic seaboard to stop shipments of oil to Germany, Standard's President Farish "sent large amounts of petroleum to Russia and thence by Trans-Siberian Railroad to Berlin long after Roosevelt's moral embargo." Farish also shipped oil to Vichy North Africa, and "fueled the Nazi-controlled L.A.T.I. airline [which flew spies, patents, and diamonds for foreign currency as well as Nazi propaganda] from Rome to Rio via Madrid, Lisbon, and Dakar." Standard did not even have the excuse that "if we don't, somebody else will" because they were the only company with "the high-octane gasoline that enabled the lumbering clippers to make the 1,680-mile hop across the Atlantic."

On February 27, 1942, after Pearl Harbor and the United States declaration of war against the Axis, Thurman Arnold, the head of the Antitrust Division of the Department of Justice, along with Secretary of the Navy Franklin Knox and Secretary of the Army Henry Stimson, entered Standard Oil's Rockefeller Plaza headquarters and confronted Standard President Farish, saying he (Arnold) had proof that "by continuing to favor Hitler in rubber deals and patent arrangements, the Rockefellers, Teagle, and Farish had acted against the interests of the American government." Arnold demanded that the patents handed by Schmitz to Standard's Howard at The Hague be turned over to the government, and he called for a $1.5 million fine. Farish replied that Standard was fueling the United States Army, Navy and Air Force and implied they might not continue to do so if the government pursued its case against the company. Arnold was forced to back down, and Farish ended up having to pay a token $1000 fine, leading Secretary of the Interior Harold Ickes to write in his diary April 15 that [as paraphrased by author Charles Higham], "[W]hen the light was thrown on a situation like this, it made it easier to understand why some of the great and powerful in the country were Nazi-minded and were confident of their ability to get along with Hitler. After all, he added, they had been doing business with Hitler right along. They understood each other's language and their aims were common."

The next month, on March 26, Arnold appeared before Senator Harry S Truman and his Senate committee investigating war spending, and he produced documents showing that Standard and I.G. Farben had "carved up the world markets, with oil and chemical monopolies established all over the map," and he specifically accused Standard Oil of denying synthetic rubber to the U.S. Navy. He also "charged that cables showed Standard's arrangements with Japan that were to continue throughout any conflict or break in trade." To a reporter's question, "Is this treason?" Truman answered in the affirmative. On May 2 Irving Lipkowitz, also in the Antitrust Division of the Justice Department, found evidence that "Standard had deliberately retarded production of the vital war material acetic acid in favor of the Nazis." On May 6, John R. Jacobs, Jr., of the Attorney General's department, testified that as a result of deals between I.G. Farben and Standard Oil, the United States had been prevented from using a method of producing synthetic ammonia, vital for explosives production, and the U.S. had been similarly restricted in producing hydrogen from natural gas and from obtaining a product called paraflow that was needed for high altitude airplane lubrication. Jacobs produced a document showing that on September 1, 1939, the day Germany invaded Poland, Standard Oil cabled I.G. Farben offering to buy its 20% interest in the patents they shared. The Standard Oil memo read: "Of course what we have in mind is protecting this minority interest of I.G. in the event of war between ourselves and Germany as it would certainly be very undesirable to have this 20 percent Standard-I.G. pass to an alien property custodian of the U.S. who might sell it to an unfriendly interest." It is clear that for Standard Oil, the identity of the "unfriendly interest" was not Germany, even if there was "war between ourselves and Germany." If the war was indeed caused by competing American and German industries, we can be pretty sure that these giants of the oil and chemical industry were not the culprits. The stereotype image of wars being fought over oil certainly cannot explain why America's leading oil company was so indifferent, if not outright hostile, to America's efforts to win the war. In fact, on September 22, 1947, Judge Charles Clark, in a ruling against the company (the appeal of which was denied) said, "Standard Oil can be considered an enemy national in view of its relationships with I.G. Farben after the United States and Germany had become active enemies."[276]

Henry Ford and Adolph Hitler were fans of each other. Hitler praised Ford in Mein Kampf, and each year on Hitler's birthday Ford sent the Nazi leader 50,000 Reichsmarks. In a 1923 interview, Hitler dubbed Ford "the leader of the growing fascist movement in America" and in 1938 Hitler awarded Ford the Grand Service Cross of the Supreme Order of the German Eagle, an honor which the American did not turn down despite having been given advance notice of the award and ample opportunity to do so. Ford purchased the Dearborn Independent newspaper and in 1920 began publishing weekly anti-Semitic columns which he later published as a book, The International Jew: The World's Foremost Problem in 1927. Ford believed in controlling his workers the same way the Nazis did: with a mixture of paternalism and harsh authoritarianism. He employed company police, labor spies, and violence in a protracted effort to prevent unionization. Ford not only shared Hitler's anti-Semitic world view, but he also had good reason to feel that his industrial empire was safe under the Nazis. Göring assured a director of the German Ford subsidiary, Carl Krauch (also with I.G. Farben), that, "I shall see to it that the German Ford Company will not be incorporated in the Hermann Göring Company." Krauch testified to this in 1946 under interrogation, and added that "Thus, we succeeded in keeping the Ford Works working and operating independently of our [the German] government's seizure." In 1940 Ford Motor Co. "refused to build aircraft engines for England and instead built supplies of the 5-ton military trucks that were the backbone of German army transportation" and Ford even shipped tires to Germany when there was a shortage in the U.S.

Ford also operated a 60-acre automobile factory in the German-occupied section of France in 1940, located at Poissy eleven miles from Paris. This plant, controlled by Edsel Ford from Dearborn, Michigan (and by Carl Krauch and Hermann Schmitz in Berlin) produced airplane engines and trucks for the German military. During the war, the manager of the French Ford plant, Maurice

Dollfus, and Edsel Ford communicated by letters which shed light on the Ford family's outlook. On January 28, 1942, in his first letter after Pearl Harbor, Dollfus informed Edsel Ford that the factory was ahead of the French automobile manufacturers in supplying the enemy and that he was getting help from the Vichy government to protect American shareholders' interests. He also reported that he was starting a company in North Africa for the Nazis. Ford replied on May 13 that "It is interesting to note that you have started your African company and are laying plans for a more peaceful future." Dollfus wrote on February 11, 1942 that Ford in France made a profit for the year of 58 million francs, which included payments from the Nazis. On June 6 Dollfus wrote that the British Royal Air Force had bombed the plant four times, and so he had scattered machinery and equipment all over the country, and that the Vichy government had "agreed to pay for all damages" and that this was "approved by the German government." Ford replied July 17 that he was pleased with the arrangement and that his father joined him in sending best wishes to Dollfus and the staff, in the hope they would continue in the good work. Meanwhile, on May 29, 1942, "Ford Motor Company in Edgewater, New Jersey, had shipped six cargoes of cars to blacklisted José O. Moll of Chile. Another consignee was a blacklisted enemy corporation, Lilienfeld, in Bolivia."

In April 1943, Treasury Secretary Morgenthau and economist Lauchlin Currie investigated Ford's operation in France and concluded that "their production is solely for the benefit of Germany and the countries under its occupation" and that the Germans have "shown clearly their wish to protect the Ford interests" because of the "attitude of strict neutrality" maintained by Henry and Edsel Ford, and that "the increased activity of the French Ford subsidiaries on behalf of Germans receives the commendation of the Ford family in America."

The Ford family's association with Nazis, far from being an exceptional fluke, was representative of the American automobile industry. The du Pont family owned 37% of General Motors. Lammot du Pont served on the Board of Directors of General Motors from 1918 to 1946 and his older son, Pierre, was made president of GM in 1920 while his younger son, Irénéé, sat on the board of directors of the auto company between 1921 and 1924. Like the Fords, and despite the fact they were Jewish, the du Ponts were anti-Semitic and in the 1930s they funded native American Fascist organizations like the

American Liberty League. In 1936 "Irénéé du Pont used General Motors money to finance the notorious Black Legion. This terrorist organization had as its purpose the prevention of automobile workers from unionizing. The members wore hoods and black robes, with skull and crossbones. They fire-bombed union meetings, murdered union organizers, often by beating them to death, and dedicated their lives to destroying Jews and communists. They linked to the Ku Klux Klan...[Irénéé] personally paid almost $1 million from his own pocket for armed and gas-equipped storm troops modeled on the Gestapo to sweep through the plants and beat up anyone who proved rebellious."

In 1933 GM's President, William Knudsen, traveled to Germany to meet with Göring, who assured him there would be no German annexation of GM operations in Germany. "By the mid-1930's, General Motors was committed to full-scale production of trucks, armored cars, and tanks in Nazi Germany." The company's vice president, Graeme K. Howard, wrote the book *America and a New World Order* in 1940 which praised Hitler and advocated appeasement with the Nazis. James Mooney, GM's head of its European operations, also strongly advocated appeasement, telling U.S. diplomat George Messersmith on December 22, 1936 in Vienna, "We ought to make some arrangement with Germany for the future. There is no reason why we should let our moral indignation over what happens in that country stand in the way." The next day, Messersmith reported to the Acting Secretary of State on Mooney's views, writing that, "It is curious that Mooney and Col. Sosthenes Behn [chief of American International Telephone and Telegraph Corporation...both give this opinion. The factories owned by ITT in Germany are running full time and in double shifts and increasing their capacity for the simple reason that they are working almost entirely on government orders and for military equipment. The Opel works, owned by General Motors, are [also] working very well [in the same way]."

In 1938 Mooney received the Order of the Golden Eagle from Hitler. In 1939 Mooney traveled to Berlin and then to London to enlist U.S. Ambassador Joseph Kennedy's support for a peace plan that would, according to Mooney's notes [paraphrased here by Higham], involve giving Germany "a half to one billion gold loan through the BIS, a restoration of Germany's colonies, a removal of embargo on German goods, participation in Chinese markets. On Germany's side there would be armaments limitations, nonaggression pacts, and free exchange." Higham notes that, "Whatever Mooney's motives, these were pure Nazi objectives, nothing else."

On June 26, 1940, Mooney, along with other American business leaders including Edsel Ford, gave a party for Gerhardt Westrick, the International Telephone and Telegraph Corporation's chief in Germany, who had traveled to the United States in March. Westrick's law partner until 1938, Dr. Heinrich Albert, was the head of Ford in Germany, and Westrick "represented in Germany not only Ford but General Motors, Standard Oil, the Texas Company, Sterling Products, and the Davis Oil Company." The party hosted by Mooney and Ford was to "celebrate the Nazi victory in France." During his stay in the United States, Westrick gave an interview to *The New York Times* in which he expressed views shared by the Nazis and the American business leaders he represented: He said the U.S. should loan the Nazi government $25 billion at one and one a half percent interest, with the money shipped to the Bank for International Settlements, and he called for a peace presided over by Wall Street, the Reichsbank, and the Bank of Japan.

When asked his opinion of Mooney in 1941, Messersmith wrote on March 5, "Mooney is fundamentally fascist in his sympathies. Of course he is quite unbalanced...he is obsessed by this strange notion that a few businessmen, including himself, can take care of the war and the peace. I am absolutely sure that Mooney is keeping up this contact with the Germans because he believes, or at least still hopes, that they will win the war, and he thinks if they do that he will be our Quisling." In response to FBI questioning by L.L. Tyler in mid-October 1940, Mooney said, "Besides, Hitler is in the right and I'm not going to do anything to make him mad. I know Hitler has all the cards" and added that [as paraphrased by Higham] "Germany needed more room; and that if we tried to prevent the expansion of the German people under Hitler, it would be 'just too bad for us.' " Shortly after making these statements, Mooney was promoted to assistant to the company's president for defense liaison work in Detroit.[277]

The last of the top 10 wealthiest families' corporations that we consider here is the Mellon family's Aluminum Corporation of America (Alcoa). In May 1941, Congressman Pierce of Oregon charged that Alcoa's sabotage of American war production had cost the U.S. "10,000 fighters or 1,665 bombers [because of] the effort to protect Alcoa's monopolistic position..." Secretary of the Interior Ickes, on June 26, said, "If America loses this war, it can thank the

Aluminum Corporation of America." These accusations sprang from the fact that, as George Seldes wrote in 1943, "By its cartel agreement with I.G. Farben, controlled by Hitler, Alcoa sabotaged the aluminum program of the U.S. air force. The Truman Committee [on National Defense, chaired by then-Senator Harry S. Truman in 1942] heard testimony that Alcoa's representative, A.H. Bunker, $1-a-year head of the aluminum section of O.P.M., prevented work on our $600,000,000 aluminum expansion program."[278]

The pro-Fascist American businessmen cited above are only some of the ones that Higham and others have written about. Clearly many of the largest and most powerful industrialists in America did not fear Germany or Japan as a threat to their business profits. They understood how to do business with Fascists and expected business would be very good.[279] For these businessmen, the American war effort was something that they either disagreed with or treated as an inconvenience. Insofar as this sector of the American business elite is concerned, the evidence certainly does not suggest that competing economic interests of Allied and Axis bankers or industrialists provided the motive for the war.

Kid Gloves For Traitors

Most Americans are not aware of the pro-Fascist sympathies of many American corporate leaders during World War II. The reason is that the FDR and subsequent administrations kept a lid on this information and never prosecuted the corporate executives who could have been charged with crimes such as trading with the enemy in times of war. On the contrary, these men were often given important roles in the wartime government: Standard Oil's William Farish served on the War Petroleum Board, and General Motors President William S. Knudsen headed the Office of Production Management. The government treated the Fascist leanings of corporate leaders merely as an embarrassment to be hidden from public view. President Roosevelt and his cabinet and other advisors were highly sensitive to how the general public perceived the government and corporate leadership class. Their prime concern was preserving the power of this class over American working people, which was a far more fundamental problem than ensuring high profits. These politicians were experts at manipulating public opinion and using the rhetoric of war to control domestic rebellions. They understood, in many cases with far greater sophistication than business leaders, that the purpose of the U.S. entry into

World War II was to provide an ideological cover for actions that were in fact meant to defeat working class movements at home and abroad. The appearance of an "all out war against Fascism" was more important than its reality. If U.S. banks and industry were making money by supplying war materials to the "enemy"—so what? The important thing was that ordinary Americans did not hear about it and become cynical about their leaders' real motives. Thus, whenever the "dirty little secret" of corporate indifference to the military outcome of the war leaked out, government officials acted shocked and pretended to take strong action, but did not do so for real. Two examples illustrate the pattern.

On March 26, 1943, Congressman Jerry Voorhis introduced a resolution in the House of Representatives calling for an investigation of the Bank for International Settlements, including "the reasons why an American retains the position as president of this Bank being used to further the designs and purposes of Axis powers." When the resolution was not considered by Congress, Congressman John Coffee objected, stating, "The Nazi government has 85 million Swiss gold francs on deposit in the BIS. The majority of the board is made up of Nazi officials. Yet American money is being deposited in the Bank." Objections to the BIS had become strong enough that when the International Monetary Conference met at Bretton Woods, New Hampshire, on July 10, 1944, one economist there called for the BIS to be dissolved. The Chase and the First National banks and others tried to silence the criticisms of the BIS, but then New Hampshire's Senator Charles Tobey addressed the meeting on July 18 and said, "What you're doing by your silence and inaction is aiding and abetting the enemy." Under these circumstances Secretary of the Treasury Morgenthau and Secretary of State Hull (who had approved of the BIS until now) decided that the U.S. delegation to the Conference would officially approve the dissolution of the BIS, and the Conference voted to dissolve it. But it was all for show. Despite the Bretton Woods Resolution, the BIS was never dissolved.[280]

On February 26, 1943 the economist Henry Waldman, alarmed that U.S. companies were providing gasoline and petroleum products to Spain via the Spanish tanker fleet—in quantities equal to the full capacity of the Spanish fleet—and that Spain was helping thereby to fuel the Nazis, wrote to the *New York Times*, "Here we are, a nation actually assisting an enemy in time of war, and not only that, but stating through our Ambassador, that we stand ready to continue and extend such help...Spain is [an enemy] and yet we aid her."

Under Secretary of State Sumner Welles handled this problem by announcing on March 11 that "adequate guarantees have been furnished to satisfy the British and United States governments that none of these quantities of oil will reach Germany or German territory." Welles did not reveal that the "guarantees" were merely the empty promises of Spain's fascist General Franco.[281] The oil going to the Nazis was never the real problem, but word of the fact getting to the public was.

Anti-Fascist Business Leaders

By ignoring the existence of the pro-Fascist sector and looking only at the anti-Fascist sector of American business leaders, one can form the impression that the United States entered World War II strictly for objectives stemming from capitalist competition with Fascist elites. These objectives were articulated most clearly by the Council on Foreign Relations (CFR), whose role in shaping United States post-war objectives was examined closely by G. William Domhoff in The Power Elite and the State: How Policy is Made in America. Domhoff is one of the leading scholars who advocates that private business leaders use the government to secure their economic interests. To those who ascribe loftier goals to the American government, Domhoff is of course controversial. However, to those who advocate the competition theory of the war's origin, Domhoff makes their case as strongly, perhaps, as it can be made, based on enormous research into the various meetings and memoranda of organizations like the CFR. From this perspective, then, let us see what Domhoff says.

The CFR is generally acknowledged to be a major influence on American Foreign policy, and is described by a Domhoff source to be: "the province of internationally oriented bankers and corporate executives in New York and surrounding areas, as well as of academic experts and journalists...[I]ts funding for projects comes from large foundations directed by business leaders who are members of the council in significant numbers." The CFR enjoys great influence on government decision-making because "Its studies are conducted by respected scholars. Its leaders are known to be highly informed about foreign affairs. Many members had close social and business relations with central [government] decision-makers when they were in private life. Government officials are often members of council discussion groups. Then too, many members have served in government positions or as government advisers."[282]

Domhoff recounts the important CFR studies, papers, and memoranda to government leaders that related to defining the "national interest" and post war planning between 1940 and 1942. The earliest CFR planning was by its Economic and Financial Group, which in four papers dated March 9, 1940, concluded that there had been no serious consequences of the war on the United States up to that date. On April 6 it wrote five papers "primarily descriptive in nature, dealing with the possible impact on American trade of price-fixing and monetary exchange controls by the belligerents." Another paper May 11 warned that "a way would have to be found to increase American imports in order to bring about a necessary increase in exports." After the Nazi invasion of France in May and its subsequent attack on Great Britain, the CFR "turned the attention of both the State Department and the council to the problem of stabilizing the economies of Latin American countries that previously had depended upon their exports to continental Europe." On June 10 the State Department suggested setting up a single trading organization to market all of Latin America's agricultural surplus but the CFR had concluded on June 7 that such a trading organization would not work because [Domhoff's paraphrase] "it would be weak in needing raw materials and unable to consume the agricultural surpluses of Canada and the southern half of Latin America" and that "economic isolation in the Western Hemisphere would cost the United States almost two-thirds of its foreign trade." Later the council concluded that "any Western Hemisphere cartel for selling to Germany was doomed to failure because the self-sufficiency of the German bloc was such that it could not be forced to trade with the Western Hemisphere."

At this time the council "began to define the national interest in terms of the minimum geographical area that was necessary for the productive functioning of the American economy without drastic controls and major governmental intervention." On June 28 one report "concluded that the Far East and Western Hemisphere probably bore the same relationship to the United States as America had to Europe in the past—a source of raw materials and a market for manufactures." Other studies concluded that "the economies of Great Britain and Japan could not function adequately in harmony with the American economy without a large part of the world as markets and suppliers of raw materials" and "United States problems could not be solved if Japan excluded the American economy from Asia."

On October 19, 1940 Secretary of State Hull's special assistant, Leo Pasvolsky, asked the CFR to "suggest blocs that it thought might result from the war, and then see what could be done in economic terms within each area.

There would be two cores to start on; the first, Germany and the minimum territory she could be assumed to take in the war; the second the United States. Working outward from these cores, one could build up several possible blocs on a political basis, and then examine their economic potentialities." By December 14, the CFR had reached a general consensus on three points: 1) There was a need to plan "as if there would be a Germanized Western Europe for the immediate future; however, everyone agreed they preferred the defeat of Germany and the integration of Western Europe into the Western Hemi-sphere-Asia-British Empire bloc that was now being called the 'Grand Area.' 2) 'The Grand Area could not be broken into two democratic blocs [a British and an American] because of the danger that Great Britain might try to main-tain its empire and exclude the United States from free trade and investment within it." 3) "[I]mportant American economic and strategic interests in Asia were being threatened by Japanese expansionism." In evaluating whether these economic/competitive concerns suffice to explain the U.S. entry into the war, note that the CFR was able to plan around a "Germanized Western Eu-rope" and merely "preferred" the defeat of Germany. Also note that when it came to fear that a powerful nation might "try to maintain its empire and ex-clude the United States from free trade and investment within it," the CFR was referring to Great Britain, not Germany or Japan.

On June 22, 1941 the CFR formally defined the national interest as: "(1) the full use of the world's economic resources—implying full employment and a reduction in business cycle fluctuation; and, (2) the most efficient use of the world's resources—implying an interchange of goods among all parts of the world according to comparative advantages of each part in producing certain goods." The Political Group of the CFR added that the most important aim was "the decisive defeat of the Axis aggressors as rapidly as possible."

The CFR's report was preceded by an introduction which stated: "State-ments of war aims have two functions: propaganda and definition of national interests." From the point of view of propaganda, framing the national interest in terms of economic interests such as the CFR's focus on raw materials and markets was useful. A war waged for such interests is easily portrayed as a war for goals that benefit all Americans, since everybody depends on a well-functioning economy. On the other hand if the goal of the war were de-fined as "controlling the working class" it would obviously be a propaganda di-saster. Therefore, to the extent that the CFR formulated war goals with propaganda in mind, it had every incentive to stress the economic/competitive issues and no incentive to mention social control. It is therefore telling that after studying in great detail the CFR's role in shaping U.S. policy in this period, and despite the fact that he advocates the theory that the U.S. government serves the interests of big business (against the view that the government is guided by general ideological beliefs and acts independently of private business interests), Domhoff feels obligated to introduce in the concluding section of his chapter on this period (*Defining the National Interest: 1940-42*) a theme which he does not mention at all in the preceding part of the chapter—avoiding social upheaval. He writes: "[T]he new definition of the national interest was in good part economic in the sense that it was concerned with the full functioning of the American capitalist system with minimal changes in it. The goal was to avoid depression and social upheaval on the one hand, and greater state control of the economy on the other."

As earnest as the CFR reports sound, one has to wonder if they were the reason for or the rationalization of the U.S. entry into the war. For one thing, some of the CFR memoranda sound more like propaganda (or themes offered for use as propaganda) than private assessments of economic interests. For example, a report of the council's Economic and Financial Group dated January 15, 1941, says: "Toward the Philippines we have special obligations of a historical and moral nature." Another odd fact about the CFR in this regard is that some of its prominent members were in fact pro-Nazi. Much of the financing of the CFR came from the Rockefeller family through its foundation, and Rockefellers have been prominent on the CFR. The CFR's project on post-war planning and defining the national interest began September 12, 1939 and on December 6 the Rockefeller Foundation[283] gave it $44,500 for that specific project.[284] Yet John D. Rockefeller II put the distinctly pro-Fascist Walter Teagle and William Farish in charge of Standard Oil of New Jersey.[285] Similarly, Allen Dulles was an international lawyer in 1936 who represented Avery Rockefeller and Baron Bruno von Schröder who, along with Kurt von Schröder of the BIS and Gestapo, were the major owners of a company called Schröder, Rockefeller and Company, Investment Bankers. Dulles was also a director of this company, which was part of a larger company that *Time* magazine disclosed as being "the economic booster of the Rome-Berlin Axis."[286] Dulles (future head of the OSS, later CIA) was instrumental in trying to secretly create a Japanese-Anglo-Nazi alliance against the Soviet Union—an idea originally proposed by the British Lord Cadogan and foreign secretary, Lord Halifax, in 1939. By 1942 the proposal had gained support from the Vatican, and from Walter Schellenberg, the new Nazi SS intelligence head, who was in touch with Dulles' business partner, Karl Lindemann, the chief of Standard Oil of New Jersey's German subsidiary. On April 3, 1943, Dulles met (illegally and in violation of FDR's unconditional surrender policy) with the Nazi intelligence chief's personal emissary, Prince Max von Hohenlohe of the SS. "Dulles emphasized that German industry must be preserved and a *cordon sanitaire* established against the Soviets."[287] Yet Dulles was a co-leader of the CFR's Security and Armaments Group, helped to develop the CFR's definition of the U.S. national interest between 1940 and 1942,[288] and later rose to become a Vice President of the CFR from 1944 to 1946.[289]

Why did the Rockefellers fund the CFR? What was Allen Dulles doing leading the CFR? Why would Dulles help the CFR plan a war against his business partners and secret allies? If the competition theory of the war's origin is true, and the U.S. entered the war simply because American capitalists feared that Fascism was encroaching on their access to raw materials and markets and therefore had to be defeated, then how does one explain not only that some of America's wealthiest and most powerful corporate leaders wanted to make peace with the Fascists and do business with them, but that pro-Fascists played such a prominent role in the CFR—the chief organization through which corporate aims influenced government decision making in matters of war and foreign policy? It is the social control theory—not the competition theory—of the war's origin that offers an explanation for this paradox: for America's business leaders the goal of defeating the Fascists was never the most important goal—some preferred it and others did not; what united them (within the CFR and as a class) was their desire for the U.S. government to do whatever was necessary to prevent a social upheaval, an upheaval that they all realized was a far greater threat than the Fascists with whom many of them were doing business. The "war against Fascism" was promoted, or at least tolerated, by the American business elite, not because of economic or moral objections to Fascism which only some of them had, but because the war served to control the working class at a time when little else seemed capable of doing so.

Domestic Versus Foreign Causes Of Wars

In the competition framework with its associated implicit view of ordinary people as passive bystanders, it seems far-fetched to claim that Allied and Axis leaders on the eve of World War II were more concerned about preventing domestic revolution than they were about protecting and expanding their empires, and absurd to suggest that they launched the war in order to prevent domestic revolution. But the notion that national leaders start wars for domestic rather than external reasons is not considered absurd by academic researchers who try to approach this question with a spirit of objectivity and with tools such as statistical inference. In academic circles the competition view is referred to as "realism" and it has come under fire as not being in accord with empirical observations. An article in the peer-reviewed Journal of Conflict Resolution says,

> A major tenet of realism, long the dominant paradigm in international relations, is that domestic factors have little impact on foreign policy decisions, particularly in the realm of the "high politics" of security issues. Realists argue that decisions affecting the security, and especially the survival, of states are based on the requirements of the external situation and are directed at protecting the *national* interest. In particular, decisions to engage in foreign conflict are based upon careful considerations of the external environment, not on the political needs of domestic actors...This realist assumption has long been suspect, however, and a number of recent studies of international conflict have found evidence of linkages between domestic factors and foreign conflict...Indeed in his classic work, Wright claimed that "foreign war as a remedy for internal tension, revolution, or insurrection has been an accepted principle of government."[290]

The same article notes that rulers have long been aware of the usefulness of war as a means of preventing domestic revolution, and cites, as one example of this, Russian (Czarist) interior minister Plehve's statement on the eve of the Russo-Japanese War in 1904: "What this country needs is a short victorious war to stem the tide of revolution."[291]

An earlier article in the same journal looked at the United States government's use of force in foreign conflicts between 1949 and 1976 and reported:

> Ostrom and Job (1986) found that domestic, political factors are more influential on the president's decision to use military force than characteristics of the international environment. These results pose a serious challenge to the realists' assumptions regarding the motives of states

and the separability of domestic and foreign policy...Can a realist theory of America's use of military force be sustained in light of our findings? The answer at this stage must be: only with considerable effort...We are left then with significant discrepancies between the realist view of international politics and the influences that seem to have encouraged U.S. presidents to use military force in the post war period.[292]

Another article in this journal by a professor at the Center for International Affairs at Harvard University found post-WWII evidence that democratic (so-called) governments were more likely to use war for domestic reasons than totalitarian governments:

> It is hypothesized that democratic leaders will respond to domestic unrest by diverting attention by using force internationally. On the other hand, authoritarian leaders are expected to repress the unrest directly, and these acts of repression will make them less likely to use force internationally. An analysis of the initiation of force by the challenging states in 180 international crises between 1948 and 1982 strongly supports these hypotheses...My results indicate that the diversionary initiation of force is generally a pathology of democratic states...In particular, my finding that democratic states are more likely to respond to domestic unrest by initiating force at the international level than authoritarian states raises troubling questions.[293]

Why Did They Do It? Why Does It Matter?

Why did national leaders lead their people into a war that killed tens of millions of people? Nobody will ever be able to say with absolute certainty; we can only try to infer from our limited knowledge of history what explanation makes the most sense. I have made the case for the social control theory (that the Second World War had its roots and origins primarily as a joint strategy for control of the working classes of Europe, the U.S., and Japan), placing emphasis on the generally overlooked fact that working people were challenging corporate power to an unprecedented degree just before the war, and arguing that elites must have been preoccupied by this problem and certainly understood that war was a potential, though dangerous, solution. I have shown that the competition theory (that war was an instrument of capitalist competition between national elites who viewed competing capitalists in foreign nations, not working people at home and abroad, as the serious threat) cannot explain the anomaly of America's largest corporations and banks being owned and controlled by pro-Fascists seeking to avoid war with Germany and Japan. And I have shown that academic studies of the wars since World War II support the idea that they were more a response to domestic unrest than to concerns rooted in foreign affairs, a finding that lends further support to the plausibility of the social control theory regarding World War II itself. I believe the social control theory fits the facts better than competing theories.

The question of leaders' motives in waging the Second World War has a profound significance for our lives today. If the competition theory is true, it suggests that elites are the sole makers of history—they fight each other and wage wars in a world where ordinary people are merely passive victims of their rulers' actions. It means elites are the only actors on the stage of history and there is no force that can sweep them away. On the other hand, if the social control theory is true, it means that ordinary people are the force that makes history, that working people in their struggle to shape the world with their values of solidarity and equality and democracy are such a powerful force and are so threatening to elite rule that elites on occasion are compelled to resort to war as a last ditch and desperate effort to control them. It means there is a force in the world that has revolutionary potential, that there is a basis for hope in the possibility of revolution to defeat elite rule and make a far more equal and democratic society. This is why the question is important. The next section about Allied war objectives in Europe and Asia will shed light on the answer.

SUMMARY

In Germany and Japan, the elite's fear of working class revolution made them opt for Fascist methods of social control based on an extremely racist and nationalist ideology. The elite in these countries used racism primarily to recruit fanatics to attack the working class and repress disobedience in the name of "national defense" or "national glory." This method of social control required an aggressive war-making foreign policy, which is why the Fascist leaders risked initiating wars even when they knew they lacked the material capability to win unless victories were immediate.

The Soviet Union, which claimed to be the only socialist nation, was in fact, from the very beginning of the October 1917 revolution, a brutal dictatorship of the Communist Party over not only the former exploiting classes, but over the workers and peasants as well. The authority of the Communist rulers, and their ability to influence the Left all over the world as well as many working people in their own country, was based on their claim to be applying a "science" of revolution—Marxism—which required that they exercise power undemocratically for the purpose of increasing economic production at all costs. Long before the Second World War, Stalin had formed a tacit alliance with Western capitalism. Stalin only fought Hitler because he was unsuccessful in his efforts to form a lasting alliance with the Nazis, and when Hitler attacked the Soviet Union he had no choice but to fight back.

In the United States, FDR faced a working class rebellion that not only fought specific companies, but the U.S. government itself. FDR used New Deal reforms to contain and control the working class but they were not very effective. Needing to put the working class on the defensive, FDR secretly provoked Japan to attack the United States in order to get the United States into war on a nationalist footing, which enabled him to use the war as a pretext to demand sacrifice and obedience from the working class.

Notes

1. Tim Mason, *Nazism, Fascism and the Working Class: Essays*, Press Syndicate of the University of Cambridge, Cambridge, England, 1996, pp. 35.

2. Gabriel Kolko, *Century of War: Politics, Conflicts, and Society Since 1914*, The New Press, New York, 1994, p.149.

3. The *Freikorps* was an irregular reactionary military force that originated at the end of the First World War. As John Weiss recounts in *Ideology of Death*: "Frightened by the growing disobedience of front-line [German] troops in the summer of 1918, the generals would not publicly admit their impotence. With radical discontent rising at home and socialist workers' councils proliferating, the high command released only divisions they knew would resist the left. Aware the Allies would not allow the use of force by the army, military authorities encouraged officers to form irregular units, armed and often uniformed, into what was called the Freikorps. Recruiting civilians, Freikorps units, many virulently anti-Semitic, fought pitched battles and guerilla warfare to maintain German control over Poland and the Baltic states and hold off the Bolsheviks during the Russo-Polish War... By 1920 there were about 300,000 Freikorps irregulars fighting in the east and against leftists and strikers at home... The army funded and organized the Freikorps, and secret government monies were also available. Army leaders saw the Freikorps as the nucleus of a new Wehrmacht (armed forces), and regular troops often marched with them. Unarmed opponents were often shot; Jews were always at risk. Industrialists and landowners often contributed to Freikorps units, and landed aristocrats provided rest havens on their estates for the warriors, who in return disciplined radical farm workers." [pp. 217, 224]

4. Sergio Bologna, *Nazism and the Working Class—1933–93*, [paper presented at the Milan Camera del Lavoro, 3 June 1993], section 13, p. 29.

5. *Ibid.*, section 14, p. 31.

6. *Ibid.*, section 15, p. 39.

7. William L. Shirer, *The Rise and Fall of the Third Reich: A History of Nazi Germany*, p. 231.

8. William Sheridan Allen, *The Nazi Seizure of Power: The Experience of a Single German Town 1930-1935*, Quadrangle Books, Chicago 1965, paperback edition, p.115.

9. Bologna, *Nazism and the Working Class—1933–93*, section 12, p. 24.

10. *Ibid.*, section 15, p. 35.

11. *Ibid.*, section 15, p. 37.

12. Shirer, pp. 222-3.

13. "Unlike all other parties, Social Democratic leaders refused all offers to combine with anti-Semites in election runoffs, even though in the few cases where the offer was made, it would have helped them. For ordinary workers the capitalist was the enemy, Jewish or not;..." The Communists were not only opposed to anti-Semitism but were portrayed by the Nazis as being allied with Jews against Germans. "A famous [Nazi] poster shows a proletarian street fighter protecting a Jewish financier sitting on a bag of gold labeled 'War, revolution, inflation profits of eastern Jews.' The poster asks, 'Is this your battle against capitalism, Marxist?'" [John Weiss, *Ideology of Death*, pp. 145, 284.]

14. Shirer, p. 241.

15. *Ibid.*, pp. 246-7.

16. *Ibid.*, p. 249.

17. "On November 23, 1932, at a meeting of the famous and influential industrialists of the Langnamverein, with some fifteen hundred members, 'One observer reported that most of the industrialists he had talked with favored Hitler's appointment as chancellor.' In the same month, agrarian landowners and important figures in 'banking, finance, retailing, and export industries' wrote a joint letter to Hindenburg asking that Hitler be brought into the government...Prominent business figures—Siemens, Bosch, Schacht, Thyssen, Krupp, and others—pressed Hindenburg, writing that the Nazis, 'through the overcoming of class contrasts, create the essential basis for a rebirth of the German economy.'" [John Weiss, *Ideology of Death*, p. 302]

18. Shirer, p. 244.

19. *Ibid.*, p.245.

20. *Ibid.*, pp 249-51.

21. *Ibid.*, pp 271-3.

22. *Ibid.*, pp. 271, 282-3.

23. John Weiss, *Ideology of Death: Why the Holocaust Happened in Germany*, Ivan R. Dee, Chicago, 1997, p. 307.

24. Shirer, pp. 374-5.

25. Weiss, p. 363.

26. Mason, p. 238.

27. *Ibid.*, p. 239.

28. Bologna p. 49.

29. Mason, p. 239.

30. *Ibid*, p. 105.

31. Bologna section 12, p. 26.

32. *Ibid.*, section 16, p. 47.

33. Ian Kershaw, *Popular Opinion & Political Dissent in the Third Reich: Bavaria 1933-1945*, Clarendon Press, Oxford, England, 1999, p. 100.

34. Detlev J.K. Peukert, *Inside Nazi Germany*, Yale University Press, New Haven, 1987, pp. 152-3.

35. Mason, p. 48.

36. *Ibid.*, p. 113.

37. *Ibid.*, p. 119.

38. *Ibid.*, pp. 118-19.

39. *Ibid.*, pp. 119-20.

40. *Ibid*, pp. 126-7.

41. *Ibid.*, p. 123.

42. *Ibid.*, p. 49.

43. *Ibid.*, p. 115.

44. *Ibid.*, p. 122.

45. David Kaiser, *Politics & War: European Conflict from Philip II to Hitler*, Harvard University Press, Cambridge, Massachusetts, 2000, p. 380.

46. Mason p. 123.

47. *Ibid.*, p. 124.

48. Kaiser, pp. 380-2.

49. Foreign workers were either drafted like soldiers or made prisoners. Some volunteered for the labor draft at first, but quickly it became compulsory. In France it was called the STO (Service du Travail Obligatoire: Compulsory Work Service). As prisoners or drafted labor, foreign workers were exploited even more ruthlessly than German workers. The Nazis also tried very hard to turn German workers against the foreign laborers, not always succeeding however, as the following excerpts from an account by a French man deported for his political beliefs and forced to work in an aircraft factory in Oranienburg near Berlin for two years (1944/45), demonstrate. This man was held in a concentration camp at night while sent to work in the factory by day. "...And the workers who struggled daily against the Nazi dictatorship. In our Halle 2, in the Heinkel factory, they were a score of organized workers amongst around 200 German civilian workers and more than double of this figure of

unorganized German workers, perhaps less courageous, but among whose (sic) nevertheless we have found good friends when after a long period of working together they had learned to know us better. Could these workers be considered as 'responsible' for the Nazis crimes?

"The comrade prisoners of the Kolonne 8 in our workshop at Heinkel certainly will remember for a long time of (sic) the German comrade Paul W. (I call him comrade because it would be impossible for me to give him another name), who from the first day of work in this 'commando' tried to look for political left militants. And if he did everything to help us as his comrades in other Kolonnes in the hall did it with other prisoners, it was not for pity's sake, as some Nazi supporters, but for solidarity. The loaf he brought once a week for all the prisoners French, Polish or Russian working with him, the share of his daily sandwich he left deliberately for us, the German or French daily papers he put in our pockets or in our drawer, all that with the constant risk to join us in the camp, can we forget it? And he knew (he did not hide this fact from us militants) that most of the prisoners working with him would have hanged him once the war were over only because he was a German. One day he had a row with some patriotic petty bourgeois telling them he did not like at all patriotism from any country.

"Could we forget this good old riveter in our Kolonne 8 later moved to the Kolonne 2 who brought every time the first fruits from his garden, and many other things? He was yet rather a fearful man but he managed anyway to bring us daily papers.. And again in this Kolonne 8, this old German craftsman mobilized in this factory, who took the side of the prisoners several times when they were treated badly by the 'vorarbeiter'; he also left part of his poor sandwich and dared to tell us his hate for the Nazis though not a member of the anti-Nazi organization in the factory.

"And at the other end of the Kolonne this brave but a bit crazy worker who was so nice with us and with whom I could talk very openly in total brotherhood; and this young worker of the Kolonne 6 who was arrested when he tried to post a letter for a prisoner and got 6 months in jail and all the night workers from other parts of the factory who at midnight brought full pans of soup to the prisoners working with them.

"And F., who when he had become confident enough to explain that Hitler had come to power with the help of workers divided, and recall[ed] this communist vote with the Nazis to pull down the socialist government in Berlin. Most of these German workers had a financial interest in our work but very few pushed us to work more. Only the middle management, most of them Nazis hidden in the factory, party members and some sympathizers tried to push us to work harder. All other German workers were constantly lectured by the Nazi leaders of the factory, by the leaders of the Labor Front, by the foremen, all party members. Very often , the civilian German workers told us to beware of some worker who was more or less an informer.

"And yet they always had to be very careful not to become too confident because they knew that amongst the prisoners there was some criminals, members of the lumpen proletariat and some young aristocrats for whom any worker even of their own nationality was scum. Even so , they helped us..." [quoted inside a letter from Henri Simon to the *Discussion Bulletin*, September-October 2001, http://www. libertariansocialism. 4t.com/db/db010910.htm].

50. Mason p. 127.

51. Andrew Gordon, *Labor and Imperial Democracy in Prewar Japan*, University of California Press, Berkeley and Los Angeles, California, 1991, pp. 238-9.

52. *Ibid.*, p. 279.

53. Shakaishugi Kenkyûû Socialist Studies October 1921 p. 12 cited by http://www. spunk.org /texts/places/japan/sp001883/japbib.html

54. Gordon pp. 108-9.

55. *Ibid.*, pp. 132-3.

56. *Ibid.*, p. 229.

57. *Ibid.*, pp. 135-6.

58. *Ibid.*, p. 150.

59. *Ibid.*, pp. 168-71.

60. *Ibid.*, pp. 176-180.

61. *Ibid.*, p. 183.

62. *Ibid.*, p. 184.

63. *Ibid.*, p. 243.

64. *Ibid.*, p. 244.

65. *Ibid.*, p. 245.

66. *Ibid.*, p. 249.

67. *Ibid.*, pp. 249-50.

68. *Ibid.*, p. 252.

69. *Ibid.*, p. 254.

70. *Ibid.*, pp. 257-9.

71. *Ibid.*, p. 268.

72. *Ibid.*, p. 262.

73. *Ibid.*, pp. 267-8.

74. *Ibid.*, pp. 290-1.

75. *Ibid.*, p. 276.

76. *Ibid.*, p. 276.

77. *Ibid.*, p. 277.

78. *Ibid.*, p. 288.

79. *Ibid.*, p. 302.

80. *Ibid.*, pp. 302-3.

81. *Ibid.*, pp. 303-4.

82. *Ibid.*, p. 302.

83. *Ibid.*, p. 324.

84. Kolko, *Century of War*, pp. 302-3.

85. Before Hitler's rise to power, Stalin told the German Communists to campaign mostly against the social democrats (SDP), not the Nazis. In the early years of Hitler's regime, Stalin did not consider Hitler a threat and even believed he would play a useful role for the Soviet Union by keeping the Western powers pre-occupied with fighting each other. Then, in 1935 he adopted the United Front Against Fascism strategy, identifying Hitler as the main threat and the Western "democracies" as allies in opposing him. But suddenly, in the summer of 1939, Stalin signed the Nazi-Soviet Non-Aggression Treaty with Hitler and gave material and then military assistance to the Nazis, shocking and disorienting rank-and-file Communists around the world. Lastly, Stalin turned against Hitler when Hitler invaded the Soviet Union in 1941.

86. Robert Service, *A History of Twentieth-Century Russia*, Harvard University Press, Cambridge, Massachusetts, 1998, p. 33.

87. *Ibid.*, p. 36.

88. *Ibid.*, pp. 37-8.

89. *Ibid.*, p. 39.

90. Nicolas Werth, *A State against its People: Violence, Repression, and Terror in the Soviet Union*, in *The Black Book of Communism: Crimes Terror Repression*, Harvard University Press, Cambridge, MA, 1999, p. 48.

91. Service, pp. 47-8.

92. *Ibid.*, p. 53.

93. *Ibid.*, p. 60.

94. *Ibid.*, p. 62.

95. *Ibid.*, pp. 68-9.

96. Werth, p. 62.

97. *Ibid.*, p. 63.

98. Service pp. 48, 110.

99. Karl Marx and Friedrich Engels, *The Communist Manifesto*, Signet Classic, New York, 1998 (originally published 1848), Part, II, p. 75.

100. Adam Smith, *The Wealth of Nations*, The Modern Library edition, 1994, p.485 (first published 1776).

101. Karl Marx and Friedrich Engels, *The German Ideology*, in *Basic Writings*, p. 255, cited by David Stratman in *We CAN Change the World*, New Democracy Books, Boston, Massachusetts.

102. Karl Marx, *Capital*, *Vol. I*, Chapter 14, "The Detail Labourer and His Implements," cited in *We CAN Change The World*, by David Stratman, p. 164.

103. Karl Marx and Friedrich Engels, *The Communist Manifesto*, Part I. p. 55. This is a remarkable statement in light of the fact that the "enclosures" which drove the peasants off of the land and into the sweatshops of the industrial revolution were one of the greatest attacks on working people in the history of capitalism.

104. *Ibid.*, I. p. 65.

105. *Ibid.*, II pp. 73-4.

106. The question of what motivates human beings has an interesting history in Western intellectual thought, a brief discussion of which helps to put the Marxist view in perspective. Thomas Hobbes took the individuals he was familiar with as representative of all people, and concluded in 1651 (in his famously influential book *Leviathan* which advocated the need for a strong government to rule over people) that, "I put for a generall inclination of all mankind, a perpetuall and restlesse desire of Power after power, that ceaseth onley in Death." The Hobbesian view dominated future intellectual thought because at the time Hobbes wrote, the new capitalist social class in England, led by Oliver Cromwell, derived legitimacy from it, and because this class violently suppressed the peasant class which had a very different view about human nature and the way society should be. Hobbes' now virtually forgotten contemporary and intellectual equal, the British theological and political philosopher Gerrard Winstanley, was a leader of a peasant movement, called the Diggers, that rejected the Hobbesian view. The Diggers fought the "enclosures" that were driving peasants off the land and into the factories; they illegally farmed the "commons" land, creating egalitarian communes. Winstanley wrote: "When this universall law of equity rises up in every man and woman, then none shall lay claim to any creature, and say, *This is mine, and that is yours, This is my work, that is yours*; but every one shall put to their hands to till the earth, and bring up cattle, and the blessing of the earth shall be common to all....There shall be no buying nor selling...but the whole earth shall be a common treasury..." [Winstanley, Gerrard. *The Works of Gerrard Winstanley*. Ed. George Sabine. Ithaca, New York: Cornell University Press, 1941, p. 184; see also David Spritzler, *Winstanley & the Diggers*, http://www.newdemocracyworld.org /diggers.htm]

Following Hobbes, Adam Smith and Charles Darwin and Karl Marx all made self-interest the central premise of their theories; this was the dominant view of intellectuals during the industrial revolution. But the scientist in Darwin tempered prior belief with observation and skepticism. As is well known, Darwin explained evolution of species as the result of natural selection based on survival of the fittest individuals. But an individual's fitness can be determined by ability to survive in a hostile natural environment or by ability to compete against other same-species individuals. Darwin strongly emphasized the latter because he accepted the prevailing idea of "progress" and realized that if adaptation to the environment drove evolution then species would change over time as the environment changed but they would not "improve" because environmental changes were random. Competition with other members of one's species, however, could explain why evolution led to improvement because then the bar for survival would always be raised higher, never lowered. But despite this cultural and theoretical bias in favor of seeing a struggle of each against the other (rather than of the whole species against the environment), Darwin was struck by the anomaly of human altruism, writing, "He who was ready to sacrifice his life, as many a savage has been, rather than betray his comrades, would often leave no offspring to inherit his noble nature...Therefore it seems scarcely possible...that the number of men gifted with such virtues...would be increased through natural selection, that is, by the survival of the fittest." With great care to stress the specialness of the case, Darwin nonetheless admitted that human altruism was a fact that required a special exception to his general theory of individual competition. He suggested that human altruism evolved because an altruistic man "might thus do far more good to his tribe than by begetting offspring with a tendency to inherit his own high character." [*The Descent of Man* Vol. 1, pp. 163, 165] The scientist in Darwin could not simply dismiss empirical observations about human beings that his theory did not explain.

Marx, like Darwin, also saw himself as developing a scientific theory of evolution, but "of the economic formation of society...viewed as a process of natural history" rather than of the origin of species. In contrast to Darwin's more scientific grappling with the observation of human altruism, however, Marx built his grand theory on an explicit decision to ignore, as of no important consequence, aspects of human motivation other than self- (or class-, he made little distinction) interest. Thus in the 1867 Preface to the first German edition of Vol. 1 of Capital (same paragraph containing the above quotation) Marx says, "But here individuals are dealt with only in so far as they are the personifications of economic categories, embodiments of particular class-relations and class-interests." In consequence of this approach, Marx was forced to deny the obvious revolutionary character of peasant movements like the Diggers, writing in *The Communist Manifesto* (Part I) that peasants "are therefore not revolutionary, but conservative. Nay, more, they are reactionary." By enshrining an upper class seventeenth century view of human nature as an axiom of its entire theory, and systematically ignoring observations that do not fit the theory, Marxism departs from the scientific approach of relying on skepticism and testable hypotheses that can be refuted by observation.

Modern scientists studying evolution, such as the late Stephen Jay Gould in his *The Structure of Evolutionary Theory* (pp. 595-1024), argue that evolution cannot be fully understood without also granting an important role to species, as opposed to individual organisms, as units that are sorted out by natural selection. This perspective makes the emergence of mutual aid behaviors within a species (herding, grooming other individuals, altruism, etc.) easier to explain, as an earlier Russian naturalist, Peter Kropotkin (who was also a famous anarchist and critic of Marx), wrote about in great detail in his *Mutual Aid: A Factor of Evolution*.

107. Werth, pp. 123-4.

108. Karl Marx and Friedrich Engels, *The Communist Manifesto*, Part II. p. 75.

109. Werth, p. 65.

110. *Ibid.*, p. 66.

111. *Ibid.*, p. 46.

112. Service, p. 109.

113. Werth, p. 97.

114. *Ibid.*, p. 76.

115. *Ibid.*, p. 96.

116. Mike Malet, *Nestor Makhno in the Russian Civil War*, p. 26, excerpted on http://www.struggle.ws/russia/makhno_notes.html

117. Piotr Arshinovm, *History of the Makhnovist Movement*, excerpted on http://www.struggle.ws/russia/makhno_antisem.html

118. Service p. 108, Werth p. 72.

119. Service, p. 121.

120. Werth, p. 91.

121. *Ibid.*, p. 68.

122. *Ibid.*, p. 68.

123. *Ibid.*,p. 68.

124. *Ibid.*, p. 69.

125. *Ibid.*, p. 69.

126. *Ibid.*, p. 86.

127. *Ibid.*, p. 86.

128. *Ibid.*, p. 86.

129. *Ibid.*, p. 87.

130. *Ibid.*, p. 88.

131. *Ibid.*, p. 88.

132. *Ibid.*, pp. 89-90.

133. *Ibid.*, p. 91.

134. *Ibid.*, p. 112.

135. *Ibid.*, p. 112.

136. *Ibid.*, p. 113.

137. *Ibid.*, p. 114.

138. Service, pp. 125-6.

139. *Ibid.*, pp. 169-70.

140. *Ibid.*, pp. 170.

141. *Ibid.*, pp. 192.

142. Werth, p. 147.

143. *Ibid.*, p. 148.

144. *Ibid.*, p. 148.

145. *Ibid.*, p. 149.

146. *Ibid.*, p. 149.

147. *Ibid.*, p. 149.

148. *Ibid.*, p. 153.

149. *Ibid.*, p. 160.

150. *Ibid.*, p. 161.

151. *Ibid.*, p. 162.

152. *Ibid.*, p. 164.

153. *Ibid.*, p. 163

154. *Ibid.*, p. 164.

155. *Ibid.*, p. 165.

156. *Ibid.*, p. 167.

157. *Ibid.*, p. 167.

158. Service, p. 210.

159. Service, p. 210.

160. Werth, p. 187.

161. Werth, p. 187.

162. Werth, p. 188.

163. Werth, p. 190.

164. Service, p. 177.

165. *Ibid.*, p. 177.

166. Leibovitz, p. 219.

167. *Ibid.*, p. 255.

168. Service, p. 256. Also, Albert Meltzer in his autobiographical *I Couldn't Paint Golden Angels* recalls the effect of the Hitler-Stalin pact on a co-worker in a British hospital: "I recall the arguments I used to have with a young woman at work who worked in X-rays and who resented my criticisms of the Communist Party. She insisted I must have a personal reason for disliking Soviet Russia, but restrained her rage to a muttered 'Lies— all reckless lies,' the typical response of the bewildered idealist. One morning I looked in her office and told her Molotov, for Stalin, had just signed a treaty with Hitler. Had I known, it was not the most tactful time to break the news. She had been on night shift, was tired, and had not heard the radio. She flew into a temper and I retreated before her wrath with unused X-ray plates flying at

me. Later I thought she might have cooled down and the news was in the papers anyway. I looked in her office to find her in floods of tears. I guess many pop-frontists felt that way then." [AK Press and http://www.spunk.org/library/writers/meltzer /sp001591/ angels4.html]

169. Kaiser, p. 379.

170. Service, p. 257.

171. *Ibid.*, pp. 257-8.

172. *Ibid.*, pp. 258-9.

173. *Ibid.*, pp. 259-60.

174. *Ibid.*, p. 282.

175. *Ibid.*, p. 284.

176. *Ibid.*, p. 270.

177. Republic Steel Corporation, *War Labor Report* 325 (July 16, 1942): 340-41, cited in *Strike*, by Jeremy Brecher, p. 239.

178. John Zerzan in *Telos*, quarterly, Spring 1975, cited by Sam Dolgoff in *The American Labor Movement: A New Beginning*, originally published in 1980 by *Resurgence*, and now at http://www.normalbooks.com/ text/samdolgoff/ alm1.html

179. Matthew Josephson and Sidney Hillman, *Statesman of Labor*, p.439 cited in Sam Dolgoff, *The American Labor Movement: A New Beginning*, http://www.normalbooks. com/text/samdolgoff/ alm1.html

180. *Ibid.*,(same url).

181. Jeremy Brecher, *Strike*, South End Press, Boston, Massachusetts, 1997, p. 174.

182. "On May 3, 1941, J. Edgar Hoover sent a memorandum to Roosevelt's secretary, Major General Watson, which read as follows: 'Information has been received at this Bureau from a source that is socially prominent and known to be in touch with some of the people involved, but for whom we cannot vouch, to the effect that Joseph P. Kennedy, the former Ambassador to England, and Ben Smith, the Wall Street operator, some time in the past had a meeting with Göring in Vichy, France, and that thereafter Kennedy and Smith had donated a considerable amount of money to the German cause. They are both described as being very anti-British and pro-German.'" [Charles Higham, *Trading With the Enemy*, p. 204]

183. John Loftus and Mark Aarons, *The Secret War Against The Jews: How Western Espionage Betrayed the Jewish People*, St. Martin's Griffin, New York, 1994, pp. 256.

184. Brecher, pp. 121-7.

185. *Ibid.*, pp. 129-31.

186. *Ibid.*, pp. 138-140.

187. *Ibid.*, pp. 147-8.

188. Brecher, p. 151.

189. *Ibid.*, pp. 153- 5.

190. A detailed account of this struggle (in which the striking coal miners wore red neckerchiefs and called themselves "red necks")—*The Redneck War of 1921* by Michael M. Meador—recounts that the local sheriff actually did hire private airplanes that dropped homemade bombs on the strikers.[http://www.rootsweb.com/ ~ wvcoal/red.html]

191. Brecher, p. 160.

192. Linda Wheeler, *Routing a Ragtag American Army*, Washington Post Staff Writer, http://aspin.asu.edu/hpn/archives/Apr99/0066.html

193. During WWII Hoover went on to advise Secretary of War Stimson on how the military could use the control of food to control starving people. Stimson praised Hoover's expertise in this field, remarking "Hoover stamped out Communism in this way in central Europe." [Kolko, *Politics of War*, p. 498] See also, *The Engineer President, Presidential Moments,* http://www.americanpresident.org/KoTrain/Courses/HH/HH_Presidential_Moments.htm

194. Brecher, p. 162.

195. *Ibid.*, pp. 169-74.

196. *Ibid.*, p. 177.

197. *Ibid.*, pp. 178-84.

198. *Ibid.*, pp.185-7.

199. *Ibid.*, pp. 188-90.

200. *Ibid.*, pp. 190-92.

201. Arthur M. Schlesinger, Jr., *The Age of Roosevelt*, Vol. III, *The Politics of Upheaval*, Houghton Mifflin Company, Boston, 1960, p. 325.

202. Brecher, p. 203.

203. *Ibid.*, p. 217.

204. *Ibid.*, p. 221.

205. *Ibid.*, pp. 222-3.

206. NYT, March 19, 1937, cited in Brecher, p. 227.

207. NYT, March 18, 1937, cited in Brecher, p. 227.

208. Kevin Phillips, *Wealth and Democracy*, Broadway Books, New York, 2002, pp. 71-2, citing William Leuchtenberg, *Franklin D. Roosevelt and the New Deal* (New York, 1963), p. 80.

209. James N. Gregory, in the introduction to Upton Sinclair's *I, Candidate for Governor: And How I Got Licked*, University of California Press, Berkeley, California, 1934.

210. On May 22, 1920 Henry Ford's newspaper, the *Dearborn Independent*, ran the headline: THE INTERNATIONAL JEW: THE WORLD'S PROBLEM. Hitler praised Ford in *Mein Kampf* and in 1938 awarded him the Order of the Golden Eagle. In 1941, Ford hired Charles Lindbergh as a member of his executive staff. On

December 17, 1941, ten days after Pearl Harbor, Lindbergh told a group of America Firsters, "There is only one danger in the world—that is the yellow danger. China and Japan are really bound together against the white race. There could only have been one efficient weapon against this alliance...Germany...the ideal setup would have been to have had Germany take over Poland and Russia, in collaboration with the British, as a bloc against the yellow people and Bolshevism." [Higham, pp. 175-8, 189] "The Du Ponts' fascistic behavior was seen in 1936, when Irénéé du Pont used General Motors money to finance the notorious Black Legion. This terrorist organization had as its purpose the prevention of automobile workers from unionizing. The members wore hoods and black robes, with skull and crossbones. They fire-bombed union meetings, murdered union organizers, often by beating them to death, and dedicated their lives to destroying Jews and communists. They linked to the Ku Klux Klan." [Higham, p. 186] William S. Knudsen, President of General Motors, returning from a visit with Hitler's top Nazi, Hermann Göring, told reporters on October 6, 1933 that Germany (all of whose labor leaders Hitler had arrested) was "the miracle of the twentieth century." Knudsen implemented the speedup system at GM which caused men to die, while Irénéé du Pont "personally paid almost $1 million from his own pocket for armed and gas-equipped storm troops modeled on the Gestapo to sweep through the plants and beat up anyone who proved rebellious." [Higham, pp. 183-4, 186-7] See also, Charles Higham, *Trading With The Enemy: An Exposé of the Nazi-American Money Plot 1933-1949*, Dell Publishing Company, New York, 1983, pp. 175-7 (Henry Ford), pp.183,186 (DuPonts), p. 184 (Knudsen), pp. 132,192 (Behn).

211. For Führer they chose General Smedley Butler, former commandant of the Marine Corps, who had been awarded two Congressional Medals of Honor and was one of the most popular soldiers in America. The plan backfired when Butler refused to go along and reported it.

212. Higham, pp. 184-6.

213. "On October 20, 1942, John G. Winant, U.S. Ambassador to London, cooly reported to Dean Acheson that two thousand German army trucks were authorized for repair by the Ford motor works in Berne. On the same day, Winant reported that the British Legation and the U.S. authorities recommended the Ford Motor Company of Belgium be blacklisted because its Zurich branch, *on U.S. orders* [italics added], was repairing trucks and converting the use of gasoline for truck and cars of the German army in Switzerland...In December 1943 a further report from Minister Leland Harrison in Berne said, 'The Ford Motor Company in Zurich, acting for Cologne, supplies spare parts for the repair of Ford trucks and passenger cars to U.S. Ford Motor Company agents in Switzerland. Some of these parts are imported, which provides the enemy with clearing funds.' Thus, one year after these matters were reported in Washington, trading with the enemy was continuing. All Swiss operations functioned under the guidance of Ford's Charles E. Sorenson." [Higham, *Trading With The Enemy*, p. 182] Of Sothenes Behn, Chief of ITT in the U.S., Higham writes, "During the last period of the war Behn's work on behalf of the Ger-

man army had deeply intensified. His communications systems for the OKW, the High Command of the Nazi armed forces, had become more and more sophisticated. The systems enabled the Nazis under Schellenberg's special decoding branch to break the American diplomatic code. They also allowed the building of intercept posts and platoons in the defensive campaign against the British and American invasion of France. At the same time, Behn was indispensable in making that invasion possible." [Higham, p. 132]

214. "A presidential edict, issued six days after December 7, 1941, actually set up the legislation whereby licensing arrangements for trading with the enemy could officially be granted. Often during the years after Pearl Harbor the government permitted such trading. For example, ITT was allowed to continue its relations with the Axis and Japan until 1945, even though that conglomerate was regarded as an official instrument of United States Intelligence. No attempt was made to prevent Ford from retaining its interests for the Germans in Occupied France, nor were the Chase Bank or the Morgan Bank expressly forbidden to keep open their branches in Occupied Paris. It is indicated that the Reichsbank and Nazi Ministry of Economics made promises to certain U.S. corporate leaders that their properties would not be injured after the Fáhrer was victorious. Thus, the bosses of the multinationals as we know them today had a six-spot on every side of the dice cube. Whichever side won the war, the powers that really ran nations would not be adversely affected." [Higham, pp. 13-14]

215. In the 1530's, one group of Anabaptists under the leadership of John of Leyden gained control of the German city of Münster where they attempted to institute a government that disallowed private property and class distinctions.

216. Hugh Thomas, *The Spanish Civil War*, Harper Colophon Books, Harper & Row, New York, 1961, pp. 187, 192-3.

217. For an excellent eyewitness account of these events, see George Orwell's *Homage to Catalonia*. Also, Vernon Richards, Foreword to the 1975 edition, Gaston Leval, *Collectives in the Spanish Revolution*, Freedom Press, London 1975, trans. Vernon Richards.

218. Hugh Thomas, pp. 637, 363.

219. Arnold A. Offner, *American Appeasement: United States Foreign Policy and Germany 1933-1938*, W.W. Norton & Co., NY, 1969, p. 155.

220. *Ibid.*, p. 156.

221. *Ibid.*, pp. 156-7.

222. *Ibid.*, p. 159.

223. Charles A. Beard, *President Roosevelt and the Coming Of The War: 1941*, New Haven, Yale University Press 1948, pp. 443-4.

224. Beard, pp. 415-16.

225. Thomas Fleming, *The New Dealers' War: Franklin D. Roosevelt and The War Within World War II*, Basic Books (Perseus Books Group), New York, 2001, pp. 79-80.

226. Fleming, p. 16.

227. *Ibid*, p. 16.

228. Beard, p. 180.

229. *Foreign Relations*, 1941, Vol. IV, pp. 839-40., and at ftp://ftp.purdue.edu/pub/Liberal-Arts/History/pha/pearl.harbor/misc/turner_1.txt

230. Beard, p. 457 footnote (citing *Foreign Relations of the United States: Japan, 1931-1941*, *II*, 556 f.), & p. 494, 488.

231. Fleming, p. 18.

232. Fleming, p. 19.

233. Beard, p. 418.

234. Fleming, p. 23, Jonathan G. Utley, *Going to War With Japan: 1937-1941*, University of Tennessee Press, Knoxville, 1985, p. 174.

235. Jonathan G. Utley, *Going to War With Japan: 1937-1941*, University of Tennessee Press, Knoxville, 1985, p. 174, note pp. 223.

236. Charles A. Beard, *President Roosevelt and the Coming Of The War 1941: A Study In Appearances And Realities*, Yale University Press, New Haven, 1948, p. 517.

237. The historian Charles Beard wrote of this ultimatum: "American citizens who had any knowledge of American diplomatic history and foreign affairs worthy of mention could readily detect the significance of the memorandum as soon as it was published...First of all, it revealed that President Roosevelt and Secretary Hull had categorically rejected a Japanese proposal in November for a modus vivendi...The memorandum made it patent that they had not chosen to follow the methods long recognized in diplomacy as calculated to arrive at a modus vivendi; in other words, they had not limited the issues to primary and essential terms...At no time in the history of American diplomatic relations with the Orient, if published records are to be trusted, had the Government of the United States proposed to Japan such a sweeping withdrawal from China under a veiled threat of war and under the pressure of economic sanctions likely to lead to war. Not even the most brazen imperialist under Republican auspices had even ventured to apply this doctrine officially in the conduct of relations with Japan." [*President Roosevelt and the Coming Of War 1941*, pp. 235-6]

238. Robert Stinnett, in *Day of Deceit: The Truth About FDR and Pearl Harbor*, draws on previously classified documents to make a compelling case that in fact FDR even had information the day before the December 7 attack that Pearl Harbor was the target.

239. Fleming, p. 23, citing Waldo Heinrichs, *Threshold of War: Franklin D. Roosevelt and American Entry into World War II*, New York, 1988, 135, 177-179.

240. Beard, p. 419. The standard account of how the war between the United States and Japan started ignores all of the evidence that the leaders of these nations saw im-

portant benefits in being at war. For example, Jonathan G. Utley, in *Going To War With Japan: 1937-1941*, takes it as a premise that war is never the goal and writes: "The purpose of diplomacy is to find a way for nations with conflicting interests to resolve their differences other than on the battlefield, and if not to resolve those differences at least to learn to coexist with them. By this criterion, American foreign policy managers failed. During a period of more than four years they were unable to guide either American or Japanese policy in a direction that would avoid war." [p. 179] Utley cannot bring himself to consider the far more plausible hypothesis that wars happen because top national leaders want them to happen.

241. Fleming, p. 34.

242. *Ibid.*, p. 26.

243. *Ibid.*, p. 32.

244. *Ibid.*, pp. 35-6.

245. *Ibid.*, p. 1.

246. *Ibid.*, p. 82.

247. *Ibid.*, p. 238.

248. Martin Glaberman, *Wartime Strikes*, Bewick Editions, Detroit, MI, 1980, pp. 2-3.

249. Brecher, p. 238.

250. Fleming, p. 241.

251. *Business Week*, pp. 83-84, cited in Brecher, p. 238.

252. Fleming, p. 294.

253. Art Preis, *Labor's Giant Step*, Pioneer Publishers, New York, 1964, p. 236, quoted in *Wartime Strikes* by Martin Glaberman p. 119.

254. *Ibid.*, p. 272.

255. *Ibid.*, p. 272.

256. *Ibid.*, p. 428.

257. *Ibid.*, p. 429.

258. *Ibid.*, p. 430.

259. *Boston Globe*, August 26, 2001.

260. Fleming, p. 268.

261. *Ibid.*, p. 181.

262. *Ibid.*, p. 175.

263. *Ibid.*, pp. 174-6.

264. *Ibid.*, p. 270.

265. *Ibid.*, p. 465.

266. *Ibid.*, pp. 423-4, 434.

267. *Ibid.*, pp. 373-4.

268. *Ibid.*, pp. 466-7.

269. *Ibid.*, p. 267.

270. *Ibid.*, p. 267.

271. *Ibid.*, p. 267, citing Henry L. Feingold, *The Politics of rescue: The Roosevelt Administration and the Holocaust*, New Brunswick, N.J., 1970, p. 197.

272. Higham, pp. 23-40.

273. *Ibid*, pp. 41-50.

274. Kevin Phillips, *Wealth and Democracy*, Broadway Books, New York, 2002, p. 72 (based on Ferdinand Lundberg, *America's Sixty Families 1937*).

275. Ivy Lee was a master of public relations who had earlier counseled John D. Rockefeller Sr. to develop a reputation as a philanthropist when the nation was outraged at the way the tycoon broke a coal strike in Colorado by massacring coal miners and their wives and children in Ludlow.

276. Higham, pp. 53-82.

277. *Ibid*, pp. 175-95.

278. George Seldes, *Facts and Fascism*, 1943, p. 262, [http://www.cybertap.com/gem/pages/Elkhorn/Elkhorn_002.htm]

279. The notion that business interests need their home governments to have empires (as opposed to needing anti-working class regimes regardless of which flag flies over them), and that this explains foreign policy of nations, does not accord with reality. Even the British Empire before World War I, the classic example supposedly of "capital following the flag," does not bear out the theory. "[I]mperial possessions were not the main destination of British investment taken as a whole: for the period between 1865 and 1924, only around a quarter of investment went to the Empire, compared with 30 percent for the British economy itself and 45 per cent for foreign economies." [Niall Ferguson, *The Pity of War*, p. 37, citing Davis and Huttenback, *Mammon and the Pursuit of Empire: The Political Economy of British Imperialism, 1860-1912*, Cambridge, 1986] A slight variant of the "capital following the flag" theory was advanced by the United States government under the phrase, "Open Door Policy." But the history of this phrase indicates that it was never taken seriously by U.S. leaders as a motive for waging war. The historian Charles Beard writes of the "Open Door": "This old phrase used by Republicans to justify the intervention of the Government of the United States in Oriental affairs on behalf of economic interests was never more than a kind of shibboleth. Various powers, including Japan, had agreed to observe or respect it, but none of them, not even the United States, had undertaken to guarantee it by political and military action. That profound student of American policy in the Far East, Tyler Dennett, writing in 1922, said of it (as of 1899): 'The United States merely demanded an open door for trade in that part of China in which American merchants were already interested, *viz.*, the area westward from Kwangtung on the South to Manchuria on the North...And as for those parts of the traditional Chinese Empire in the extreme South where France had already carved

out an empire, or along the Amur where Russia had begun the partition of China in 1860, the United States never murmured a protest...It seems clear that the United States would not have taken up arms either to enforce assent to the open door policy, or to prevent the partition of the Empire.' " When Japan invaded China's Manchurian territory and created the puppet state of Manchukuo in 1931, United States leaders were not yet seeking an excuse for waging war, which explains why President Herbert Hoover, quite candidly, informed his Cabinet that "the actions of Japan in Manchuria 'do not imperil the freedom of the American people, the economic or moral future of our people.'" [Charles A. Beard, *President Roosevelt and the Coming Of The War 1941: A Study In Appearances and Realities*, Yale University Press, New Haven, 1948, p.238-9, and citing *Americans in Eastern Asia*, pp. 648 f.] The reason Hoover could make this statement is that American capitalists were fully able to do business as easily following the Japanese Imperial flag as the American flag. As late as January 1941 the American oil company, Associated Oil Company, which later became the Tidewater Associated Company, was a partner in business with the Japanese Mitsubishi Oil Company. Tidewater's president, William F. Humphrey, planned a joint venture with Mitsubishi in Japanese-occupied China. The project was prevented, not by the fact of Japanese expansion, but by U.S. government objections. "Humphrey attempted to improve sentiment toward Japan by indicating to these government officials and businessmen that his relationship with Mitsubishi had been 'more pleasant than any other association with accounts in any other country in the world...'" [*Senator Harley M. Kilgore and Japan's World War II Business Practices*, by Robert F. Maddox, Volume 55, pp. 127-142]

280. Higham, pp. 33-6.

281. *Ibid.*, pp. 80-1.

282. Some typical business affiliations of CFR directors at this time include: Paul D. Cravath, a director of the Equitable Trust Co.; Russell C. Leffingwell, a partner of J.P. Morgan & Co.; George O. May, a partner of Coopers & Lybrand, a predecessor firm to PricewaterhouseCoopers; Owen D. Young, Chairman of the Board of General Electric Corp.; Leon Fraser, President of The First National Bank of the City of New York (as of 1945).

283. One might question whether the actions of the Rockefeller Foundation necessarily reflected the views of John D. Rockefeller II, but in fact at this time the senior Rockefeller exerted personal control over the foundation. G. William Domhoff, in *State Autonomy or Class Dominance*, writes, "The most important and tightly controlled organizations in the Rockefeller network were the three major foundations created by the family: the Rockefeller Foundation, the General Education Board, and the Laura Spelman Rockefeller Memorial," and refers to the Rockefeller Foundation being "under the watchful eyes of close Rockefeller advisors like Raymond B. Fosdick, Arthur Woods, Clarence J. Hicks, Beardsley Ruml, and Walter Teagle" (the last of whom, as we have seen, worked to promote a positive image of Nazis in the United States [pp. 120-22]).

284. G. William Domhoff, *The Power Elite and the State: How Policy is Made in America*, Aldine de Gruyter, New York, 1990, pp. 107-144.

285. The pro-fascist leanings of the Rockefeller family were not limited to its senior member. John D. Rockefeller II's son, Nelson Rockefeller, a CFR member, was appointed by FDR in 1940 to head the Office of Inter-American Affairs and be Assistant Secretary of State for American Republic Affairs; in reality he was in charge of U.S. intelligence operations in Latin America where his family had tremendous business interests. Rockefeller's economic preoccupation in Latin America was keeping the British, not the Germans, out. According to John Loftus and Mark Aarons, when Rockefeller discussed taking on his new government responsibilities with FDR aide Harry Hopkins, he "proposed that while Hitler and Churchill fought each other to death, the United States should be ready to pick up the pieces by seizing the opportunity to increase the economic influence of American businessmen...All through the war, at least while Rockefeller was in charge, everything the Germans wanted in South America they got, from refueling stations to espionage bases. The British, on the other hand, had to pay in cash. Behind Rockefeller's rhetoric of taking measures in Latin America for the national defense stood a naked grab for profits. Under the cloak of his official position, Rockefeller and his cronies would take over Britain's most valuable Latin American properties. If the British resisted, he would effectively block raw materials and food supplies desperately needed for Britain's fight against Hitler." [*The Secret War Against the Jews*, pp. 164-5]

286. Higham, p. 43.

287. Loftus and Aarons, p. 89.

288. Domhoff, p. 118.

289. webpage: http://www.cfr.org/about/pdf/ar_2002/090-92.pdf

290. Diana Richards *et.al.*, *Good Times, Bad Times and the Diversionary Use of Force: A Tale of Some Not So Free Agents*, Journal of Conflict Resolution, 37, 1993 p. 505-535. The Wright citation is Wright, Q., 1965, *A Study of War*, Chicago: University of Chicago Press.

291. Lebow, R.N., *Between Peace and War*, 1981, Baltimore: John's Hopkins University Press.

292. Patrick James *et al*, *The Influence of Domestic and International Politics on the President's Use of Force*, Journal of Conflict Resolution, 35: 1991 pp. 307-28.

293. Christopher Gelpi, *Democratic Diversions: Governmental Structure and the Externalization of Domestic Conflict*, Journal of Conflict Resolution, 41 (2) 1997 pp. 255-282.

III ALLIED WAR OBJECTIVES IN EUROPE AND ASIA

IN THE STANDARD STORY THE TOP PRIORITY OBJECTIVE of the Allied leaders during the war in Europe and Asia was to defeat the Fascist military forces, thereby freeing other nations from brutal oppression and enabling them to create democratic societies. In the competition theory of the war that I have criticized above, the Allied leaders still had the primary goal of defeating the Fascists, but their reason had nothing to do with either helping or controlling ordinary working people whom, according to the competition theory, the elites considered to be only passive bystanders in a war that was a struggle between the world's elites. According to this theory, the war would have happened whether or not the working class actions described in this book had taken place, and whatever actions the wartime leaders took against working people during the war were quite incidental to the motives driving the war. In contrast, the social control theory advocated here says that Allied leaders were primarily concerned with preventing working people at home and abroad from making revolutions and creating a more equal and democratic world; fighting the Fascists was strictly subordinate to that goal, and served as the pretext for actions that in fact had nothing to do with defeating Fascism. To investigate Allied war aims we will look closely at events during the war in Italy, Greece, France, Yugoslavia, China and the Philippines, where there were armed, working class anti-Fascist Resistance movements. We will see that Allied leaders actually attacked the working class anti-Fascist forces in these countries, demonstrating that their top priority was not defeating the Fascists, but preventing the working class from seizing power. The Allied fight against the Fascists was a secondary objective, pursued to protect and expand their elite control of workers and resources around the world, but never pursued at the expense of allowing workers themselves to take power. World War Two continued the pattern set by the Allies' hostility to Spanish workers fighting the fascistic General Franco in 1936-7.

ALLIES ATTACK ANTI-FASCISTS IN ITALY

The small anti-Fascist groups that opposed the Fascist dictatorship of Benito Mussolini in Italy before 1943 grew stronger rapidly in 1943 and afterwards. In March 1943 there were Communist-led workers strikes in northern Italy.[1] "During the late winter of 1944 well over a half million and perhaps closer to a million workers participated in strikes in the north, some lasting as long as eight days in Turin, despite the presence of German and Fascist guns."[2] In March 1945 there were 182,000 resistance fighters according to U.S. intelligence estimates, with 500,000 potential recruits. The resistance was strongest in the north, but even in the southern city of Naples "a spontaneous mass uprising liberated" the city from the Fascists three days before Allied troops entered on October 1, 1943. The Resistants were nearly all from the industrial working class and the peasantry, led by a number of political parties of which the Communist Party was the largest and, in fact, most conservative. An umbrella Resistance organization called the Committee of National Liberation for Northern Italy (CLNAI) formed in 1944 united around their desire for a radical transformation in society. American intelligence reports at the end of 1943 called the situation in the north "revolutionary."[3]

Realizing that the Allies were going to win the war, the Italian Fascist Grand Council, together with monarchists (the King, Victor Emmanuel had supported the Fascists from the beginning) and other military officers, all led by Marshal Pietro Badoglio (the leader of the Italian invasion of Ethiopia when Mussolini ruled), deposed and arrested Mussolini on July 25, 1943. Immediately these Fascists appealed to Churchill and Roosevelt for help in preventing an imminent working class revolution. Churchill told Roosevelt in August 1943 that, "There is nothing between the King and the patriots who have rallied around him...and rampant Bolshevism." to which Roosevelt replied that what was needed in Italy was "first, disarmament [of the Resistance], and, second, assurance against chaos."[4] General Eisenhower, in July 1943, publicly proclaimed that in Allied-occupied Italy: "No political activity whatsoever shall be countenanced during the period of military government" and "banned all publications or public meetings without the consent of the Allied Military Government of the Occupied Territories."[5] Badoglio hoped that the Allies would land north of Rome and rescue him from the anti-Fascist movement in the north. To his dismay, the Allies invaded Italy from the south on September 3, leading Badoglio and his followers to "desert" Rome "for the southeast tip of Italy, leaving most of Italy to the Nazis."[6]

Hungry and often armed men began joining the Communist Party in huge numbers. "Long lines formed in the streets to join the party." Membership quadrupled between the end of 1943 and July 1944. But On April 1, 1944 the leader of the Italian Communist Party, Palmiro Togliatti, who had just returned from two decades in the USSR and who was strictly obedient to Stalin, declared that his party would cooperate with Badoglio and that after the war it would seek power only by legal parliamentary means. Many Resistance members in the north found Togliatti's declaration "intolerable."[7] Other parties in the Resistance that were more radical than the Communist Party grew at this time. The Action party and the Socialists were not controlled by Stalin, and they organized one quarter of the Resistance fighters in the north and most of the city workers around demands for "prompt elimination of the monarchy, immediate land and economic reforms of the most far-reaching nature, a socialist republic rather than a parliamentary fiasco of the nineteenth-century variety, workers' control, and a new society based on the structure of the Committee of National Liberation at the grass-roots level."[8]

On June 4, 1944 the Allied forces entered Rome and were greeted by "armed Italians, often in red shirts, waving revolutionary banners" who frequently had "set up their own local administrations." The Partisans, as these revolutionary Italians were known, were surprised at what happened next. "The Allied armies pushed some Partisans aside, and even threatened them with the firing squad; they arrested many and threw them into prisons." The Partisans were ordered to surrender their arms or be imprisoned. Some gave up their weapons, but many did not,[9] especially because the Allied Military Government kept many ex-Fascists and their collaborators in office, including Fascist police and *carabinieri* who were used against the people in numerous protests and riots.[10] By early 1944 the Allied Military Government was relying on 180,000 former Fascist soldiers and *carabinieri* to suppress the "liberated" Italians.

In the north, the Allies' "war against Fascism" turned into a barely disguised alliance with Fascism. In the summer of 1944 the Allies controlled Rome and the south of Italy, and the Resistance alone confronted the Germans in northern Italy, tying down as many as 14 Axis divisions at one time. On November 13, 1944, the supreme Allied commander in Italy, General Alexander, whose forces were south of the Resistance forces that confronted the Nazis, made a radio broadcast appealing to the Resistance forces to cease their activities, and he announced that the Allies could not help them during the winter. "Alexander was fully aware that his statement would act as a virtual invitation to a Nazi and Fascist offensive, which predictably occurred and battered the poorly equipped partisans, causing death, defections, and demoralization."[11]

By May of 1945 German military units in northern Italy, on the initiative of local commanders, began surrendering because it was clear they had lost the war. Anglo-American political authorities, however, feared that, "there is a real danger of extreme Communist elements taking control" and because of this fear Allen Dulles, then head of the U.S. Office of Strategic Services (later the CIA) tried to *prevent* the Nazis from surrendering to the Italian resistance. Dulles "began secret negotiations with the Nazi commander in northern Italy" as a result of which "the Germans agreed to remain in their existing positions and surrender their arms only to those forces the Anglo-Americans designated...Until the Anglo-American armies arrived, the Nazis were to...provide for 'the general maintenance of law and order.' In effect, the Allies attempted to rely on the Nazis to forestall, as best they could, the Resistance's consolidation of total power." In this grotesque act, the Allied leaders demonstrated that when it came to Fascist power versus working class power, they had no hesitation in choosing the former. Ordinary German soldiers, on the other hand, proved to be more supportive of democracy than Allied leaders: they "refused to risk their lives to keep radicals out of power, and their units began to disintegrate."[12]

ALLIES ATTACK ANTI-FASCISTS IN GREECE

Before the war, Greece was ruled by the dictator, Ioannis Metaxas, under the reign of King George II. These rulers were "pro-Nazi in sympathy"[13] prior to Mussolini's invasion of Greece October 28, 1940. After the invasion the king and his "royal government" fled to England and backed "British power in the Mediterranean" in exchange for British aid in returning to Greece and British recognition of Greek border claims. Metaxas and the army stayed and officially resisted the Fascists, although "without the support of many leading generals, who preferred to surrender."[14] Hitler followed Mussolini into Greece April 6, 1941.

A popular resistance rapidly developed especially in the mountainous north. A National Liberation Front called EAM was the largest of several resistance organizations and the only one to have an army (ELAS) in all regions of Greece. The EAM included the Communist Party as well as virtually the entire spectrum of opposition to the Fascists; it was very decentralized and acted largely by local initiatives, and as a result the Communist Party, itself split over strategy questions, had only modest influence on the organization. By the time the British occupied Athens (Oct 14, 1944) the EAM's labor organization "controlled the entire [Greek] working class and helped lead strikes in the occupied territories throughout the war."[15] Despite Nazi control of the major cities, the EAM by 1943 "administered from two thirds to four fifths of Greece and claimed one and a half million members out of a total population only five times that figure—a claim, even if exaggerated, that probably was not far from the unknown truth."[16]

Nine tenths of the 20,000 to 70,000 members of EAM's army (ELAS) were peasants and workers. The EAM "administered most of the villages," even collecting taxes and supplying schools and relief. While not anti-capitalist (the Communist Party was the most conservative element inside EAM in this respect), the EAM nonetheless "introduced a degree of democracy hitherto unknown in Greek society" and won enormous popularity, in particular "the fervent devotion of the youth and women."[17] It's army engaged in sabotage and some attacks on the Fascists. All of the resistance organizations opposed the monarch and wanted a republican form of government. Great Britain, however, wanted to maintain the monarchy and the undemocratic pre-war government. For that reason, Great Britain provided arms to only one small conservative resistance organization, the EDES, led by Colonel Napoleon Zervas, which was "busy with various nationalist causes, such as driving the Cham minority out of Greece, as well as resistance to the invader."[18]

When Italy surrendered in September 1943, Italian soldiers in Greece just handed over their weapons to the Greek Resistance, indicating their true leanings. As a result, there were now "35,000 to 40,000 well-armed ELAS Resistants."[19] Confronted with this situation, British leaders viewed a sudden German *withdrawal* from Greece as the real danger, because it would mean that the Greek people would become the rulers of Greece instead of elites fronting for the British. "In the event of sudden German withdrawal...London ordered a permanent force of 5,000 men with armor and high firepower and mobility to be held in readiness to enter and hold Athens immediately."[20]

On March 3, 1944 the "EAM announced the formation of a 'Provisional Governmental Committee' to run the part of Greece under their control." The British-sponsored Greek government in exile was stationed in Egypt, with a Greek army and navy. On March 31, fourteen Greek military officers, representing a large majority of the officers, asked for "the inclusion of the EAM in a new government," for which they were arrested. Then from "April 3 to 5 a large part of the Greek army in Egypt, including five ships of the navy, rioted and struck for a republican government and collaboration with [EAM's] Governmental Committee in Greece...The Greek soldiers quickly took up arms and mounted defenses around their camps, and a number of ships refused to obey British orders." The British ambassador, Reginald Leeper, wired, "What is happening here among the Greeks is nothing less than a revolution." The British attacked the soldiers and "threw about 20,000 Greeks into prisoner-of-war cages." Roosevelt publicly told Churchill, "I join in the hope that your line of action toward the problem may succeed in bringing back the Greeks into the camp of the Allies."[21]

On September 14, 1944 Hitler ordered German troops to leave Greece, knowing it was the last thing the British wanted. The British Supreme Allied Commander for the Mediterranean met with the ELAS commander who agreed to place his forces under the orders of British General Ronald M. Scobie representing the Allied high command. Scobie informed the ELAS commander that ELAS was "forbidden... to take the law into their own hands" and that ELAS "Security battalions will be treated as enemy organizations...or instruments of the enemy."[22]

At the beginning of October, German troops began leaving Greece and British troops parachuted in, to discover "50,000 to 75,000 well-armed ELAS troops in charge and the EAM administering Greece...with efficiency and order and the support of the majority of the population."[23] "The last German solider left Greece on November 10,"[24] but the British continued their military buildup to the end of November "not to fight the Nazis but to settle Greek political problems." ELAS was cooperating with the British, and Churchill even acknowledged that he was "confident the Russians seem really to be keeping their hands off this country," but the problem, as Reginald Leeper, British Ambassador to the exile Greek government, put it was that he had "doubts as to whether the national leaders of the organizations are really able any longer to control their men."[25] Ordinary people in Greece felt that now that they controlled their own country, why give it to the British? On December 2 the Greek exile government prime minister, Papandreau, dissolved the ELAS. The EAM announced a general strike for the 4th and also "asked for and was granted permission to hold a protest demonstration early the following Sunday morning in Athens."[26] Unarmed demonstrators marched to Constitution Square in the center of Athens and were fired upon by police with British troops standing nearby. Twenty-four people were killed and 150 wounded including women and children. "By the evening of the 4th" ELAS forces were engaged in "savage battles throughout Greece" against British forces and were getting the "upper hand," especially in Athens.[27] On December 5, Churchill sent General Scobie these instructions:

> Do not hesitate to fire at any armed male in Athens who assails the British authority... It would be well of course if your commands were reinforced by the authority of some Greek Government...*Do not however hesitate to act as if you were in a conquered city where a local rebellion is in progress.*[28]

The British rushed in 16,000 more troops which "barely held on to the center of Athens" and "were quickly isolated in the rest of Greece, sniped at in Piraeus" and found themselves "on December 11, with food nearly exhausted and the ELAS making advances everywhere." Field Marshall Alexander predicted the possibility of "a first class disaster."[29]

On December 13, Roosevelt wired Churchill that "I regard my role in this matter as that of a loyal friend and ally whose one desire is to be of any help possible in the circumstances."[30]

The British were saved by the Communist Party using its influence to get ELAS to back down even though they held military supremacy. An "important Communist member of EAM asked Scobie for his armistice terms" on December 12 and was told they were "disarmament in Athens and Piraeus."[31] "Four days later, while they still held military supremacy, the ELAS offered to withdraw their forces from the two cities as part of a general disarmament,...the British being saved from total defeat."[32] Stalin did his part to help the British prevail by not uttering a single word of criticism of the British strangling of popular democracy in Greece. In fact, Churchill wrote on December 11, "I am increasingly impressed, up to date, with the loyalty with which, under much temptation and very likely pressure, Stalin has kept off Greece in accordance with our agreement."[33]

In the streets of Athens and throughout Greece, the true conflict in World War II was revealed to be not the Allies versus the Fascists, or even the "Democracies" versus Stalin, but elite rule versus democracy.

ALLIES ATTACK ANTI-FASCISTS IN FRANCE

The relationship of the Allied leaders to the French anti-Fascist Resistance was hostile. But the hostility did not manifest itself in direct military attacks, as in other countries, but rather indirectly as support for pro-Nazis and lack of support for the Resistance. A key factor in making a direct attack on the Resistance by the Allies unnecessary was the fact that the most important leadership of the Resistance, the French Communist Party, was the only party with substantial working class support, and it insisted on obedience to Allied leaders, even when that meant repudiating the anti-capitalist ideas which had attracted most of its members to join the Party in the first place.

When the Germans invaded France in May 1940, the French government and military quickly capitulated, to the disgust of many French citizens. The Germans allowed a French collaborationist government to form in the south of France in Vichy, under the leadership of Marshal Henri Petain. The Vichy government represented the anti-working class elements of French society who were most anti-British, anti-Soviet Union, and anti-Semitic, and they enforced Nazi regulations that subjected Frenchmen to forced labor and subjected Jews to genocidal anti-Semitic policies. The Vichy government promoted pro-Nazis in the French police departments and imposed death sentences as directed by the Nazis. Though officially neutral in the war, the Vichy government continued to administer French colonies in southeast Asia as collaborators with the Japanese invaders. Also, Vichy continued to administer French territories and colonies in Africa where many French Europeans lived as colonists.

Frenchmen opposed to Vichy who lived in France itself joined the Resistance, also known as the French Forces of the Interior (FFI) composed of numerous groups, the largest of which was the Communist Party's *Francs-Tireurs et Partisans* (FTP). By June 1944 Allied intelligence estimated that there were 200,000 FFI fighters in France.[34] Shortly before the D-Day invasion the Resistance fighters "tied down as many as eight German divisions in action."[35] Those outside of France joined the Free French forces and the army in Africa.

General Charles DeGaulle, in exile in London, became the accepted leader of the external forces. The interior forces consisted mainly of people in or close to the Communist Party, and a smaller number known as the *maquis* who were non-political unarmed people who refused to cooperate with the Fascists, as well as followers of other smaller political parties. The people who supported DeGaulle were mainly patriotic military officers, politicians from the vanquished Third Republic, and members of the upper occupational and social classes and they were generally anti-Communist as was DeGaulle most emphatically. While many people in the upper classes feared that the Communist Party might lead a working class revolution or create a Bolshevik style dictatorship unfriendly to the French upper classes, the Party actually was, as Stalin insisted, only against the Fascists and strictly opposed to any revolutionary activity against capitalism. This was made quite evident later in the war when the leader of the party, Maurice Thorez, returned to France from exile in Moscow at the end of November 1944, and banned strikes, demanded more labor from the workers, and endorsed the dissolution of the Resistance itself on the grounds that the Allied invasion made it unnecessary.[36]

But despite the non-revolutionary nature of the Communist Party leadership, the Allies worried about a Resistance movement of working people, armed, following a party calling itself "Communist," and so decentralized that nobody could be relied upon to completely control them from above. The British supported DeGaulle as the best way to ensure that the Communist Resistance would be prevented from taking power. FDR and his advisors, especially Secretary of State Hull, however, feared that the British were using DeGaulle to create an Anglo-French economic bloc that would compete with American interests after the war, and so the Americans backed the Vichy government itself for a number of years hoping to make it one that could rule France after the war.

The first manifestation of a pro-Vichy U.S. policy occurred in February 1941 when the United States concluded the Murphy-Weygand agreement with Vichy "that gave America a distinctive position in the French North African economy for the first time."[37] The agreement was so blatant that the British protested this aid to a tacit ally of Germany. The Vichy Governor of North Africa was Admiral Francois Darlan who fully cooperated with the Nazis. The U.S. made a deal with Darlan in November 1942: he would not attack U.S. troops in North Africa, and the U.S. would respect "his civil authority and officials in North Africa," and even "outfit his military forces."[38] The "Darlan deal" was denounced by many Americans who were disgusted to see their government giving aid to pro-Nazis. Realizing the danger if ordinary Americans suspected that their leaders had any goals that pro-Nazis shared, Secretary of the Treasury Morgenthau, in a meeting with Secretary of War Stimson and Archibald MacLeish from the Office of War Information, denounced the deal angrily stating, "There is a considerable group of rich people in this country who would make peace with Hitler tomorrow...The only people who want to fight are the working men and women, and if they once get the idea that we are going to favor these Fascists...they're going to say what's the use of fighting just to put that kind of people back into power?"[39] Morgenthau "predicted sit-down strikes and production slowdowns would soon be sweeping the country."[40] Washington defended the deal by arguing that without it they would have had to fight French as well as German forces in North Africa, but in private military authorities knew it was unlikely that French soldiers would actually fight for the Nazis if so ordered. When Darlan was assassinated on December 23, "Eisenhower, acting on instructions from Roosevelt, insisted" that Vichy replace him with the French General Henri Giraud, which they did. The Giraud administration was "neo-Fascist in character" with support from local bankers and industrialists, and it kept the anti-Semitic laws on the books. Then the Vichy government announced that Marcel Peyrouton—the former Vichy Minister of the Interior who had been in charge of enforcing the anti-Semitic laws and making political arrests for the Nazis—would be the Governor of Algeria, and the State Department, Eisenhower and FDR all approved the appointment, on the grounds that, as Eisenhower wrote, "Abrupt, sweeping or radical changes, bringing into office little known or unqualified administrators, could create serious difficulties for us."[41]

By January 1943 DeGaulle's popularity among the French people as a symbol of the fight against the German occupation was firmly established; "all of the major underground organizations in France endorsed" his French National Committee (although only a minority of them were Gaullist in ideology.) In contrast, the contempt that Frenchmen felt for the Vichy regime was so strong that U.S. leaders gave up on the tactic of relying on the Vichy government to contain the working class. Yet "even as late as February 1944, [FDR's Chief of Staff Admiral] Leahy advocated leaving [Vichy's Marshall] Petain as head of France after D-Day."[42] In May 1943 Secretary of State Hull voiced the problem he had with supporting DeGaulle: "The issue at stake is not only the success of our future military operations, but the very future of France itself. DeGaulle has permitted to come under his umbrella all the most radical elements in France."[43]

One incident that made DeGaulle look more worthy of U.S. support occurred during the Corsican uprising of September 1943, when French Communist Resistance fighters and French soldiers from Algeria drove the Germans out and liberated the "first occupied territory." "On October 8, soon after the shooting had stopped, DeGaulle [went to the island and] pushed the Communists aside, [leaving] his own administration behind to run affairs entirely by themselves."[44] As the historian Kolko puts it, "By June 1944 the Americans and English needed someone who could repeat the Corsican precedent in France itself, for the FFI [Resistance] was in many areas on the scene before Anglo-American troops could arrive. Many of the FFI were Communists..."[45]

As D-Day in June of 1944 approached, the Allies' concern with the Resistance in France focused on two problems—whether to give them any arms, and how to keep them from assuming power in the projected Allied occupational government. The U.S. leaders favored rearming the "French army in North Africa when it was seemingly under the control of [the Vichy neo-Fascist General] Giraud, but when DeGaulle took over the Americans decided to delay [arms] shipments," supposedly because he might use them to consolidate his power in France. The arms that the British dropped to the Resistance in France were of a "quantity and quality...that made it impossible for the Resistance to plan for more than sabotage" and never did Allied leaders supply the Resistance in urban areas with sufficient arms that would have enabled them to take over cities on their own before a conventional conquest by Allied forces. Also, the Allies gave the non-political *maquis*, who had only 50,000 fighters, more arms than the 200,000 political, largely Communist, Resistance fighters; and "they never knowingly sent arms to urban and Communist-controlled groups."[46]

In the summer of 1944 DeGaulle succeeded in obtaining partial recognition from the United States, and he managed to get all of the Resistance organizations to formally accept his leadership. The Resistance had been fueled in large measure by the Communist Party's call for a national insurrection to take place at some unspecified time. Everyone felt that with the Allied troops closing in on Paris, that time was fast approaching, and Frenchmen passionately wanted to free themselves from the Nazi yoke to reclaim their self-respect after the disgrace of having seen their leaders capitulate so quickly to the Nazi invaders. The Resistance leaders inside France called for Resistants to "strike where the enemy was weak and to take over civil authority on a provisional basis;" and the leaders appealed continually to DeGaulle for Allied arms to enable them to carry out the large scale insurrection. The units of the Resistance that were at this time fighting German troops outside of Paris were doing it entirely with weapons they captured from the Germans. DeGaulle told Resistance leaders that he would only get them arms if they swore an oath of obedience to him that would convince the Allies that the Resistance would do exactly as they commanded. The arms were never forthcoming. After mid-July, Resistance leaders realized that DeGaulle was "recruit[ing] his own forces, especially among the police and former pro-Vichy officers in Paris and elsewhere." DeGaulle then told Resistance leaders that "a national insurrection was 'impossible.'" At the same time, Maurice Thorez, the leader of the Communist Party which had recruited hundreds of thousands of members with an appeal for a national uprising, broadcast from Moscow that Resistants should only "aid the Anglo-American advance rather than preempt the need for it" with any uprising.[47]

On July 14, Bastille Day, "over 100,000 Parisians spontaneously demonstrated in the face of German guns, and on August 10 the railroad workers went on strike."[48] On August 15 the Paris police went on strike after the Nazis moved to disarm them, and their weapons fell into the hands of the Resistance. "On August 17 and 18 the subway, post office, and other workers went on strike," and the Resistance leaders issued "detailed instructions on street fighting and tank destruction as well as objectives to attack in the event of an insurrection," and on the morning of the 19th they issued a "call for a general uprising." Fighting broke out and more guns fell into the hands of the Resistance. The Germans were "resigned to losing" Paris and were preparing to withdraw to the north and east. The German general in Paris, Dietrich von Choltitz, possibly with a view to securing good treatment from the Allies after the German defeat, agreed "to give the city to the Allied military but not to the Resistance." Eisenhower was at this time with American forces less than twenty-five miles away, with the intent of by-passing Paris and encircling it rather than engaging in costly street fighting and then having to figure out how to supply the city with food and fuel, the supplies of which had been so disrupted by war that famine was imminent. But the possibility of the Resistance taking the city themselves persuaded him to change plans, and he sent an American and a French division to Paris where, on August 25, they accepted General Von Choltitz's surrender and handed the military governorship to DeGaulle's leading military aide, General Pierre Koenig.[49]

In the southwest of France the Resistance was "moving into the vacuum the Germans left in their swift retreat" and "American troops landing in the south of France in August found the Resistance, including a preponderance of Communists, firmly in control of the civil administration." The main concern of Allied leaders was that 200,000 Resistants remained armed, and that there were rumors that they were "planning a revolution in the southwest." Already, the Resistance had shot "at least 11,000" collaborators, and they were showing signs of acting independently of central moderating authority. Eisenhower decided that the best way to control the Resistants and prevent them from threatening the capitalist social order in France would be to enroll them into DeGaulle's regular army with orders to sit tight. The Allied commander gave DeGaulle enough military equipment "to enroll 137,000 former FFI members [Resistants] into...[his regular] army," where they were "given a high proportion of outmoded equipment and assigned to the most menial tasks, many in isolated regions far from the fronts, bases which many bitterly dubbed 'concentration camps.'" To doubly ensure the Resistance would be contained, "Eisenhower also transferred one French division to DeGaulle at the end of August expressly for the purpose of maintaining internal order...." By the end of 1944 the Resistance had been eliminated as a threat to Allied power.[50]

Had the goal of Allied leaders been to defeat the Fascists as quickly as possible they would have armed the Resistance and supported the national insurrection. Instead they backed the collaborationist Vichy government and its neo-Fascist colonial rulers in Africa, they deprived the Resistance of arms and corralled them in an army that gave them menial tasks far away from the front, and they actually diverted an entire division just to control them. The Allies' relation to the Resistance was driven by their actual top priority goal, which was to make sure that working people did not have arms in their own independent organization and seize real democratic control over their own lives.

ALLIES ATTACK ANTI-FASCISTS IN YUGOSLAVIA

Yugoslavia's population consisted of different national-ethnic groups: Serbs, Montenegrins, Macedonians, and Croats. Before the war and the occupation by German and Italian troops, the wealthy and elite class of people were represented by a king—King Peter—with an authoritarian government whose strong man was Minister of War General Draza Mihailovic. When the Germans and Italians invaded, King Peter fled to London, leaving Mihailovic in Yugoslavia.[51] Mihailovic, whose forces were known as Chetniks ("a small group of officers, noncommissioned officers, and men of the Yugoslav royal army, almost exclusively Serbs, who refused to surrender at their post near the town of Doboj in northern Bosnia at the time of the collapse of the Yugoslav army in mid-April 1941"[52]), "fought little, and then only against the Germans in Serbia and never the Italian occupation army." By early 1943 the Chetniks were discredited as "resistance" fighters because they were on friendly terms with the Italian forces and were not only "supplying information on the Partisans [Communist resistance fighters led by Josip Broz Tito] to the Germans" but also "were preoccupied with fighting and containing Tito's growing power."[53] Whereas Mihailovic appealed to upper class Serbs with Serbian nationalism, Tito called for a Pan-Slav nationalism with federal principles and he emphasized the goal of an egalitarian classless society.[54] Tito was a Communist unwilling to follow Stalin's directives and his movement was extremely popular and a source of alarm to all of the Allied leaders, including Stalin. "By October 1943 [the Partisans] had tied down twenty-five German and eight Bulgarian divisions in the Balkans" and had arms acquired from the Italian surrender in September and 200,000 full-time combatants.[55] The Partisans did this without help from Stalin who refused to send them military aid or even to read their proclamations over Moscow radio, prompting Tito to send a telegram to Stalin that began, "If you cannot send us assistance, then at least do not hamper us."[56]

The British and the American leaders used different tactics to influence events in Yugoslavia. The British tried to play the King and Tito against each other, feeling that Tito could be turned into a pro-British and anti-working class ruler. The basis for their optimism on this score was Churchill's assessment of Tito's movement, which he delivered to the House of Commons February 1944: "The Communist element had the honor of being the beginners, but as the movement increased in strength and numbers, a modifying concept

and unifying process has taken place and national conceptions have super-
vened."[57] The British also knew that Stalin was an anti-working class force and
for this reason, in October 1943, they began encouraging the Soviet Union to
send a mission to both Tito and Mihailovic to try to moderate Tito's
pro-working class position.[58] Stalin gave it his best, ordering Tito to tone down
his anti-capitalist message and just talk about anti-Fascist unity. "Stalin ad-
vised Tito to take back King Peter. 'The blood rushed to my head,' Tito recalled." Stalin also "insisted that the Yugoslavs not frighten the British into
thinking that they planned a Communist revolution, not merely in the sense
of hiding the intention, but in prohibiting it."[59]

The U.S. feared that Tito was too much a working class force that was
not submissive to Stalin, and so they supported Mihailovic but not Tito, maintaining a mission with the King's General even until November 1944 "by
which time virtually all admitted his full collaboration with the Axis." The
U.S. knew exactly what it was doing. The State Department and OSS (predecessor of the CIA) "ignored the detailed reports of Mihailovic's repression
against the Partisans"[60] and "reported that Tito had the backing of a majority
of the population, including even the Serbs...In July 1944 the State Department insisted on continuing the arms drops to Mihailovic, and attempted to
see if they could find some way to prevent Tito's forces from entering Serbia."[61]
The American military leaders issued orders prohibiting arms being sent to
Tito. A State Department memo to Secretary of State Hull read, "The Department has made it clear that we disapprove of any plan for building up the Tito
forces at the expense of the Serbs." American leaders were so determined to deprive Tito of arms that in August, the Joint Chiefs of Staff, the State Department, and Admiral William Leahy even attempted to track down if rumors of
such arms shipments were true.[62] American arms were meant to be used by
Mihailovic, an Axis collaborationist, against the Partisans who were the only
Yugoslavs fighting the Fascists.

ALLIES ATTACK ANTI-FASCISTS IN CHINA

When Japan invaded China in 1937, the government of China, led by Chiang Kai-shek and the Kuomintang (KMT) party, allowed the Japanese to occupy the coastal provinces but retreated westward without giving Japan the large territory it had expected to secure within one month. By 1944 Japan's grip on China was still so fragile that it was forced to devote one million soldiers to hold its coastal regions and fight a "stabilized" war "periodically entering and sacking" the rice-growing areas of central China.[63] The American military objective in the Far East was to secure land close enough to Japan to stage an attack on that nation. China was the obvious choice because the Japanese hold there was weakest. But, as the historian Kolko writes: "The desire to avoid war on the Asian mainland became the central limiting fact of American political and military strategy in the Far East during the last two years of the war—the reality that caused Americans to fight island by island rather than combat the greatly overextended and vulnerable Japanese troops in China."[64] Instead of hitting the Japanese where they were weakest, the United States attacked heavily defended Japanese positions on one island after another in the Pacific—at enormous cost in American lives—attempting to obtain land from which to stage the final attack. Why? The answer, as we shall see, is that Franklin Roosevelt chose not to fight in China because it would have meant helping Chinese peasants who were fighting to overthrow powerful landowning elites and create a more democratic and equal China.

Roosevelt had the choice of giving all out support to the Chinese Communists, who were mobilizing peasants in a serious fight against the Japanese, or supporting Chiang Kai-shek, who refused to fight the Japanese but who did fight the Communists and who represented the warlord landowning elite in China. Stalin had the same choice. Both leaders chose to support Chiang Kai-shek and not the Communists. Stalin gave Chiang Kai-shek more than $50 million by mid-1940 (and never gave the Communists any military aid) because he wanted a weak China on Russia's border that would not challenge his authority as a "revolutionary" leader.[65] FDR similarly wanted to make sure that armed peasants fighting for more democracy and equality did not take power.

The Chinese KMT government's conscription of soldiers was in fact a money-making racket that killed peasants; it had virtually nothing to do with forming a fighting army. "Press gangs conscripted peasants out of the fields, tied them and transported them away" in a deadly forced march. "The county magistrate would arrest ten men for each conscript needed and permit all but one to buy their freedom—if they could."[66] The commander of American forces in China, General Albert Wedemeyer, described his view of China's conscription army in a memo to Chiang Kai-shek:

> Conscription comes to the Chinese peasant like famine or flood, only more regularly—every year twice—and claims more victims. Famine, flood, and drought compare with conscription like chicken pox with the plague...Hoe and plow rest in the field, the wife runs to the magistrate to cry and beg for her husband, the children starve...Later they are too weak to run away. Those who are caught are cruelly beaten. They will be carried along with broken limbs and with wounds in maimed flesh in which infection turns quickly into blood poisoning and blood poisoning into death. As they march they turn into skeletons; they develop signs of beriberi, their legs swell and their bellies protrude, their arms and thighs get thin... From this point of view the conscripts' bodies have a great value... A Chinese conscript's pay can be pocketed and his rations can be sold. That makes him a valuable member of the Chinese Army and that is the basis of the demand for him. Because of this demand, the journey has no end. Being sick, he has to drag himself along... Dysentery and typhoid are always with them. They carry cholera from place to place... If somebody dies his body is left behind. His name on the list is carried along. As long as his death is not reported he continues to be a source of income, increased by the fact that he has ceased to consume. His rice and his pay become a long-lasting token of memory in the pocket of his commanding officer. His family will have to forget him.[67]

The basic ration of Chinese soldiers was not enough to live on and they rarely even saw the money they were "paid"; as a result they had to survive by looting, thereby becoming objects of hatred among the peasants where they were camped. The American Joint Chiefs of Staff at the end of 1943 estimated that "at most, not more than one-fifth of the Chinese Army is currently capable of sustained defensive operations and then only with effective air support."[68] By the war's end, General Wedemeyer "estimated that only five of the approximately three hundred Chinese divisions were effective military units, and American officers commanded three of those in India."[69]

Chiang Kai-shek made no moves to reform the army, he "refused to engage in offensive operations," and he "usually retreated before Japanese advances."[70] In 1942 General Joseph Stilwell "suspected that Chiang was prepared to reach a detente with the Japanese in order to fight the Communists, and that he preferred a German victory over Russia..."[71] By 1943 Stilwell realized that Chiang had an "undeclared truce with the Japanese" because "every time they advanced the Chinese withdrew and then returned to their former positions when the Japanese voluntarily permitted them to do so."[72] By the beginning of 1944 Chiang had positioned a half million KMT troops, "the best of the generally miserable lot," against the Communists in the northwest, and he told the U.S., "For me the big problem is not Japan but the unification of my country. I am sure that you Americans are going to beat the Japanese some day, with or without the help of the troops I am holding back for use against the Communists in the Northwest. On the other hand, if I let Mao Tse-tung push his propaganda across all of Free China, we run the risk—and so do you Americans—of winning for nothing."[73]

Chiang Kai-shek threatened to surrender to the Japanese as a form of blackmail to extract huge cash transfers from the U.S. treasury. He demanded a "loan" at the end of December 1941, and in February 1942 the U.S. granted the KMT government a loan of $500 million (about $5 billion in today's dollars) without any binding terms and conditions, and it went into the pockets of the KMT ruling clique.[74] In 1943 Chiang demanded a one billion dollar (about $10 billion in today's dollars) gold "loan"[75] to which Treasury Secretary Morgenthau replied, "They are just a bunch of crooks."[76] On September 26, 1944 General Stilwell wrote, "Chiang Kai-shek has no intention of making further efforts to prosecute the war... he believes he can go on milking the United States for money and munitions by using the old gag about quitting if he is not supported...he will only continue his policy and delay, while grabbing for loans...for the purpose of maintaining his...suppression of democratic ideas with the active aid of his gestapo."[77]

To maintain the alliance with Chiang Kai-shek, Roosevelt, "over the objections of the Joint Chiefs of Staff," recalled General Stilwell back from China and "compelled him to keep silent on the realities in China."[78] Patrick J. Hurley, FDR's personal representative in China, told Acting Secretary of State Edward Stettinius at the end of December 1944 that "the policy of the United States in China is (1) To prevent the collapse of the national government, (2) To sustain Chiang Kai-shek as President of the Republic and Generalissimo of the Armies..."[79]

The alternative to an alliance with Chiang Kai-shek was an alliance with those Chinese who were in fact fighting the Japanese—the Communists. According to an American military attache in Chungking reporting in November 1943, "the Communists had a regular army of half a million men, an equal number of guerrillas, and perhaps a million militiamen."[80] Unlike the KMT army, the Communist army "did not loot, but grew its own food and worked with the peasants. Its morale was high, its commitment great."[81] The Communists had genuine support among China's peasants and for this reason American officers feared that if a civil war between the KMT and the Communists broke out "the defection of Chiang's troops to the Communists" was possible.[82] The Chinese Communists differed with Soviet-style Marxists in claiming to represent the bulk of the peasantry in addition to the small industrial working class, whereas the Bolsheviks claimed to represent the industrial working class and only the poorest peasants. But aside from this, the Chinese Communists held the same fundamental Marxist views that led the Bolsheviks in the Soviet Union to be anti-democratic. In practice, they did whatever they felt was necessary to maintain their support among the poorest peasants, and secondarily they tried to keep wealthy peasants and even capitalists in their united front against the Japanese. When they needed an influx of new soldiers they would emphasize a strong land reform policy, only to reverse themselves later. The Party leadership always worried about lower level cadres recruited from the peasantry being too radical, and they tried to impose Party discipline on them; but the peasants often "forced the issue" and the Party would yield to avoid losing their support.[83] The net result was a large and popular movement to fight the Japanese, but a movement with internal conflict between democratic forces from below and anti-democratic forces from the Party.

The Communists not only organized millions of Chinese peasants to fight the Japanese Fascists, but they also organized Japanese soldiers—most of whom were themselves peasants—to fight the Japanese Fascists. The Communists won over large numbers of Japanese prisoners to see the commonality between Chinese and Japanese peasant aspirations, and in fact after early 1944 many Japanese prisoners formed organizations and operated radio stations to urge Japanese soldiers to change their allegiance.[84] Knowledge of this was one of the main reasons that Japan's former Premier and an intimate of Emperor

Hirohito, Prince Konoye, in February 1944, urged the Emperor to surrender, warning him, "What we have to fear is not so much a defeat as a Communist revolution which might take place in the event of a defeat."[85]

American military and civilian officials in China visited the Communists in Yenan and were favorably impressed. The Army mission in Yenan concluded that the Communist area was, in it's own words, "a different country... the most modern place in China" and they described the conditions as (Kolko's words) "far better than those under Chiang's regime."[86] Hurley, FDR's personal representative, even concluded that the Communists were "the only real democrats in China" and Ambassador Gauss "thought it was now likely that they would eventually prevail."[87] The U.S. and the Communists even came to an agreement in which the U.S. would "arm 25,000 [of their] guerrillas and many more militia,"[88] but Chiang Kai-shek vetoed the plan, and since the alliance with the KMT was a higher priority than anything else, it never happened. The fact that the U.S. was allied with Stalin shows that the reason the U.S. did not support the Chinese communists had nothing to do with opposition to communist dictatorship; the reason was that U.S. leaders, notwithstanding the advice of their military commanders, did not trust Mao-tse Tung to maintain control over Chinese working people as much as they trusted Stalin to control the Soviet working class, and they preferred to keep a more reliable pro-capitalist like Chiang Kai-shek in power.

This basic strategic decision to make fighting the Fascists secondary to preventing workers or peasants from seizing power not only meant risking a Japanese victory in China, but also guaranteed that U.S. soldiers would have to confront Japanese forces where they were strongest, not weakest, on tiny Pacific islands, where 6,821 marines and nearly nine hundred American sailors were killed in the fight to take Iwo Jima alone.[89] American soldiers could have been sent to fight alongside Chinese peasants whose fight for democracy and equality, though hindered undoubtedly by the role of their Communist leaders, was nonetheless so inspiring to Japanese peasant soldiers that it actually caused some of them to defect to the Chinese side and certainly weakened the resolve and discipline of the others. Instead, American soldiers were sent to fight the Japanese on barren islands where there was no popular movement to make the Japanese soldiers question their loyalties, and where they fought to the death. On Iwo Jima, for example, 20,000 Japanese died fighting to hold the eight square mile island, and only 1,083 were captured alive.[90]

ALLIES ATTACK ANTI-FASCISTS IN THE PHILIPPINES

The Japanese invaded the Philippines and defeated U.S. troops under General MacArthur in 1941. Prior to this the nation of islands (the largest of which was Luzon) was one in which "the export, import and banking sectors were predominantly American-owned," while local Filipino business groups were "intimately associated with American interests" and constituted a small elite that ran the Philippines with a corrupt and inefficient government. In the countryside, a civil war was raging that had begun in the 1930s between a class of large landowners who were concentrating land ownership in their hands, and the peasants who were losing their land and becoming tenants. The large landowners had forced the agrarian economy into becoming a "lopsided... extractive and agricultural raw-materials industry" which by 1940 resulted in a long-term major "food deficit."[91]

When the Japanese invaded, the local politicians willingly collaborated with them, and the Japanese just left the existing ruling class in power. The government of President Sergio Osmena fled to Washington but kept relations with the collaborationist government in the Philippines, and the U.S. government, specifically its psychological-warfare services, "never attacked the local collaborators" on the islands.[92]

During the Japanese occupation, the landless peasantry organized into armed bands, the largest of which was the People's Anti-Japanese Army (the Hukbalahap, or Huks) which fought the Japanese and also fought for more equality and democracy in the countryside. The peak strength of the Huks was approximately 100,000 and they "controlled vast sections of the nation." The Huks were primarily Communist led but their leaders also included liberal politicians. They fought against tenancy and they "created new organs of self-government in local areas, and a radically new society." And, "function[ing] mainly as an armed peasantry seeking to end its misery" they "killed over 20,000 Japanese and puppet troops." Some American military officers were assigned to work with the Huks, and they "soon grew to respect the Huks" and their revolutionary goals and became quite resentful that the higher level U.S. leaders were hostile to them. The Huks gave aid to American intelligence and military operations, but the U.S. created "non-political" militias that were officially anti-Japanese but which "often clashed with the Huks." American leaders were so much more concerned with preventing a social revolution in the Philippines than with driving the Japanese off the island, that they actually fought the one force on the island that was seriously fighting the Japanese Fascists.[93]

In 1944 when MacArthur re-invaded the Philippines, the U.S. granted independence to the Philippines without giving up U.S. economic domination of the country or the right to military bases. This arrangement was approved by the conservative collaborator class, but not approved by the peasants. In November 1944 "when Osmena landed on Leyte with MacArthur [he] immediately issued a statement exonerating" the collaborators, or as he put it, "those public officials who 'had to remain at their posts to maintain a semblance of government..' "[94] The U.S. then proceeded to reverse the social revolution for which the peasants had fought so hard. MacArthur "pressed the Filipino collaborationist police into the service of the United States and the United States military authorities arrested and held the two major Huk leaders..."[95] McArthur also broke up Huk meetings throughout 1945. During this time the landlords got laws passed that gave them back the land that peasants had fought to reclaim, and they received military aid from the U.S. to use in their fight against the Huks. MacArthur chose Manuel Roxas to succeed Osmena and to be the first president of the newly "independent" nation. Even the American intelligence agency, the OSS, described Roxas as being "in the peculiar position of an exonerated collaborationist" behind whom stood "some economically powerful groups."[96]

SUMMARY

U.S. and British leaders consistently chose to side with Fascist collaborators when that seemed necessary to prevent armed working people from seizing power. Stalin used his influence over Communist parties in the Resistance movements to try, not always successfully, to make sure that they only fought Fascists and never aimed for democratic revolution. Were it not for Stalin's counter-revolutionary role during the war it is very likely that working people in Europe and Asia would have seized power with their new-found strength in the anti-Fascist movements.

But British and American leaders were wary of Stalin's intentions and also worried that even if he wanted to he might not be able to control Communist parties in other countries. This is why British and American leaders did not hesitate to directly attack the Resistance forces violently, as in Greece and the Philippines, or indirectly as in China where they backed Chiang Kai-shek's armies which mainly fought Mao Tse-Tung's Communists, in Italy where they gave German forces the green light to attack the Resistance, and in Yugoslavia where they armed the Chetniks, led by the King's Nazi collaborator, who fought Tito's Communists. In France, where the Communist Party leadership followed Stalin's lead most loyally and where there was no competing party advocating revolution, the Resistance posed less of a threat of fighting for working class power and yet the United States still chose to support the Vichy collaborationist government as a means of containing the Resistance. The Japanese were weakest where they were overextended in China and the Philippines, where there were large populations of peasants who wanted to fight them. With total Allied backing of the peasants and their revolutionary goals which inspired them to fight, the Japanese could have been defeated not only militarily but politically in China and the Philippines. Japan's peasant soldiers (as we will see in more depth in the next section) could have been convinced to turn their guns around, and in fact the Chinese Communists did win converts from the Japanese troops in the context of a peasant social revolution. From the point of view of defeating the Fascists quickly and with the least loss of life, this strategy would have made the most sense. Allied leaders never considered this strategy, however, because their war aims were not primarily to defeat the Fascists; their aim was to defeat the working class. As a result, American soldiers were sent to a string of barren islands like Iwo Jima to be slaughtered by the thousands in a fight against Japanese peasant soldiers who, in isolation from revolutionary "enemy" peasants, saw no choice but to fight to the death.

Notes

1. Gabriel Kolko, *The Politics of War: The World and United States Foreign Policy, 1943-1945*, Pantheon Books, New York, 1968, 1990, p. 47.

2. *Ibid.*, p. 48.

3. *Ibid.*, p. 48.

4. *Ibid.*, p. 45.

5. *Ibid.*, p. 56.

6. *Ibid.*, p. 45.

7. *Ibid.*, p. 54.

8. *Ibid.*, p. 55.

9. *Ibid.*, p. 61.

10. Kolko, *Century of War*, p. 294.

11. *Ibid.*, p. 299.

12. *Ibid.*, p. 300.

13. Kolko, *Politics of War*, p. 172.

14. *Ibid.*, p. 172.

15. *Ibid.*, p. 175.

16. *Ibid.*, p. 175.

17. *Ibid.*, p. 175.

18. *Ibid.*, p. 174.

19. *Ibid.*, p. 177.

20. *Ibid.*, p. 177.

21. *Ibid.*, pp. 178-9.

22. *Ibid.*, p. 183.

23. *Ibid.*, p. 183.

24. *Ibid.*, p. 184.

25. *Ibid.*, p. 184.

26. *Ibid.*, p. 188.

27. *Ibid.*, p. 188.

28. *Ibid.*, p. 188.

29. *Ibid.*, p. 189.

30. *Ibid.*, p. 190.

31. *Ibid.*, p. 189.

32. *Ibid.*, p. 198.

33. *Ibid.*, p. 191.

34. *Ibid.*, p. 80.

35. *Ibid.*, p. 84.

36. *Ibid.*, pp. 87, 95.

37. *Ibid.*, p. 65.

38. *Ibid.*, p. 66.

39. Fleming, p. 168.

40. *Ibid.*, p. 168.

41. Kolko, *Politics of War*, p. 67.

42. *Ibid.*, p. 69.

43. *Ibid.*, p. 70.

44. *Ibid.*, p. 82.

45. *Ibid.*, pp. 82-3.

46. *Ibid.*, pp. 80-81.

47. *Ibid.*, pp. 86-7.

48. "Prior to the invasion of Normandy in June 1944, Britain's leaders sought to stop or forestall the massive bombing of French rail yards, which they thought might produce many more victims than the British suffered from German raids on England. As many as 160,000 Frenchmen could be killed or wounded, they argued, but American planners dismissed their concerns. Indeed, French railroad workers played an especially prominent role in the Resistance and were now being designated as prime targets..." [Kolko, *Century of War*, p. 185]

49. Kolko, *Politics of War*, pp. 88-91.

50. *Ibid.*, pp. 92-3.

51. "The Nazi invasion of Yugoslavia in April 1941, resulted in the replacement of a unified state by a puppet regime in Serbia and an ideologically-fascist Independent State of Croatia under the Ustasa regime. This regime claimed for Croatia most of the ethnically mixed Bosnia-Herzegovina as well as the Serb-dominated eastern Slavonia and Krajina. To cleanse those areas of ethnic Serbs, the Ustasa committed atrocities, the brutality of which was most potently symbolized by the death camp at Jasenovac, later to also become symbol for Yugoslavia's 1990s disintegration." [Laurie West Van Hook, *Ethnicity in Exile: Coping with the Yugoslavs in World War II*, http://wwics.si.edu/ees/reports/2001/230wes.htm]

52. Jozo Tomasevich, *War and Revolution in Yugoslavia: The Chetniks*, (Stanford: Stanford UP, 1975), pg. 122, cited by Sarah O'Keeffe in Case Studies in Serbian Historical Consciousness:The Kragujevac Massacre and Stjepan Filipovic's Valiant Last Stand, http://www.geocities.com/sqokeeffe/front.htm

53. Kolko, *Politics of War*, p. 131.

54. "The split between the two forces was in part ideological, but primarily ethnic, with Mihailovic's Chetnik guerrilla army reflecting the interests of the urban and well-to-do Serbs, and Tito's a much broader, dynamic South Slav pan-nationalism encompassing all of Yugoslavia's numerous minorities." [Kolko, *Politics of War*, p. 131]

55. *Ibid.*, p. 132.

56. *Ibid.*, p. 135.

57. *Ibid.*, p. 133.

58. *Ibid.*, p. 132.

59. *Ibid.*, p. 137.

60. *Ibid.*, p. 133.

61. *Ibid.*, p. 134.

62. *Ibid.*, p. 134.

63. Kolko, *Century of War*, pp 310-11.

64. Kolko, *Politics of War*, p. 204.

65. Len Deighton, in Blood, *Tears and Folly: An Objective Look at World War II*, writes, "The Communists were forced into the 'alliance' with Chiang because they received no support or encouragement from Moscow...A turbulent China suited Stalin who was not eager to see a strong united China whether it was communist or not." [Castle Books, 1999, Edison, NJ, p. 512]

66. Kolko, *Politics of War*, p. 201.

67. *Ibid.*, pp. 200-1.

68. *Ibid.*, pp. 202-4.

69. *Ibid.*, p. 202.

70. *Ibid.*, p. 204.

71. *Ibid.*, p. 205.

72. *Ibid.*, p. 210.

73. *Ibid.*, p. 205.

74. *Ibid.*, p. 210.

75. *Ibid.*, p. 211.

76. *Ibid.*, p. 209.

77. *Ibid.*, p. 214.

78. *Ibid.*, p. 215.

79. *Ibid.*, p. 225.

80. *Ibid.*, p. 216.

81. *Ibid.*, p. 238.

82. *Ibid.*, p. 216.

83. Kolko, *Century of War*, p. 331.

84. Kolko, *Politics of War*, p. 551.

85. *Ibid.*, p. 550.

86. *Ibid.*, p. 223.

86. *Ibid.*, p. 224.

88. *Ibid.*, p. 224.

89. Martin Gilbert, *The Second World War: A Complete History*, Henry Hold & Co, New York, 1989, p. 643.

90. *Ibid.*, p. 643. In the first American assault on the Pacific island of Guadalcanal, when Americans attacked a garrison defended by 250 Japanese soldiers, only three of the Japanese soldiers "allowed themselves to be taken prisoner; in every engagement, the Japanese fought to the death, or, at the last moment, killed themselves to avoid capture." Describing the experience of Marines attacking four smaller islands during the Guadalcanal landing, Major-General Alexander A. Vandegrift wrote to the Marine Commandant in Washington, "I have never heard or read of this kind of fighting...These people refuse to surrender. The wounded will wait till men come up to examine them, and blow themselves and the other fellow to death with a hand grenade." On Tarawa Atoll, more than five thousand Japanese defended against approximately the same number of American soldiers. "At the end of seventy-six hours of savage fighting, only one Japanese officer and sixteen men, and 129 Korean labourers, were still alive. A thousand Americans—a fifth of the invasion force—had been killed in overcoming the fanatical resistance of the five thousand." [*The Second World War*, by Martin Gilbert, pp. 350, 476]

91. Kolko, *Politics of War*, p. 604.

92. *Ibid.*, p. 604.

93. *Ibid.*, p 605.

94. *Ibid.*, p. 605.

95. *Ibid.*, p. 606.

96. *Ibid.*, p. 606.

IV WHY THE ALLIES BOMBED CIVILIANS

T HE AXIS BOMBING OF CITIES AND OTHER METHODS of mass slaughter are not hard to explain since these methods reflected obvious Fascist values. The Allies' use of mass killing, however, is not so easy to explain. Nobody denies that the Allies engaged in barbaric bombing of Japanese and German cities, or that they used conventional and nuclear bombs to deliberately create fire-storms that would kill the maximum number of civilians. But why did they do it?

In the official story of the war, the Allies had to bomb German and Japanese civilians because the citizens were virtually all united behind their Fascist rulers and only by killing them in large numbers could the Allies succeed in destroying their will to keep fighting and thereby convince their governments to surrender. This view rests on two prior assumptions which are generally just taken for granted, but which are factually wrong. The first assumption is that German and Japanese civilians were fundamentally on the side of their Fascist leaders, or at least that Allied leaders believed they were. The second assumption is that the top priority goal of the Allied leaders was in fact to make the Axis nations surrender, and as we have seen, this was simply not true—their chief goal was to prevent working class revolutions. As we will see now, the historical record demonstrates that the first assumption is not true either.

To investigate the first assumption we will examine eye witness accounts of attitudes and opinions of German and Japanese civilians during the war, and see that many, arguably most, working class Germans and Japanese vehemently opposed their Fascist governments and would have helped to overthrow them if, instead of being bombed, they had been provided with support that was inspiring for being genuinely pro-working class, and substantial in material and military terms. Allied leaders did not provide Japanese and German anti-Fascists with such support because this would have contradicted their actual, but unstated goal. The bombing was the end result and necessary outcome of an effort by Allied leaders to turn their own populations against the entire people of Germany and Japan, demonized as evil and savage entities whose defeat had to be "unconditional" and against whom "there can never be successful compromise"; it was the culmination of a deliberate effort to destroy working class solidarity in the world by making the mass killing of workers in some countries the goal of workers in other countries. The war against Fascism was the excuse, not the reason, for the barbaric bombings.

ANTI-FASCIST SENTIMENT IN JAPAN DURING THE WAR

On March 9, 1945 172 American B-29 bombers dropped 1,165 tons of incendiary bombs on densely populated Tokyo for the purpose of creating a firestorm that would kill tens of thousands of civilians. After the bombing raid, the U.S. Strategic Bombing Survey estimated that more than 87,000 Japanese died, more than 40,000 were injured, and more than one million were made homeless.[1] Similar firestorm bombing raids were subsequently carried out against the cities of Nagoya, Osaka, Kobe, and Yokohama. American leaders viewed the atom bombs dropped on Hiroshima and Nagasaki as just a more efficient way to do what they were already doing with conventional bombs—kill as many civilians as possible. As President Truman wrote in his "Potsdam diary" after ordering the use of atomic bombs, the Japanese were "savages, ruthless, merciless and fanatic" and "when you have to deal with a beast you have to treat him as a beast."[2] About 140,000 people died quickly in Hiroshima and another 60,000 from radiation poisoning in the next five years.[3] In Nagasaki 70,000 people died either immediately or from burns and injuries the first year, and radiation poisoning eventually brought "the death toll to 140,000."[4]

Did Dropping The Atom Bomb On Japan Save American Lives?

U.S. leaders told Americans that the massive killing of Japanese civilians was necessary to force them to surrender and thus avoid tremendous American casualties in a land invasion. This was a lie. Major General Curtis LeMay, commander of the Twenty-First Bomber Command responsible for destroying Japan's military targets, gave an interview after the war explaining why he knew, in the spring of 1945, that the war would end before the scheduled November 1945 landing could begin:

> General Arnold made a visit to our headquarters in the late spring of 1945 and he asked that question: When is the war going to end?...We went back to some of the charts we had been showing him showing the rate of activity, the targets we were hitting, and it was completely evident that we were running out of targets along in September and by October there wouldn't really be much to work on, except probably

railroads or something of that sort. So we felt that if there were no targets left in Japan, certainly there probably wouldn't be much war left.[5]

General Henry ("Hap") Arnold, Commander of the Army Air Forces, wrote of this event in his diary, in June 1945:

> LeMay's staff showed how Japan's industrial facilities would be completely destroyed by October 1st. 30 large and small cities, all to go, then Japan will have none of the things needed to supply an Army, Navy or Air Force. She cannot continue her fighting after her reserve supplies are gone. October 1st—we will see.[6]

General Douglas MacArthur, Supreme Commander of the Allied Forces in the South West Pacific Area (including Japan) during the war, stated in a press conference in 1963: "We did not need the atomic bomb against Japan."[7] MacArthur later wrote that by June 1945:

> My staff was unanimous in believing Japan was on the point of collapse and surrender. I even directed that plans be drawn 'for a peaceful occupation of Japan' without further military operations.[8]

This opinion was not merely held by Army/Air Forces commanders. Admiral William Leahy in 1950 made the following statement:

> It is my opinion that the use of this barbarous weapon at Hiroshima and Nagasaki was of no material assistance in our war against Japan. The Japanese were already defeated and ready to surrender because of the effective sea blockade and the successful bombing with conventional weapons....My own feeling was that in being the first to use it, we had adopted an ethical standard common to the barbarians of the Dark Ages. I was not taught to make war in that fashion, and wars cannot be won by destroying women and children.[9]

In 1963, Dwight Eisenhower wrote about the moment when Secretary of War Stimson informed him the atomic bomb would be used:

> During his recitation of the relevant facts I had been conscious of a feeling of depression and so I voiced to him my grave misgivings, first on the basis of my belief that Japan was already defeated and that dropping the bomb was completely unnecessary, and secondly because I thought that our country should avoid shocking world opinion by the use of a weapon whose employment was, I thought, no longer mandatory as a

measure to save American lives. It was my belief that Japan was, at that very moment, seeking some way to surrender with a minimum loss of 'face.'[10]

Some have argued that top American leaders ignored military leaders and used the atomic bombs in order to obtain a Japanese surrender before the Soviet Union had time to enter the war against Japan and win occupation rights after the war. But if a quick surrender were the goal, the U.S. would have dropped the unconditional surrender policy and made it clear to the Japanese rulers that the Emperor would be allowed to remain on the throne, since everyone knew this was the only thing left that prevented the Japanese rulers from surrendering. In fact, the U.S. insisted on unconditional surrender and thereby delayed the eventual surrender which, in the end, did keep the Emperor on the throne.[11]

To understand why the civilian leaders of the U.S., President Truman and Secretary of State James Byrnes in particular (who would later run for governor of South Carolina on a "segregationist, anti-civil rights platform"[12]), would use atomic bombs when their military leaders felt it was not militarily necessary, we need to look at things from a working class point of view, and start by asking a question that is seldom asked. Were the civilians targeted by these bombs (both the atom bombs and the earlier incendiary bombs) Fascists or anti-Fascists? And why didn't American rulers seem to care?

Hardly "One Hundred Million Hearts Beating As One"

The Fascist Japanese government and military leaders tried to instill in ordinary Japanese people a willingness to die for the Emperor and sacrifice themselves in battle for the glory of Japan. They saturated the newspapers and other media with evocations of the ideals of loyalty and self-sacrifice to the "Yamato" race, ideals that came from an ancient but tiny Samurai warrior elite who themselves did not often honor these ideals in practice.[13] The propaganda about Japan being "One hundred million hearts beating as one" was meant not only to stifle dissent in Japan but also to inspire fear in Allied armies.

Japanese soldiers were ordered to sacrifice themselves and die with honor or else be branded a coward and a traitor. Some soldiers, especially those from the small and elite Samurai warrior caste, fought and died with fanatical loyalty to the Emperor. But most soldiers obeyed because of fear and coercion. John Dower, in *Embracing Defeat*, recounts how in May 1946 a veteran wrote a letter to *Asahi*, a leading newspaper in Japan, recalling the " 'hell of starvation' he and his fellow soldiers had endured on a Pacific island and the abuse they suffered at the hands of their officers." The veteran described how enlisted men "had died of starvation at a far greater rate than officers" and said they "had been killed by the tyranny of their own leaders." Referring to an old Samurai saying in which killing an enemy at the time of one's own death is described as "taking a souvenir to hell," the veteran said, "Most of his comrades died wishing to take not an enemy but one of their officers with them as their souvenir."[14] Dower also reports that, "Several months later, a report in the *Asahi* about an abusive officer 'lynched' by his men after surrender triggered eighteen reader responses, all but two of which supported the murder and offered their own accounts of brutality and corruption among the officer corps. One veteran confessed that he frequently had felt like attacking his officers, but restrained himself because he feared adverse consequences for his family back home."[15]

The government's "Die for the Emperor and the Yamato race" propaganda in Japan during the war was not terribly successful, even based on accounts from before the surrender. As early as 1942 Japanese police records show there was a growing contempt for the authorities, even for the Emperor himself.

The following letter was addressed to police in Osaka in 1942:

It is only the privileged classes and military who live extravagantly, leaving the sacrifices to the common people alone. Abolish aristocratic government. If you truly wish to speak of one hundred million hearts beating as one, then practice communism thoroughly and treat everyone equally. Don't mouth such utter nonsense as the "Yamato movement." The people's hearts are turning more and more against the government.[16]

In 1943 at several local meetings in rural Kochi at which the government's agrarian policy was being discussed, a forty-nine year old farmer declared:

I feel no gratitude for having been born in Japan. Being born in Japan is regrettable, I think, and I loathe the emperor.
Soldiers are killers. Students who get orders are embryo killers. They say soldiers die on the battlefield saying *Tenno Heika Banzai* [Long live the emperor], but it isn't so. Invariably they die filled with loathing.[17]

A sixty-eight year old woman in a small rural community concluded in August,1943:

If the United States or the like faced this sort of situation, they'd immediately turn the gun on their emperor, and it would be good if Japan did so too.[18]

"By mid 1944, before the air raids began,"an official of the Home Ministry's "Special Higher Police"—the notorious "Thought Police"—privately described the social situation as "like a stack of hay, ready to burst into flame at the touch of a match."[19]

The Thought Police recorded graffiti found on the "walls of public and private places between December 1941 and early 1944." The following is a small sample.[20]

December 1941:

Kill the emperor.

Why does our fatherland dare to commit aggression? Ask the leaders why they're waging aggressive war against China.

Look at the pitiful figures of the undernourished people. Overthrow the government. Shoot former Prime Minister Konoe, the traitor.

January 1942:

Absolute opposition to the imperialist war.

Soon we won't be able to eat. Those who feel good being called soldiers of industry are big fools.

March 1942:

End the war. In the end we'll lose and the people will suffer.

Her Majesty the Empress is a lecher.

Sumitomo Metal is a cheating company that wrings the sweat and blood out of us workers for a pittance. Kill those guys who decide on salaries.

June 1942:

No rice. End the war.

End the war. Give us freedom.

Destroy the aristocracy—those consuming parasites.

August 1942:

Overthrow the government. Raise wages.

November 1942:

Stop the war.

February 1943:

Kill the dumb emperor.

Kill Tojo

March 1943:

Ridiculous to be a soldier—35 sen a day.

June 1943:

2,000 yen to whoever lops off the emperor's head. 2,000 yen...for the empress.

July 1943:

Kill the rich.

For what purpose have you all been fighting for seven years?

Not exactly one hundred million hearts beating as one.

In September 1943 a twelve-year-old boy addressed a postcard reading "stupid emperor" to the imperial residence. The next month a mother, whose two sons had been killed in the war, cursed the emperor as "heartless" and trampled his likeness underfoot before burning it. The same month a nineteen year old student wrote a letter to his mother saying, "What's all this about being the Emperor's children! If that were so the Emperor would take care of his poor unfortunate children, but he doesn't...It would be good if the Emperor and all just died off."[21] These kinds of outbursts of emotion revealed to the police that even people who had no formal connection to subversive organizations were, under the surface, seething with anger at the authorities.

A secret Home Ministry survey "on the eve of Japan's surrender" reported:

> As we survey recent occurrences of statements, letters, and wall writings that are disrespectful, antiwar, anti-military, or in other ways inflammatory, from April 1942 to March 1943... the total number of incidents was 308, an average of slightly less than 25 incidents a month. From April 1943 to March 1944...the total number was 406, an average of 34 incidents a month. Compared to this, from April 1944 to March 1945...the total was 607, an average of slightly less than 51 incidents a month, thus showing a rapid increase.[22]

After the surrender, a Kyoto journalist reported that "his paper received two hundred letters per day during the war," and that "the great majority became critical as the war progressed and included 'much denouncing of officials and the military for their alleged failure to share the people's hardships.' "[23] (The letters were not published.) The Japanese government was so frightened of losing support for the war that they began arresting people for expressing even the slightest deviation from ultra-patriotism. A parent was arrested after being overheard saying, "I learned my child was killed in Singapore. However much one may speak of the country, can a parent help but weep?" One of the most common types of comment investigated by the police was that "it made little difference at all to the common person whether or not Japan was victorious." One company employee was recorded as saying: "No matter what country's control we come under, it's all the same." Likewise, a farmer was arrested for saying that "farmers would not be adversely affected by Japan's impending defeat, only officials and politicians would be in trouble."[24] Some people welcomed defeat with slogans such as "Win, America, Win." One anonymous letter to military officials read, "Japan is the enemy."[25] One unsigned letter addressed to Prime Minister Tojo in March 1943 read:

> I am the child of someone killed in the war in North China. It is the army and navy ministers, starting with Tojo, who cruelly killed my precious father and elder brother on the battlefield. Fools! What do you mean by holy war and peace? Look at how miserable my family is. My father died in the desolate fields of North China. My brother is unemployed. My grandmother can barely swallow the wretched rice she is forced to eat. Our baby is skinny as a praying mantis and cries piteously.[26]

Police dossiers included many letters that explicitly denounced the Emperor. A typical one read:

> The war is a cruel thing where many people and talented people are killed and injured, so we shouldn't wage war. Why are we waging war and who is doing it? The emperor is doing it. If there were no emperor the war wouldn't be necessary.[27]

Fighting Fascism On The Job

Opposition in Japan to the authorities was not only of an individual nature. Between January 1943 and November 1944 there were 740 industrial labor disputes and another 612 potential disputes that were thwarted in an overt police state that made any open protest extremely dangerous.[28] The most prevalent form of protest took the form of mass absenteeism from work, even before the bombing of urban areas commenced in late 1944. Between October 1943 and September 1944 absenteeism in Japan's undamaged plants was 20 percent.[29]

The "Thought Police" came to believe as defeat drew closer that Japan faced a revolutionary upheaval. In February 1945 Prince Konoye Fumimaro, who had been Prime Minister from 1937 to 1941, "personally urged the Emperor to effect a surrender quickly in order to save Japan 'from a communist revolution'" and explained exactly why he believed that "Japan seemed ripe for revolutionary transformation."[30] Two months later the Thought Police reported on the rural population, warning that "the germination of an impending class struggle is a real matter for anxiety."[31]

Contrary to people like Admiral William "Bull" Halsey of the Pacific Fleet, who was fond of saying that "The only good Jap is a Jap who's been dead six months"[32] there were many good Japanese people living in the cities that were firebombed by the U.S. government. Many of the victims of American bombs were as anti-Fascist as any American. In fact, many of the Japanese bombing victims were more anti-Fascist than the Allied commander in the Pacific, General MacArthur, because they wanted to do away with the Emperor whereas MacArthur kept the emperor on the throne. The Japanese government used the powers of a police state to control the population; but the fact that there was so much expressed opposition to the government in the face of harsh repression and unrelenting propaganda indicates that most of the ordinary Japanese people killed by the firebombing would be more accurately described as anti-Fascist than pro-Fascist. Furthermore, this was no secret to U.S. intelligence, especially in the Foreign Morale Analysis Branch of the U.S. Office of War Information, who knew very well that one hundred million hearts were not beating as one; in 1945 they specifically concluded that "the country was beset by serious internal tensions."[33]

Could the American and British leaders have allied with the anti-Fascists inside of Japan instead of adopting a strategy of killing as many of them as possible? We will take this question up after next looking at what ordinary Germans were thinking during the war years.

ANTI-FASCIST SENTIMENT IN GERMANY DURING THE WAR

On July 27-28 1943, the British Operation Gomorrah sent 278 bombers with incendiary bombs to destroy the city of Hamburg. The resulting firestorm incinerated 45,000 people[34]—more than the total British civilian deaths for the whole of the Blitz.[35] American bombers then followed the British bombers and tried to bomb military targets, but the pilots said the smoke was so thick they couldn't see anything and admitted most of their bombs fell on civilians.[36] "FDR thought Hamburg was an 'impressive demonstration' of air power's potential and hoped it would soon be applied to Japan." He said that such bombing was necessary to force the Germans and Japanese to change their militaristic philosophy.[37] In a letter to Secretary of War Stimson in September 1944, FDR said, "the German people as a whole must be punished for the Nazis' 'lawless conspiracy against the decencies of modern civilization.' "[38] Winston Churchill told the British public in 1941 that bombing was making "the German people taste and gulp each month a sharper dose of the miseries they have showered among mankind."[39]

Over nine hundred American bombers bombed Berlin on February 3, 1945 "in the first act of [Operation] Thunderclap... killing an estimated 25,000 civilians"[40] with high explosives and incendiary bombs. A few days later Munich and Leipzig were similarly bombed. From the 13th to the 15th it was Dresden—60,000 dead and 30,000 injured.[41] An RAF officer "gave an interview to an AP reporter, frankly admitting both the Americans and British were aiming at killing and dehousing civilians...[and] that 'Allied air bosses' had decided to adopt 'deliberate terror bombing.' "[42] Dresden had "no war industries worth mentioning except a small factory that made lenses for gunsights."[43] By May 1945 British and American bombing "had killed a minimum of 300,000 German civilians, only about a third of the number British planners had counted upon."[44]

According to the official story, German civilians were the enemy and only by killing them in large numbers could we defeat the Fascists. Does this view fit the facts?

There are two main sources of eye-witness accounts of the attitudes and opinions of ordinary Germans towards the Nazi regime during the war: reports by the Gestapo and other Nazi security agencies, and reports to the Social Democratic Party in exile from numerous members who remained in Germany. One book based on these voluminous sources is *Popular Opinion &*

Political Dissent in the Third Reich—Bavaria 1933–1945, by Ian Kershaw,[45] Professor of Modern History at the University of Sheffield, UK. Kershaw documents in great detail tremendous popular opposition to the Nazi regime during the war, which is summarized here.

Although the Nazi Party never achieved an electoral majority in Germany and had power given to it by the German elite in 1933, it did initially attract support from peasants and the middle class (each of these groups made up about one third of the population), based on promises to them that it didn't keep. As for German industrial workers (the remaining third of the population), the Nazis made only half-hearted efforts to win their support because the Nazis realized that workers understood the Party's true anti-working class aims very clearly. By the time Germany was at war, however, even peasants and the middle class were bitter that the Nazi regime had given them the opposite of what it had promised. The peasants felt more exploited than ever and were furious at Nazi actions they saw as purely immoral, and the middle class felt betrayed because they were treated with greater contempt by the Nazis than by the old rulers in the preceding Weimar Republic.

The Anti-Semitism Question

Because of the profound importance of the Holocaust, the question of whether most Germans supported the Nazi extermination of the Jews needs to be addressed before we look at the opinions various classes of people had about the regime in other respects. Kershaw writes,

> Our examination of popular opinion on the Jewish Question has shown that in its anti-Jewish policies the Nazi regime acted not in a plebiscitary [i.e., popular] fashion, but with increasing autonomy from popular opinion until the extermination policy in the east was carried out by the SS [*Schutzstaffel*] and SD [*Sicherheitsdienst*, or Security Service] as a 'never to be written glorious page of our history,' as Himmler put it, whose secret it was better to carry to the grave. The very secrecy of the 'Final Solution' demonstrates more clearly than anything else the fact that the Nazi leadership felt it could not rely on popular backing for its extermination policy.[46]

Anti-Semitism was an important part of Nazi organizing, but not for the stereotype reason that we have been taught by countless movies and books—that it "mobilized the German masses behind Hitler." In truth, anti-Semitism did not mobilize the masses; but the Nazi leadership did use it effectively to recruit fanatical supporters from a gangster criminal element and from some teachers and civil servants. The main people attracted to the Nazi's anti-Semitism (not counting the very wealthy upper class who financed the Nazis and published anti-Semitic propaganda without necessarily believing it themselves) were those who had very little wealth in capitalist Germany and had only the traditional prestige and status of their job. They saw this prestige threatened by worker's demands for equality from below and by the growing domination of big capitalists from above.

The Nazis cleverly used the stereotype of the "Jewish Bolshevik" and the "Jewish capitalist" to give a seemingly coherent world view to such people's fears. But for the majority of the population, workers and peasants and middle class white collar workers, anti-Semitism did not resonate; and knowing that, the Nazis did not use it to win support among the general public in elections before Hitler's appointment as Chancellor. In fact, when it came to winning votes, the Nazis actually had to downplay anti-Semitism. In *Germans Into Nazis*, Peter Fritzsche writes: "Germans do not appear to have voted for the Nazis because they blamed the Jews for their troubles... [A]ntisemitism played only a secondary role in National Socialist [Nazi] election campaigns. It was not the main feature in electoral propaganda or in the pages of the leading Nazi newspaper, *Volkischer Beobachter*."[47] William F. Allen reports the same thing in the town of "Thalburg" just prior to the Nazi takeover: "Social discrimination against Jews was practically non-existent in the town...If Nazi anti-Semitism held any appeal for the townspeople, it was in a highly abstract form, as a remote theory unconnected with daily encounters with real Jews in Thalburg. Thalburg's [Nazi] leaders sensed this, and in consequence anti-Semitism was not pushed in propaganda except in a ritualistic way."[48]

Kershaw draws the same conclusion from his in-depth examination of Nazi and Socialist reports of German opinion in Bavaria. He writes that "One can speak of anti-Semitism functioning as an integrating element [i.e., binding people to the Nazi leaders]. But this was mainly within the ranks of the Nazi Movement itself, above all within the SS... Party activists needed activity: and anti-Semitism went a long way towards providing the SA and, in practical terms, otherwise useless sections of the Party with something to do, at the same time binding them propagandistically more closely to the apparent 'aims' of Führer and Movement."[49] Nazi appeals to right the wrongs that England and France had done to Germany with the punitive Versailles Treaty after World War I, and Nazi claims to represent "all the people," and their promises of a fairer economic deal to peasants who had been evicted from their farms during the Great Depression and promises to civil servants of greater respect under a Nazi regime, these were the kinds of things that convinced people to vote for the Nazis. And this explains why the Nazi's one attempt to mobilize the entire German people behind violence against Jews backfired on them. This was the state-organized pogrom, known as "Crystal Night."

The prelude to "Crystal Night" began with the Nazis using incremental legislation to pressure Jews to leave Germany. The Nazis wanted the Jews to be out of the sight and out of the minds of other Germans so that the "Final Solution" would be easier to accomplish. The mass killing of Jews was not only a secret but deliberately carried out in Poland and Russia away from German civilians. Only on one occasion in their twelve year rule did the Nazis try to involve the German people as a whole with openly visible, government-sponsored physical violence against the Jews, and that was the infamous "Crystal Night." On November 9-10, 1938 all across Germany, Propaganda Minister Goebbels ordered Nazis to attack Jewish homes, synagogues and stores ("Crystal Night" refers to the broken glass) and to terrorize and kill Jews. Goebbels hoped to incite a national pogrom against the Jews. How did ordinary Germans react?

In Bavaria, one Gestapo report said that the "violence and destruction not only met with little sympathy, but was 'condemned deep into the ranks of the Party.' "[50] In Franconia Jewish eye-witness accounts reported that the small town of Lohr was "'very angry about these atrocities' [and] one woman protested openly and was threatened with arrest."[51] Kershaw adds this account:

> Catholics in [the town of] Gaukonigshofen made what was described as 'a true pilgrimage' to the burnt-out synagogue on the Sunday after the pogrom, making open show of their disgust. Peasants from the neighboring villages boycotted a public house in Ochsenfurt when they heard that the son of the owner had taken part in the destruction in Gaukonigshofen. In Hochberg... the peasants protested in vain at the burning of the synagogue by...sixteen SA men, expressed regret and disgust over what had happened, and viewed the sudden death of one of the participants six months later as a just punishment of God. In Fischbach in Swabia, in the Augsburg area, even the mayor had taken a stance against the intended burning of the synagogue, declaring that 'we are no incendiarists,' and was actually able to prevent the destruction taking place.[52]

In Prichsenstadt...a farmer ordered a taxi and accompanied a Jewish lady in his village to Schweinfurt to warn her husband that he was being sought out for arrest. The farmer was denounced by the owner of the taxi and spent a fortnight in prison as a result. In Schweinfurt, 'Christian neighbors' brought the children of a Jewish family fresh milk and bedding. In Burgsinn Jews were given money, fresh clothing, bread, and other foodstuffs by local inhabitants. An 'aryan' in Unteralterheim near Wurzburg prevented the house of a Jewish neighbor from being destroyed by threatening the SA men with a revolver if they did not disappear. They left. Peasants in Nordlingen gave a Jewess, whose husband had been arrested, a sack of potatoes and asked whether she was otherwise well provided for.[53]

A Jewish emigrant wrote a few days after the violence in Munich: "The mood among the Christian population in Munich is wholly against the action. I encountered the most expressive sympathy and compassion from all sides. It had been generally presumed that the houses would be attacked on the Friday evening (11 November). Aryan people from the area, unknown to me, offered to accommodate my family for the night. Despite the ban on sales to Jews, grocers asked Jews whether they needed anything, bakers delivered bread irrespective of the ban, etc. All Christians behaved impeccably."[54]

Kershaw found from records of a Munich 'Special Court' that "A master cobbler from Ruhpolding was denounced by SA men for saying that the demolition of property amounted to robbery of the Jews by the Führer. A salesman, once a Party and SA member, was accused of telling three soldiers in a Munich public house that burning the churches of the Jews was a wrongful act, and that in his view all men were equal...[and] a Munich police officer...was also denounced for condemning the burning of the synagogues as a scandal."[55]

One anonymous letter from an apparently conservative Nazi sympathizer in Schweinfurt and addressed to Goebbels ended with: "One could weep, one must be ashamed to be a German, part of an aryan noble people, a civilized nation guilty of such a cultural disgrace. Later generations will compare these atrocities with the times of the witch-trials. And nobody dares to say a word against them, though 85 per cent of the population is angry as never before. Poor Germany, wake up properly at last!"[56]

The revulsion at Crystal Night was so widespread, that even the Nazi's SD (Security Agency) admitted in its general retrospective survey that the "actions against the Jews" was not successful because: "From a basic liberal attitude many believed they had openly to stand up for the Jews. The destruction of the synagogues was declared to be irresponsible. People stood up for the 'poor repressed Jews.' "[57] Kershaw notes that these recorded reactions to Crystal Night in Bavaria were "little different in essence from those registered all over Germany."[58]

The notion that the Holocaust could only have happened because most ordinary Germans wanted to kill the Jews is not supported by the weight of scholarly evidence. Yet Daniel Goldhagen, the author of *Hitler's Willing Executioners: Ordinary Germans and the Holocaust*, advances this thesis, and has received acclaim for it in the *New York Times*, *Time*, and other corporate media. Goldhagen makes fraudulent use of historical evidence to argue for his thesis. For example, Goldhagen cites "ritual murder" accusations leveled against Jews as evidence for rampant antisemitism in Germany before the First World War. He writes, "...in Germany and the Austrian Empire, twelve such trials [for ritual murder] took place between 1867 and 1914."[59] Goldhagen, however, omitted the remainder of the sentence which appears in his source; it reads "eleven of which collapsed although the trials were by jury." As Norman Finkelstein and Ruth Bettina Birn point out,[60] honest use of the evidence by Goldhagen would have contradicted his thesis. Indeed, even the evidence that Goldhagen does present in his book contradicts his thesis. For example, Goldhagen describes how Nazi SS guards marched starving Jewish women prisoners to death in zig-zag paths across the German countryside in 1945, and how, despite twelve years of Nazi propaganda declaring Jews to be sub-human enemies of the German nation, and despite threats from the guards to shoot anyone who offered the Jewish prisoners aid, German civilians in the towns of Ahornberg, Sangerberg, Althutten, and Volary offered food and water to the Jews. Goldhagen mentions the townspeople who came to the aid of the Jews in order to highlight the anti-Semitism of the SS guards who threatened them. He seems unaware of the fact that in so doing, he inadvertently undermines his own thesis.[61]

One remarkable fact that illustrates the limited extent of anti-Semitism in Germany during the Nazi era is the story of the Wessel family. Horst Wessel was a fanatical 22 year old Nazi storm trooper who was murdered in 1930. The Nazi propaganda chief, Goebbels, made him a martyr, and the Nazis put the words of a poem by Wessel to song, creating their unofficial anthem, the infamous Horst Wessel song. A 1934 Hitler Youth song included the lyrics, "We follow not Christ but Horst Wessel." As a child Horst had a friend named Margot, a Jew. During the war, Margot and her husband Martin Weissenberg survived in Berlin despite intense efforts by the Gestapo to rid the city of all Jews. They survived because of the aid given to them by, of all people, Horst Wessel's sister! In *The Last Jews in Berlin*, Leonard Gross tells the story. "When the Nazis took power it was his [Horst's] sister who prevailed upon the Weissenbergs to send their children to England, provided them with food, clothing and medicine from her own scarce reserves, warned them when actions against the Jews were imminent, and once got them away from a hiding place minutes before the arrival of the Gestapo."[62]

Peasants Turned Against The Nazis

For peasants, the rearmament and then the war itself meant a drastic shortage of labor. "On average, medium-to-large peasant holdings required the labor of between one and three Dienstboten," who "were usually youngish, unmarried and were hired for a year each Candlemas (February 2)."[63] By 1943 men who would have been Dienstboten were either working in armaments factories or fighting at the front. Peasants were required by the Nazis to engage in the "battle for production" which meant they had to produce food without the necessary labor, and then they had to sell only to Nazi appointed middlemen who paid far less than the price to the ultimate consumer. There was, says Kershaw, an "acute sense of exploitation among the peasantry, prompting deep antipathy towards the Party and regime, aloofness from the 'great events' of the war itself, and overwhelming preoccupation with material self-interest—above all else the difficulties of acquiring sufficient farm labor."[64] Referring to rural Germany in the fall of 1941, Kershaw writes, "Detestation of the Nazi regime was by this time almost universal in country areas."[65]

Soon after Hitler invaded Russia in July 1941, the *Landrat* (a government official) of one district wrote that there was "not the least understanding for the realization of plans for world domination...The overworked and exhausted men and women do not see why the war must be carried still further into Asia and Africa." and he "warned that the extraordinary physical and psychological pressure was creating a depth of bitterness which should not be underestimated. He added, 'I have only one wish, that one of the officials in Berlin or Munich...should be in my office sometime when, for example, a worn-out old peasant beseechingly requests allocation of laborers or other assistance, and as proof of his need shows two letters, in one of which the company commander of the elder son answers that leave for the harvest cannot be granted, and in the other of which the company commander of the younger son informs of his heroic death in an encounter near Propoiszk.' "[66]

The Nazis used foreign workers from Poland and other conquered lands as farm laborers, and insisted that the German farmers treat them as an inferior race. As Kershaw recounts, "On farms in particular, where foreign workers often lived in the farmhouse and ate at the same table as their employer, it was a wholly impossible task to uphold the level of apartheid which the authorities wanted. Reports complained of the 'very noble' treatment of prisoners-of-war and of the all too friendly behavior of many peasants towards their foreign laborers. In some places prisoners-of-war were given new clothes for going to church on Sundays; others were presented with watches and other gifts."[67]

A report from the SD (Nazi SS Security Service) in April 1943 stated, "The mood of the farming population is very poor at present. The most varied things are complained about and cursed terribly...The mood is especially 'charged' among smaller peasants...In the countryside the general opinion is that they are playing fast and loose with the peasants. The local peasant leaders, mayors etc., are in a dreadful position. If things go much further they will not be able to pacify the people any longer. One would then have to reckon that anyone not standing aside would be done to death. Things have already gone so far that people make no secret of saying: it's immaterial to us what happens. If we get another government, we'll back it. Things can't get any worse."[68]

One of the most dramatic examples of how the Nazis failed to win over peasants to the regime's anti-human racist world view was enormous opposition by peasants to the Nazi euthanasia action. Shortly after the war began, Hitler gave a secret order to doctors that they should kill patients who were a drain on the Aryan race due to injury or physical or mental handicap. In two years more than 70,000 people were killed by this action.[69] As people realized what was going on, they grew alarmed and angry and a number of their Church leaders wrote letters condemning the action and gave sermons denouncing it. The unrest in Wurttemberg in the summer and autumn of 1940 was sufficient to persuade top Nazi Heinrich Himmler to close down the extermination center in Grafeneck.[70] One Nazi report, written by a Nazi who did not realize that the euthanasia action was secretly ordered by Hitler himself, said, "Whoever gave the advice to carry out these measures in this way must have a poor knowledge of the mentality of the people. They [these measures] are all the more keenly discussed and condemned and [they] destroy, as hardly anything else, confidence also in the Führer personally...The people reject in their feelings the thought that we have the right to gain financial and economic benefit from the elimination of national comrades who are no longer capable of working."[71] Church leaders, Kershaw writes, "were responding to popular opinion as much as leading it" when they articulated the protests. When Bishop Galen of Munster gave a sermon "thunderously denouncing the 'murder' of the mentally sick as opposed both to the Law of God and to the laws of the German State," local Nazi leaders moved to hang him. But "Goebbels pointed out, however, that 'if anything were done against the bishop, the population of Munster could be regarded as lost to the war effort, and the same could confidently be said of the whole of Westphalia.' "[72] At this point Hitler gave the order to halt the euthanasia action.

For Catholic German peasants, the Church represented morality. They saw the Church articulate their rejection of the Nazi euthanasia, and they viewed any attack by the Nazis against the Church as gravely immoral. Unfortunately, the Church used its influence over the peasants in an effort to rally them to support Hitler's brutal invasion of the Soviet Union by publicly applauding it as "truly a crusade, a holy war for homeland and people, for faith and Church, for Christ and his most holy Cross."[73] But when the Nazis eliminated crucifixes from the public schools, which had always been closely affiliated with the Catholic Church in areas that were predominantly Catholic, peasants viewed it as an attack on human values by a selfish power-hungry immoral regime which they began referring to as "Bolshevik." There were protest demonstrations, petitions, refusals to send children to school, and civil disobedience. "In Parsberg a sizeable crowd gathered outside the school repeatedly demanding the replacement of the crucifix and threatening to use force if necessary to put the cross back in its place.[74] When the Nazi "District Leader" attempted to address the crowd his "words were drowned out...Comments were heard about fighting Bolshevism at the Front and seeing it reared at home, and threats of resignation from the Party and the [Nazi] women's organization...In neighboring Velburg... a crowd estimated at 500 strong assembled... and demanded from the [Nazi] Mayor...who had removed the crosses from the school, the keys to the classrooms in order to replace the crucifixes. On his refusal the crowd pushed menacingly into his house, and the mayor, reaching for his pistol, was pinned down. His wife gave out the keys and the protestors promptly replaced the crucifixes and then dispersed."[75] These kinds of actions occurred all over Germany. In Bavaria, Reich Governor Epp wrote in January 1942 that "the 'crucifix question' had caused extraordinary ill-feeling in town and countryside, creating 'almost a revolutionary mood, which we are in no need of at this time.' "[76]

In the last years of the war, Kershaw writes, "The escalation of repression [by the Nazis of German peasants] in the post-Stalingrad phase [of the war, when the Nazis suffered their first major defeat in Russia] was sufficient to deter any but the near lunatic. Like most other Germans, however deep their dislike of Nazism, Bavarian peasants were anxious in this phase to keep as low a profile as possible, their one end in view being to outlive the regime, experience the end of the war—and to see the Americans arriving before the Russians."[77]

German peasants may not have been as sophisticated as FDR, who called all Germans a bunch of evil "militarists," but they seem to have been more honest. Had Americans been able to share some meals with them, it is doubtful they would have agreed with FDR that German peasants were imbued with a militaristic philosophy so rabid that it was necessary to kill as many as possible.

Civil Servants Felt Betrayed By The Nazis

For teachers and civil servants, who contributed disproportionately to the Nazi party, the Nazi promises of greater respect turned out to be a big lie. Once the Nazis had power, they really didn't need the middle class, who produced neither guns nor butter. The labor shortage forced civil servants to work longer hours without being compensated. One of the main complaints of civil servants was that they were becoming "proletarianized" as salaries failed to keep pace with rapid increases in food prices. One report to the government described how "Serious indebtedness was not uncommon, and applications for public welfare from employees of the lower groups were often supported by 'credible assurances that they have no more than a single suit and a coat and no means of getting replacements.'" These were the people who were pressured by the Nazis to give money to Party and State collections, and to volunteer time for Party activities. At the same time, the Nazis publicly vilified "civil servants as whipping boys and scapegoats for popular resentment at parasitic and privileged 'non-producers,' " making them feel like "social pariahs."[78]

A Nazi SD report from April 1941 complained about numerous "civil servants deliberately not pulling their weight and in some cases revealing an outright oppositional stance towards the National Socialist State. Many were of the opinion that most civil servants were Nazis only on paper, from a sense of compulsion."[79] Kershaw writes, "From 1943 onwards, in the conditions of 'total war,' the alienation of the middle class mingled with that of other groups of society to deprive the regime of any extensive base of popular support. The mounting terror of the last war years within Germany was testimony to the fact that the legitimacy of the National Socialist regime had dissolved, even among the section of society which had provided the core of its social base...The two years or so following the invasion of Russia formed the crucial period in which the middle class turned irredeemably against the Nazi regime."[80] By 1944 the "growing alienation of most civil servants from the regime" was evidenced by "the decline in the use of the 'Heil Hitler' greeting even in top Bavarian government offices in the later war years."[81]

No doubt many of these people were killed by the firestorms of Operation Thunderclap and Gomorrah, but far from being dangerous militarists they were probably some of the least powerful people in Germany, and as likely to be hostile towards the Nazis as supportive.

German Soldiers Feared The Nazis

The revolutionary actions of German soldiers in 1918 at the end of the first world war made the Nazis determined to prevent a similar rebellion in the second world war by making sure that every soldier knew he would be executed or imprisoned if he stepped out of line. In all of the first world war, "Germany killed only 48 of its own soldiers." But "during 1939–40 alone...the Nazis sentenced 519 German soldiers to death, the large majority for political reasons." During the war, "between 13,000 and 15,000 [German] soldiers" were legally executed by the Nazis for "various disciplinary and political reasons" and an unknown number of others summarily executed. Altogether, 3.4 percent (an enormous proportion) of the soldiers in the German armed forces who were not killed or wounded in battle were imprisoned or executed by the Nazis. Such draconian measures were made necessary by the fact that the great majority of German soldiers were not Nazi true believers. In fact, when German soldiers had the opportunity to surrender their arms to working class resistance fighters, as happened in Italy, they did so in violation of orders from their own officers, and at the war's end when German military commanders were demoralized by their defeat, "according to the official U.S. history, 'Hitler's army readily laid down their arms...' "[82]

Youths Fought The Nazis

In 1942, the Nazi Reich youth leadership lamented: "The formation of cliques, i.e., groupings of young people outside the Hitler Youth, was on the increase a few years before the war, and has particularly increased during the war, to such a degree that a serious risk of the political, moral and criminal breakdown of youth must be said to exist."[83] This Nazi was complaining about a generation who had spent the last nine years of their 14 to 18 year old lives in Nazi-controlled schools, no less!

Merely gathering together outside of official Hitler Youth activities was illegal for teenagers, but thousands did so—mainly the children of working class parents. Local groups called themselves by names like Navajos, Kittelbach Pirates, or *Fahrtenstenze* (Travelling Dudes), and they all wore an edelweiss flower badge and were known as "Edelweiss Pirates." In 1941 an Oberhausen mining instructor complained about the Kittelbach Pirates (KP), reporting to superiors that, "Every child knows who the KP are. They are everywhere; there are more of them than there are Hitler Youth. And they all know each other, they stick close together...They beat up the [Hitler Youth] patrols, because there are so many of them. They never take no for an answer. They don't go to work either, they are always down by the canal, at the lock gates."[84] The same year, a Mulheim SA (Nazi) wrote his superiors, "I therefore request that the police ensure that this riff-raff is dealt with once and for all. The HJ [Hitler Youth] are taking their lives in their hands when they go out on the streets."[85]

A Dusseldorf Hitler Youth reported to the Gestapo in April 1942: "For the past month none of the Leaders of [Hitler Youth's] 25/39 Troop has been able to proceed along the Hellweg or Hoffeldstrasse (southern part) without being subjected to abuse from these people. The Leaders are hence unable to visit the parents of the Youth members who live in these streets. The Youth themselves, however, are being incited by the so-called *bundisch* youth. They are either failing to turn up for duty or are seeking to disrupt it."[86]

The Edelweiss Pirates were famous for re-wording popular songs. One version of a popular tune they sang went:

We march by banks of Ruhr and Rhine
and smash the Hitler Youth in twain.
Our song is freedom, love and life,
we're Pirates of the Edelweiss.

Polar Bear, listen, we're talking to you.
Our land isn't free, we're telling you true.
Get out your cudgels and come into town.
And smash in the skulls of the bosses in brown.[87]

Edelweiss Pirates grew more and more bold against the regime during the war years. By the time war broke out these teenagers were engaged in small acts of sabotage, and "anti-social crimes" such as helping Jews, army deserters and prisoners of war, painting anti-Nazi slogans on the walls, and shoving Allied propaganda leaflets through people's mailboxes. A 1943 Dusselforf-Grafenberg Nazi party report to the Gestapo read, "There is a suspicion that it is these youths who have been inscribing the walls of the pedestrian subway on the Altenbergstrasse with the slogans 'Down with Hitler', 'The OKW (Military High Command) is lying,' 'Medals for Murder,' 'Down With Nazi Brutality,' etc. However often these inscriptions are removed, within a few days new ones appear on the walls again."[88] "In Cologne-Ehrenfeld in 1944 Edelweiss Pirates joined an underground group which, in the confusion of ruined streets and houses, had offered shelter to German army deserters, prisoners of war, forced labourers and prisoners from concentration camps. They got supplies by making armed raids on military depots, made direct assaults on Nazis, and took part in the quasi-partisan fighting. Indeed, the chief of the Cologne Gestapo fell victim to one of these attacks in the autumn of 1944."[89]

Workers Always Hated The Nazis

Industrial workers fought the Nazis, even violently, before they came to power and afterwards; even during the war, they remained very hostile and fought them as best they could whenever they could. Kershaw notes that reports from both the Nazi security departments as well as from the workers reporting to the SPD in exile in 1937–8 "suggest widespread discontent and antipathy towards the regime... Anti-Nazi slogans daubed on walls were a common-place in many factories. There are frequent reports that the 'Heil Hitler' greeting had disappeared almost completely among workers, whose hostile stance became ever more apparent to the isolated Nazi sympathizers among the work-force... Building sites continued to pose problems. 'A radical, anti-nationalist spirit' was reported from one site... The 300 Austrians building a barracks in Mittenwald were said to be mainly Marxists, whose anti-Regime feeling was highlighted by the singing of the Internationale which prompted the arrest of three workers... Penzberg miners, whose alienation from the regime had been continually registered by the Government President of Upper Bavaria since 1934, showed during 1938 heightened interest in the fortunes of the [anti-Fascist] Republicans in Spain, in developments in Czechoslovakia, in conditions in Russia, and even in the situation in China." Workers in one small town actually smashed the windows of the building where Nazi Party functionaries were meeting.[90]

When BMW workers in Munich "discovered hidden exits from the bunker below the factory during an air-raid practice at the height of the eve-of-war tension in September 1938, they left the factory in droves, making for home and saying 'We don't want a war.'" A few days later, during the infamous Munich Conference, when a rumor circulated that war had broken out, the workers in a munition factory stopped work and said that "they were not just going to be sent into war as had been the case in 1914."[91]

Summing up the mood of German workers on the eve of the war, Kershaw writes: "The glimpses of worker attitudes which we have extracted from a mass of documentation suggest strongly that workers not only *were* unfree, in the Third Reich, but that most of them *felt* they were unfree, exploited, discriminated against, and the victims of an unfair class-ridden society in which wealth and opportunity were unevenly divided. Far from being won over to Nazism during the boom years of 1937-9, the signs are that Nazism was further losing ground among workers during this period."[92]

The Nazis hoped that war would rally workers behind the government; but as we shall see, this did not happen. A report from 1940 on one "'entirely well-managed' explosives factory in Nuremburg" complained that 400 out of 2000 women workers regularly missed work on Mondays and Tuesdays. In another armaments factory 300 women out of 1800 were absent daily. The report cited "elements provoking unrest." The Nuremburg Defense District claimed that "only 'rigorous and swift measures' on the part of the Gestapo could 'guarantee order in the works and thereby undisturbed further running of the war economy'...[and it said that] internment of troublemakers between Saturday lunchtime and Monday morning proved...'very salutary.' "[93] The Gestapo in Bavaria reported that the number of workers involved in work stoppages and related indiscipline rose after the invasion of Russia.[94] As a result of intense police surveillance and arrests in factories, workers were openly describing the situation, according to a government security report by the District Leader of

Augsburg-Stadt, as "a communist dictatorship." " 'To have people sitting behind lock and key since the beginning of the war for next to nothing, and given over to the arbitrary treatment of leaders or their subordinates in concentration camps,' was, he concluded 'calculated only to increase the anger and discontent of the workforce...' "[95]

Allied bombing was purportedly necessary to turn Germans against the Nazi regime. But even among the small numbers of workers who had joined the Nazi party, there was already—before any bombing—growing opposition to the regime as the lies and true aims of the Nazi leaders became more apparent. "Months before the first Allied bombing raids on Schweinfurt," the Nazi SD recorded the mood of local workers in May 1943: "A certain indifference, especially among workers, towards military events contrasted with heated feelings in the large factories about new wage controls. One worker, a long-time [Nazi] SA man, felt National Socialism had let workers down. It had promised a system where earnings were a reward for achievement. But instead the Nazis had introduced an unfair wage structure where workers had to 'produce more to earn just what we used to earn.' He disbelieved propaganda that the wage structure was simply an emergency war measure and was convinced that it would remain in operation when the war was over."[96]

Allied bombing merely added bomb-related grievances to the already large list of grievances workers had against the Nazis. "Following the first air raids on Schweinfurt in the summer and autumn of 1943," the SD reported that work morale had suffered "colossally" and that workers blamed the employers for not providing safe shelters. The SD reported feelings among workers "that those up there don't care if some workers and white-collar employees have to die. The main thing is that they get to safety themselves in time." A worker in a big factory said, "One has the feeling that people are worth less today than the machines." Employers posted soldiers at the exits of factories which led to rumors that they would fire upon any worker attempting to leave the factory during an air-raid alarm. In May 1944 the SD characterized the mood of the Schweinfurt workers as "very bad" and detected "signs of their former political allegiance [i.e., anti-Nazi], in essence unchanged." The working population of Schweinfurt was of the opinion, noted the SD, "that our government should conclude peace before our entire towns and villages are destroyed, since we can't do anything against it in any case."[97]

Kershaw sums the evidence regarding the effect of the war on working class feelings this way. "This common experience produced during the war if anything a heightened and even more acute sense of social injustice among German workers than had existed before 1939. Clearly the unifying force of the war itself was insufficient to overcome the social antagonisms and political antipathies which the pre-war years had defined. Rather the contrary in fact: feelings of injustice, exploitation, and lack of social privilege seem to have been magnified by the pressures of war. As some North German workers put it in March 1945: 'We're always the stupid ones. We have no connections and have to bear all the burdens and duties of the war...There's just the same class difference today as before. Nothing has changed in that.' "[98]

Because of wrongheaded Marxist leadership,[99] German blue-collar workers failed to unite with peasants and make a democratic revolution in Germany when that was the only alternative to Nazi rule. Working class leaders allowed the Nazis to disarm workers (who had militias and weapons), and then when the leaders were hauled off to concentration camps the workers were left to deal with the Nazis as best they could.

The following glimpse of life in a German coal mine, as reported by a complaining Gestapo agent, shows how some German workers fought the Nazis even without weapons or organization. One can only hope that FDR was not successful in killing the coal miner, Lapschiess, who is described below.

October 13, 1943

We wish to inform you herewith of an incident which occurred underground here on 9.10 in Franz Otto Colliery, Duisburg Neuenkamp.

At the end of a shift the foreman S[...], Karl, b. 24.10.03 in Duisburg, who is in charge of coal-extraction from the faces of one district of the pit, ordered one of the Russian prisoners of war employed there to stay on longer and help extract a wedge of coal that had remained in the rock.

Since the Russian refused, despite repeated requests, to comply with this instruction, S[...] attempted forcibly to compel him to perform this task.

In the course of the altercation the apprentice face-worker, Lapschiess, Max, b. 23.4.03 in Gelsenkirchen, resident here at Essenbergerstr, 127, turned on the foreman and defended the POW in a manner such as to encourage the latter to strike the foreman on the head with his lamp. S[...] received a gaping wound on the face which has required stitches, and he has since been on sick leave. He is a diligent man and a member of the colliery Political Action Squad.

We should be grateful if you could make it clear to Lapschiess, who has already been in a concentration camp (1935-39), that his interference with instructions issued to the Russian prisoners of war constitutes a disturbance of the colliery's operation and that he may under no circumstances take the part of a POW.

This morning Lapschiess declared in impudent fashion to my face that he would continue to intervene if Russian prisoners of war were assaulted.[100]

It is not possible that U.S. intelligence did not know of the extent of opposition to Nazi rule among the German population. As we have seen, the opposition took forms that were often of a mass character, such as the revolt against the Nazi's euthanasia program and their seizure of school crucifixes. Working class opposition was a well known fact before the outbreak of the war, and members of the SDP inside Germany were making regular reports on public attitudes towards the regime to the party in exile, which meant the Allies had at least this source of information. The fact is that top Allied leaders wanted a nationalistic war and were determined to carry it out despite any facts that didn't fit this ideological straightjacket. Thus, as noted above, the top American intelligence officer, Allen Dulles, far from trying to evaluate the extent of German anti-Nazi leanings with his agents behind enemy lines, told them to leave notes saying "DEATH TO ALL GERMANS," a strategy designed, if anything, to weaken such opposition.

ALLIES BOMBED CIVILIANS TO DESTROY INTERNATIONAL WORKING CLASS SOLIDARITY

The question "Why did the Allies deliberately bomb 'enemy' civilians?"—people who, as we have seen, were opposed to the Fascists for the same kind of reasons working people everywhere else opposed them—is a central question because it goes to the heart of what the war was really all about. The war, as waged by both the Fascists and the Allied governments, was a colossal attack on working people in every country that was affected. Allied leaders bombed civilians who hated Fascism for reasons that had nothing to do with defeating

Fascism. For Allied leaders, as well as for the Fascists, ordinary working people were the enemy. International working class solidarity was the enemy. Workers going on strike and not obeying their masters at home were the enemy.

Bombing "enemy" civilians, because it was so extremely cruel and massive, was the most powerful effort that Allied elites could conceive to turn Allied-nation workers utterly and viciously against their brothers and sisters in other nations, and thereby consolidate the loyalty of Allied-nation workers to Allied-nation elites. Convincing working people at home that they needed to commit mass murder against German and Japanese working people was the chief goal of Allied bombing. The goal was to destroy, in the minds of working people everywhere, the very notion that working people anywhere could be anything *other* than "patriotic" and loyal to their own ruling elites, no matter how barbaric "their own" elites were to foreign peoples. Only by resorting to years racist propaganda and the big lie that conventional and atomic bombing of German and Japanese civilians saved American and British lives, could Allied leaders have persuaded many (not all!) American and British people to rejoice at the mass murder of "enemy" civilians. Terrorizing Japanese and German working people was another goal of the bombing, as well as to make of them an example of what would happen to workers anywhere in the world who might challenge American or British power, or even be so unfortunate as to merely live in a country whose government did so. From the point of view of these goals, bombing civilians was perfectly rational. The fact that "enemy" civilians were opposed to Fascism was, from the point of view of Allied leaders, not at all an argument against bombing them. In fact, if the German and Japanese workers had risen up to overthrow the Fascists with democratic revolutions, the Allied governments would have had even greater reason to attack them, just as they did when workers rose up in countries like Greece.

Notes

1. Fleming, pp. 507-8.

2. John W. Dower, *Japan In War & Peace: Selected Essays*, New Press, New York, 1993, p. 155.

3. Fleming, p. 541.

4. Fleming, p. 543.

5. Gar Alperovitz, *The Decision To Use The Atomic Bomb*, Vintage Books (Random House), New York, First Vintage Books edition, 1996, p. 337.

6. *Ibid.*, p. 338.

7. *New York Times*, 21 August, 1963, p. 30.

8. Douglas MacArthur, *Reminiscences*, McGraw Hill Book Company, New York, 1964, p.260.

9. W. D. Leahy, *I Was There: The Personal History of the Chief of Staff to Presidents Roosevelt and Truman*, Victor Gollencz Ltd., London, 1950, p. 429 and p. 514; Alperovitz, p. 3.

10. Alperovitz, p. 4, citing Dwight D. Eisenhower, *Mandate for Change: 1953-1956*, Doubleday & Company Inc., New York, 1963, pp. 312-313.

11. During the crucial weeks leading up to President Truman's decision to drop the atomic bomb on Hiroshima August 6, 1945, from July 17 to August 2, the Allied leaders were attending a conference in Potsdam, Germany. Secretary of War Stimson reported in his diary on a meeting with President Truman July 24, 1945: "I then spoke of the importance which I attributed to the reassurance of the Japanese on the continuance of their dynasty, and I felt that the insertion of that in the formal warning [the forthcoming Potsdam Declaration] was important and might be just the thing that would make or mar their acceptance [of surrender], but that I had heard from [Secretary of State] Byrnes that they [Byrnes and Truman] preferred not to put it in, and that now such a change was made impossible by the sending of the message to Chiang." In *The Decision to Use the Atomic Bomb*, Gar Alperovitz concludes, "Thus, in choosing to eliminate assurances for the Emperor, Truman and Byrnes with full awareness decided also to eliminate the one remaining option (other than the Russian attack) which in the judgment of their advisers might have produced a surrender." [Alperovitz, p. 302.]

12. *Ibid.*, p. 574.

13. Dower, *Japan in War and Peace*, p. 102.

14. John W. Dower, *Embracing Defeat: Japan In The Wake Of World War II*, W.W. Norton & Company, The New Press, New York, 1999, pp. 58-9.

15. *Ibid.*, p. 59.

16. Dower, *Japan in War and Peace*, p. 137.

17. *Ibid.*, p. 143.

18. *Ibid.*, p. 143.

19. *Ibid.*, p. 109.

20. *Ibid.*, pp. 124-28.

21. *Ibid.*, p. 139-40.

22. *Ibid.*, p. 129.

23. *Ibid.*, p. 130.

24. *Ibid.*, p. 133.

25. *Ibid.*, p. 134.

26. *Ibid.*, p. 135.

27. *Ibid.*, p. 144.

28. *Ibid.*, p. 116.

29. *Ibid.*, p. 119.

30. *Ibid.*, p. 103.

31. *Ibid.*, p. 114.

32. Fleming, p. 271.

33. Dover essays, p. 103.

34. Fleming, p. 276.

35. Gilbert p. 448.

36. Fleming, p. 276.

37. *Ibid.*, pp. 276-7.

38. *Ibid.*, p. 440.

39. Kaiser p. 390.

40. Fleming, pp. 494-5.

41. *Ibid.*, p. 495.

42. *Ibid.*, p. 495.

43. *Ibid.*, p. 496.

44. Kolko, *Century of War*, p. 206.

45. Ian Kershaw, *Popular Opinion & Political Dissent in the Third Reich: Bavaria 1933-1945*, Clarendon Press, Oxford, 1983.

46. *Ibid.*, p. 371.

47. Peter Fritzsche, *Germans Into Nazis*, Harvard University Press, Cambridge, Massachusetts, 1999, p. 159.

48. Allen, pp. 48-9.

49. Kershaw, pp. 275-6.

50. *Ibid.*, p. 265.

51. *Ibid.*, p. 266.

52. *Ibid.*, p. 266.

53. *Ibid.*, p. 270.

54. *Ibid.*, p. 270.

55. *Ibid.*, p. 266.

56. *Ibid.*, p. 268.

57. *Ibid.*, p. 271.

58. *Ibid.*, p. 271.

59. Daniel Goldhagen, *Hitler's Willing Executioners*, Alfred A. Knopf, New York, 1996, pp. 63-4.

60. Norman G. Finkelstein and Ruth Bettina Birn, *A Nation On Trial: The Goldhagen Thesis And Historical Truth*, Henry Hold & Co., 1998, New York, p. 21. The authors also state, "Indeed, precisely because Hitler knew he could not count on enthusiastic popular support, the Final Solution was shrouded in secrecy and all public discussion of Jewry's fate was banned." (pg. 53), citing Bankier, *The Germans and the Final Solution*, chapter 8; Gordon, *Hitler, Germans and the 'Jewish Question*, 182-6; Hans Mommsen, *What Did the Germans Know About the Genocide of the Jews?* in Walter H. Pehle (ed.), November 1938 (New York, 1991); Mommsen, *The Realization of the Unthinkable*, 108, 128, 131 n12; Steinert, *Hitler's War and the Germans*, 55, 140-5 passim, 335.

61. Goldhagen, pp. 348-9.

62. Leonard Gross, *The Last Jews in Berlin*, Carroll & Graff Publishers, New York, 1992, pp. 101, 206; also *The Horst Wessel Song* [http://www.us-israel.org/jsource/Holocaust/wessel.html]

63. Kershaw., p. 57.

64. *Ibid.*, p. 283.

65. *Ibid.*, p. 295.

66. *Ibid.*, p. 290.

67. *Ibid.*, p. 287.

68. *Ibid.*, p. 294.

69. *Ibid.*, p. 334.

70. *Ibid.*, p. 335.

71. *Ibid.*, p. 336.

72. *Ibid.*, p. 339.

73. *Ibid.*, p. 340.

74. *Ibid.*, p. 345.

75. *Ibid.*, pp. 345-6 .

76. *Ibid.*, pp. 352-3.

77. *Ibid.*, pp. 295-6.

78. *Ibid.*, pp. 324-5.

79. *Ibid.*, p. 325.

80. *Ibid.*, p. 329.

81. *Ibid.*, p. 328.

82. Kolko, *Centuy of War*, pp. 214-15.

83. Peukert, p. 153.

84. *Ibid.*, pp. 154-5.

85. *Ibid.*, p. 160.

86. *Ibid.*, p. 160.

87. *Ibid.*, pp. 158-9.

88. *Ibid.*, p. 160.

89. *Ibid.*, p. 164.

90. Kershaw, p. 105.

91. *Ibid.*, p. 107.

92. *Ibid.*, p. 108.

93. *Ibid.*, p. 299.

94. *Ibid.*, p. 300.

95. *Ibid.*, p. 302.

96. *Ibid.*, p. 308.

97. *Ibid.*, pp. 310-11.

98. *Ibid.*, p. 312.

99. Nazism could only have been defeated by a popular armed revolution, and there was no democratic model of revolution appealing to the majority of Germans and no revolutionary leadership committed to such a model. The Social Democratic Party had long since abandoned the goal of revolution and committed its considerable power to protecting the Weimar republic against Communist revolution. The German Communist Party offered only an anti-democratic idea of revolution which had already proved itself a disaster in the Soviet Union.

   The problem was not that the Nazis reflected the real values and goals of most Germans. The problem was that the Marxist leaders of the working class parties, the Social Democratic and Communist parties, failed to champion the revolutionary aspirations of the majority of Germans.

   If the Marxists had provided leadership for ordinary people's revolutionary goals, history might have been very different. The Social Democratic Party (SDP), however, which controlled the major trade unions, acted like a special interest group and only bargained for trade-union concessions, rather than mobilizing the working class for social transformation.

   In these years (that is, 1929-33) the German Communist Party did espouse workers' revolution (this changed in 1935), but the anti-democratic model of Soviet-style revolution could hardly have been expected to gain majority support. In the USSR at the time, having crushed the Workers' Opposition within the Communist Party, the Stalin leadership was consolidating its power, destroying any lingering illusions that the Bolshevik Revolution could lead to a promising new world.

100. Peukert, p. 142.

V CONCLUSION

W ORLD WAR TWO WAS AN ATTACK ON WORKING people by elites who tried to disguise their true aims as a war between nations. The war originated because elites in Germany, Japan, and the United States (as well as other nations beyond the scope of this discussion) believed they had no choice but to go to war in order to control their working class populations whom they perceived as threateningly revolutionary. The nature of the war, setting whole nations of workers against each other, was determined by the needs of the Allied and Axis leaders to use the threat of an external enemy to legitimize suppressing dissent at home, tightening their grip on their domestic working class (by either abolishing unions outright or turning them into instruments for controlling their membership), and attacking workers in foreign countries. On the surface it would seem that the German and Japanese rulers made a disastrous miscalculation, since "Germany and Japan lost the war." But the pre-war German and Japanese industrialists behind the wartime rulers did not lose social and political power in their countries, where they remain the dominant class today. While it is always better to win than to lose a war, the fact remains that because the German and Japanese business elite used the war to suppress their revolutionary working classes, they are still ruling over them. From the point of view of these upper classes, losing the war wasn't the worst outcome; the enormous destruction, misery and loss of life borne by "their own" people was a small price to pay, given the alternative of "their own" people taking away their power and privilege altogether.

During the war, workers in all the combatant nations tried to fight for working class values of solidarity, equality and democracy and against elite power in their own nations. They fought in many ways, from personal actions, collective actions which implicitly opposed elite rule (such as mass absenteeism in factories), to mass strikes and overt armed military resistance. The Allied leaders of the United States and Great Britain consistently made it their top priority during the war to defeat all efforts by workers to win real power, even when this meant weakening the fight against the Fascists, and even when it meant allying with the Fascists and their collaborators against workers. The Soviet Union's leaders likewise used their considerable influence in the communist parties of the world to prevent working people from fighting the capitalist powers for real control of society.

The most barbaric aspect of the war—the bombing of cities for the express purpose of killing massive numbers of civilians—was carried out, not for military strategic reasons, but for the political purpose of defeating the very notion of international working class solidarity and replacing it with the idea that workers in one nation were in a fight to the death with workers of other nations. Had the war goals of the Allies really been to defeat the Fascists in order to improve the lives of the people who were oppressed by them, then everything preceding and during the war would have been different. Allied leaders would have stressed working class solidarity and true democratic working class power at home and abroad. The war would have been a revolutionary war for real democracy everywhere and an end to class privilege and exploitation. Allied leaders would have helped working people in Germany and Japan fight the Fascists and win real democracy without capitalist exploitation even before the Fascists seized power there. The Allies would have gone all out to support the Spanish workers fighting Fascist Franco in 1936-7 instead of refusing to send them arms. The Allies would have helped Chinese peasants and Filipino peasants fight the Fascists and the local collaborators, instead of doing the opposite. They would have fought alongside of the workers and peasants in Italy and Greece and Yugoslavia and France, instead of helping Nazi collaborators and attacking the Resistance.

If the Allies had been a revolutionary working class force, working people inside Germany and Japan would have been profoundly moved to support them. This is quite evident from their expressed opposition to the Fascists under the most difficult and repressive conditions imaginable. Instead of killing as many German and Japanese civilians as possible, the Allies would have figured out ways to strengthen the ability of those people to resist, possibly dropping them weapons and setting up organizational structures. Italian workers organized major strikes in Turin under Mussolini. Strikes by German and Japanese workers took place during the war without outside help; but with entire Allied nations backing them up, the strikes could have been general strikes and even revolutions. Our armies would still have fought Fascist armies, but at the same time we would have welcomed their rank and file soldiers to join the working class forces. Such an appeal, coming from a genuine working class army, one that was known to be arming even "enemy" workers and fighting for real democracy and equality, would have resonated with many soldiers. The war would have been vastly different. There would have been far less killing and the war's duration would have been much shorter. Victory would have been vastly different. The war would have deserved to be called a "good war." World War Two was not such a war.

Some readers may find the account of World War Two presented here to be emotionally depressing because it undermines hope that we can make a better world. The "goodness" of WWII—the idea that people in the Allied nations, of all races and social classes, joined together in a great common cause of defeating Fascism, and that people acted with extraordinary selflessness and heroism for this cause—acts as a beacon of hope that this kind of noble solidarity is possible. Furthermore, it suggests that uniting people in this way for the good cause of defeating anti-democratic and immoral forces can happen again today under the leadership of capitalist leaders of the Western world who, for all of their faults, are indeed the moral and ideological descendants of the great Allied leaders of WWII. To suddenly learn that WWII was not the "good war" it has been portrayed as can understandably undermine hopes that were based upon this perception. But I believe the truth about WWII provides a greater basis for hope in making a better world than does the wrong view of it as a "good war."

First, the fact that Allied leaders had a hidden agenda which, had it been revealed, most people would have found repugnant does not in any way detract from the fact that millions of ordinary people really did act selflessly and heroically in what they honestly believed was a war to defeat Fascism and protect basic decency and freedom. This remains a basis for hope whether WWII was a "good war" or not. The World War Two generation understands that something very positive happened during the war despite the material hardship and loss. One American veteran of the war, Ray Wax, spoke of it this way: "It's a terrible thing to say, but it was the most exciting span of time that I ever spent. The most romantic...I forgot all about the boredom of being an infantryman and spending hours doing mindless tasks. But I do remember all the chances I had as a personality to do something that affected the lives of other people. There was a time of good feeling. The country felt it had done something worthwhile. The guys came back feeling they had accomplished something...In the war, I was living alongside people I cared about. I was trying to do something useful with my life...[Now] I work in an office with thirty people. I swear I really know only one or two. When it comes to feeling or real ideas, you hesitate to expose yourself, to say what you really feel or believe...I sometimes let out a howl of anger where I work, because of so many terrible things happening...I don't have as much trust in my fellow man as I once did."[1]

Second, the "good war" interpretation of WWII makes hope for a better world—a more equal and democratic world where people of all races and nationalities help each other instead of compete and even wage war against each other— conditional on the premise that, as was supposedly the case in the "good war," this better world is the goal of capitalist leaders too. If, as mounting evidence beyond the scope of this book is making increasingly clear, capitalist leaders on the contrary want a more undemocratic and unequal world based on unrelenting competition between workers of every race and nationality, then it is only possible to have hope for a better world if one believes that there is a social force that not only wants such a world but is also strong enough to win it even if it requires making a democratic revolution against the capitalists presently in power. What this book demonstrates is that there is such a force. Ordinary working people around the world were such a powerful force for a better world in the 1930s and during World War II that their elite leaders feared being overthrown by revolution. So fearful of their own working classes were Allied and Fascist leaders that they resorted to using a world war to control them. The elites knew from the experience of the First World War that war would be a terribly destructive and politically dangerous gamble, and yet they felt they had no choice because their only alternative was to allow their working classes to continue on the revolutionary course they were on, which would have meant the end of elite rule altogether. When we think of World War Two we should be outraged by the memory of how catastrophic and murderous it was. But even more importantly we should be inspired by a true understanding of the war to be more hopeful and confident that we can change the world, because the war, when the myths are stripped away, reveals the enormous fear that elites have of ordinary people and their revolutionary aspirations. The reason elites are so frightened we will change the world is because they know, even if they try to keep us from knowing it, that we can!

World War Two was not a "good war," but the millions of people who fought against Fascism were a very good force who should give us hope that we can make the world be the way they wanted it to be. Let us make sure that the only war we will ever fight in the future will be a good war, a war uniting all working people for democratic revolution.

Notes
1. Studs Terkel, *The Good War: An Oral History of World War II*, The New Press, New York, 1984, pp 308-9.

INDEX

MANUFACTURING CONSENT: Noam Chomsky and the Media

Mark Achbar, editor

Charts the life of America's most famous dissident, from his boyhood days running his uncle's newsstand in Manhattan to his current role as outspoken social critic. Included are exchanges between Chomsky and his critics, historical and biographical material, filmmakers' notes, a resource guide, more than 270 stills from the film, and, 18 "Philosopher All-Stars" Trading Cards!

A juicily subversive biographical/philosophical documentary bristling and buzzing with ideas. —*Washington Post*

You will see the whole sweep of the most challenging critic in modern political thought. —*Boston Globe*

One of our real geniuses...an excellent introduction. —*Village Voice*

An intellectually challenging crash course, laying out his [Chomsky's] thoughts in a package that is clever and accessible. —*Los Angeles Times*

...challenging, controversial. —*Globe and Mail*

...a rich, rewarding experience, a thoughtful and lucid exploration of the danger that might exist in a controlled media. —*Edmonton Journal*

...lucid and coherent statement of Chomsky's thesis. — *Times of London*

...invaluable as a record of a thinker's progress towards basic truth. —*Guardian*

MARK ACHBAR has applied a wide range of creative abilities and technical skills to over 50 films, videos, and books, as editor, researcher or production coordinator.

264 pages, 270 illustrations : Paper 1-55164-002-3 $26.99 : Cloth 1-55164-003-1 $55.99

BEYOND HYPOCRISY: Decoding the News in an Age of Propaganda

Edward S. Herman, Illustrations by Matt Wuerker

This spirited book offers abundant examples of duplicitous terminology, ranging from the crimes of free enterprise to media coverage of political events. Includes an extended essay on the Orwellian use of language in popular culture, and, numerous cartoons.

Rich in irony and relentlessly forthright, a valuable resource for those interested in avoiding 'an unending series of victories over your own memory.' —*Montréal Mirror*

Edward Herman starts out with a good idea and offers a hard-hitting and often telling critique of American public life. —*Ottawa Citizen*

Makes us think and thinking is what protects our minds, otherwise we are going to join Orwell's characters. —*Times-Colonist*

EDWARD HERMAN is an economist and media analyst, Professor Emeritus at the Wharton School, University of Pennsylvania, columnist for Z *Magazine* and author of *Triumph of the Market* (Black Rose Books).

MATT WUERKER's cartoons have appeared in Z *Magazine*, *The Los Angeles Times*, *The Washington Post*, and *The Progressive*.

239 pages, cartoons : Paper 1-895431-48-4 $19.99 : Cloth 1-895431-49-2 $48.99

BOOKS of RELATED INTEREST

KILLING HOPE: U.S. Military and CIA Interventions Since World War II

William Blum

This book looks at the effects, often devastating, that the U.S. military's and the CIA's little adventures around the globe have had on the political stability and peoples of the countries they meddled in. In not one case documented has the result been greater freedom or new found peace.

A valuable reference for anyone interested in the conduct of U.S. foreign policy. —*Choice*

Far and away the best book on the topic. —Noam Chomsky

A very valuable book. The research and organization are extremely impressive. —A.J. Langguth, former *New York Times* bureau chief

I enjoyed it immensely. —Gore Vidal

Single most useful summary of CIA history. —John Stockwell, former CIA

WILLIAM BLUM worked for the State Department until 1967 at which time he became one of the founders and editors of the *Washington Free Press*. In the mid-1970s, working with a former CIA officer, he wrote and published an expose of the CIA, its personnel and their misdeeds.

458 pages : Paper 1-55164-096-1 $28.99 : Cloth 1-55164-097-X $57.99

---

send for a free catalogue of all our titles
BLACK ROSE BOOKS
C.P. 1258, Succ. Place du Parc
Montréal, Québec
H2X 4A7 Canada

or visit our web site at: http://www.web.net/blackrosebooks

To order books:
In Canada: (phone) 1-800-565-9523 (fax) 1-800-221-9985
email: utpbooks@utpress.utoronto.ca

In United States: (phone) 1-800-283-3572 (fax) 1-651-917-6406

In UK & Europe: (phone) London 44 (0)20 8986-4854 (fax) 44 (0)20 8533-5821
email: order@centralbooks.com

Printed by the workers of
MARC VEILLEUX IMPRIMEUR INC.
Boucherville, Québec
for Black Rose Books Ltd.